The Literary Freud

Also by Perry Meisel

The Cowboy and the Dandy:
Crossing Over from Romanticism to Rock and Roll

The Myth of the Modern:
A Study in British Literature and Criticism after 1850

Bloomsbury/Freud:
The Letters of James and Alix Strachey, 1924–25 (Co-ed.)

Freud:
A Collection of Critical Essays (Ed.)

The Absent Father:
Virginia Woolf and Walter Pater

Thomas Hardy:
The Return of the Repressed

The Literary Freud

Perry Meisel

Routledge
Taylor & Francis Group
New York   London

Routledge is an imprint of the
Taylor & Francis Group, an informa business

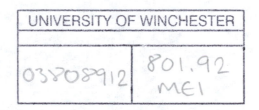

Routledge
Taylor & Francis Group
270 Madison Avenue
New York, NY 10016

Routledge
Taylor & Francis Group
2 Park Square
Milton Park, Abingdon
Oxon OX14 4RN

The canon of Freud's work is large and complex, and the tradition of humane letters is patently not to be encompassed in any formulation of its nature. I must therefore be hopelessly crude and summary in an attempt to suggest the connection between the two. Literature is not a unitary thing, and there is probably no such single entity as *the* literary mind. But I shall assume that literature is what it actually is not, a unity, and I shall deal with it in those of its aspects in which that assumption does not immediately appear to be absurd, in which it is not wholly impossible to say that literature "is" or "does" this or that.

—Lionel Trilling (1955)

Contents

Textual note

All references and citations to Freud are from *The Standard Edition of the Complete Psychological Works of Sigmund Freud*, 24 vols., ed. James Strachey (London: The Hogarth Press and the Institute of Psycho-analysis, 1953–74). All references to Ernest Jones, unless otherwise indicated, are from *The Life and Work of Sigmund Freud*, 3 vols. (New York: Basic Books, 1953–57). All other sources are provided in the list of works cited.

Preface

This book is a study of Freud's work, his reception, his sources, and his influence. It argues that Freud's texts are literary, and in a particular way. Freud's writing doubles the psychical mechanisms that it describes. One is always being asked to keep the psychoanalytic system coherent as one reads—this is Freud's tantamount demand upon his reader—just as the mind, as Freud describes it, tries to stay coherent despite the overdetermined systems that govern it. Chief among its mechanisms are the same self-dialogue and revision by means of which Freud's texts, and the arc of his career as a whole, are themselves constructed.

After an introductory reception history of Freud as literature, my reading of Freud's own career makes up the book's second chapter, a series of close readings of his major texts that takes psychical and literary representation as its principal focus. It is also Freud's own focus as he tries to represent the way the mind represents the world to itself. Like Freud's system, the psychical apparatus is designed to absorb stimulation by representing it. Representation is defensive. This is the surprising ground of continuity between early Freud and late, a continuity that I will trace in some detail from the *Project* and *The Interpretation of Dreams*, through the crucial metapsychology, and into the late phase, particularly in *Beyond the Pleasure Principle* and *The Ego and the Id*. The work of representation is central to the work of the psyche itself, as it is to the work of literature.

Inevitably, Freud's relation to literary and cultural history is also reflexive, and is the next topic the book addresses. As for Freud's "sources," Freud wins his originality in a daunting field of overdetermined prior discourses—literature, science, philosophy—the structure of which also resembles that of both his writing and the psychological subject. I take up this story in a historical chapter on psychoanalysis and aestheticism. This includes a look at Freud and nineteenth-century science and philosophical psychology, a motif which I introduce in Chapter 2 with a section on Freud's confident redaction of Henri Bergson in the *Project*, and which continues in Chapter 3 with a look at Freud's less sanguine relation to Gustav Fechner in *Beyond the Pleasure Principle*. Chapter 4 traces the histories of brain science and empiricist philosophy, particularly Hume, in the long eighteenth century, and the way in which they converge in the work of David Hartley in a startling anticipation of psychoanalysis and neuroscience alike.

As for Freud's influence on others, it, too, is structured like a literary history. Here follow chapters on Freud's influence on modernism: Strachey's *Standard Edition* (once again the subject of debate with the Penguin retranslations), and Freud's influence on Michel Foucault, a provocative but repressed relationship. Strachey and Foucault present very different but symptomatically very acute examples of Freudian influence. In the chapter on Strachey, I will begin by taking up psychoanalytic history as literary history, from Jung to Abraham and Klein, Lacan, and the French feminists. With Foucault, I will show how his criticism of Freud is in fact based on his own silent use of Freud's second model of mind to revise his first, a sleight-of-hand which allows Foucault to turn Freud—as Freud himself always does—against himself.

Last is the question—the return of the repressed, as it were—of Freud *and* literature. Does an understanding of how Freud himself writes and influences help us to read literature and influence anew? Here, a chapter on reading fiction shows how the strategies discovered in the chapter on Freud's own texts are also at work in novels. Like Freud, novels encourage their readers to disagree with them. They do so, as Freud does, in order to procure the very illusions that readers resist. Mansfield, James, and Hardy are the particular focus. A chapter on biography and literary history tests the usefulness of Freud's own dialectical way of handling influence in the case of other writers, including Conrad, Hardy, and Woolf.

A penultimate chapter meditates on the pornographic image. This is, I think, a vivid way of returning to the central literary question with which the book begins: What is representation in—and for—Freud himself? The status of the image in pornography returns us to this question with a quickened force. It will prompt another close reading of Freud's texts in order to assess both psychical and literary representation more fully than before, and also prompt an overt return to the dominant literary key of the book's earlier chapters in its final one. Here, in Chapter 10, in my discussion of Freud and Bakhtin, a satisfactory way of describing representation in Freud will, I think, emerge most clearly. Psychical identifications—a key issue throughout the book—become instances of what Bakhtin calls "stylization." These "stylizations" or "identifications" derive not only from adult social experience but from the infant's earliest experience with the parents, particularly the mother. With Bakhtin's help, the lessons of "On Narcissism" will become manifestly narratological ones. They are also social ones. Experience and its representations, even imaginary ones, or "object-relations," are one and the same thing. This is the particular terrain of fiction. The book's neurological assumptions will have already argued that life and literature—the nervous system and the novel, for example, in Chapter 7—are a continuous material field. Literature is indeed an imitation of life, but as an instance of it rather than as its copy or rendering. Psychoanalysis becomes a way of describing and assessing this material field and the dialogism that constitutes it both socially and biologically. Bakhtin will also lead us, however inadvertently, to Shakespeare, Freud's principal literary precursor, and to the ways in which even Shakespeare is treated to a Freudian measure of defensive representation.

The environment of Freud studies encourages both neural and social perspectives in any contemporary reading of psychoanalysis, literary or not. Nor are these perspectives at odds. What is ironic, however, is that it is a literary or aesthetic category that makes them continuous—representation. Representation is their common modality—identification in the social sphere, the interpretation and processing of stimulation in the neural. The distinctions taken for granted by the Freud Warriors—medicine vs. hermeneutics, brain vs. mind—well reflect their lack of sympathy for Freudian thought, which apprehends both the neural and the psychological as systems of signs. Anyone who has read A.R. Luria's *The Working Brain* (1973) will see how compatible the assumptions of a neuropsychology are with Freud's own. Luria's view of the brain as a grid of memory traces protecting the organism against stimulation shows that the brain is a motivated language with clearly defensive aims. Propped on this realm of somatic need, to use Jacques Lacan's terms, is the realm of desire—the unconscious proper, and its more familiar systems of psychological representation. They replicate at higher levels of functioning the more elementary defense mechanisms at work in the tissues. Anyone who has read Lacan will see that these psychological representations are intersubjective. Like the circuits of the brain, they make the mind dependent on its systematic connection to signification presumably "outside" itself, particularly the world of others. Whether this is because of language, or because of histology, the mind's privacy is no longer a foregone conclusion—as though it ever were in psychoanalysis.

This is also, I should stress, a study of Freud in English. It is English Freud, as I shall describe it in my chapter on Strachey, that has brought Freud his influence. It is also English Freud—the *Standard Edition*—that has raised questions about "faithfulness" in Freud's translation. To ask such questions is to make assumptions about representation that Freud—and Strachey—do not make. Patrick J. Mahony's view of translation—*Übersetzung*—is that it is something that the psyche also does (1987, vii). This is a fine way of making a quick point about the doubling effects in Freud, but an insufficient view of both translation and of Freud himself. Translation in this sense rests on a mimetic assumption—that there is something latent to be made manifest, that there is indeed something to be translated, whether on the page or in—"in"—the psyche. My argument throughout is that Freud's is not a mimetic project. His career as a whole is a careful campaign to undo precisely this ancient and problematic view of how both texts and the psyche actually work.

Such a view of Freud, however, is only a byproduct of my principal concern throughout these pages, which is simply to read Freud carefully, and to follow his reception closely. The new Freudian environment does, however, raise the stakes for the persuasiveness of a literary reading of Freud. What can it add to our reading of Freud as a whole? To situate and reevaluate representation in Freud's texts, as I propose to do, is critical to Freud's own durability, not just for literature, but also for the social and neural sciences. Other, more familiar issues are also near. What can a close reading of Freud do for a reexamination of a number of classic topoi in psychoanalytic criticism, including reader-response and the relation of biography to literary history? What can it do for an examination of less familiar topoi such as pornography that question, as psychoanalysis does, the very stability of the categories that organize them? Psychoanalysis has always surprised us. Perhaps it can do so again.

Acknowledgments

A shorter version of Chapter 2, "'Sensations' and 'Ideas,'" first appeared in *October* as "Freud's Reflexive Realism" (28, Spring 1984). A shorter version of Chapter 3, "Psychoanalysis and Aestheticism," first appeared in *American Imago* (58:4, Winter 2001). A shorter version of Chapter 4, "A Supplement to the History of Psychoanalysis and Modernism," first appeared as "Psychology" in *A Companion to Modernist Literature and Culture*, eds. David Bradshaw and Kevin J.H. Dettmar (Oxford: Blackwell, 2006).

1
Reception history

The critical tradition

The writings of Sigmund Freud have become so decisive a factor in our culture, particularly in America, that it is more difficult than ever to attribute to them the stance of a dispassionate science that simply narrates those unconscious processes of mind discovered by its founder. It is probably more accurate to say that Freud's work has itself become an example of those unconscious determinations that influence us when we least suspect it. Surely the contemporary status of psychoanalytic thinking as ideological reflex or instinct of reason should alert us to the fact that psychoanalysis no longer speaks to us so much as for us, no longer answers or confirms our condition so much as it produces it from the start. Psychoanalysis looks so like the foregone truth about life that it is easy to forget that what truth it has belongs, in the final instance, to the written achievement of Sigmund Freud himself.

Eloquent testimony to Freud's success as a lawgiver in his own right, the unconscious sway of psychoanalysis as an arbiter of modern thought and a staple of therapeutic practice represents the consummate kind of success any mythological system or set of imaginative texts can have. If it is the highest art to conceal art, to make fiction masquerade as a simulacrum of revealed or natural truth, then Freud succeeded more completely than most, more completely, probably, than any writers save Shakespeare—his principal single influence—and those earlier lawgivers who wrote the Old Testament, and who are, as the late *Moses and Monotheism* attests, the only conceivable rivals so far as Freud himself is concerned.

The burden of the present volume, then, is not to present Freud as a doctrinal figure from the point of view of either science or philosophy, nor is it to present him as a system-maker whose theories can be useful to an applied literary criticism. Rather, it is to situate Freud's achievement as a properly literary one in its own right, and one that casts Freud as both a theoretician of literature and a practitioner of it in exact and specific ways. Lionel Trilling in particular (1940) emphasizes that Freud's principal literary speculations are not to be found in the familiar psychosexual reductions that tend to characterize his own overt attempts at the psychoanalysis of art. They lie instead in his notion that the very mechanism of the mental agencies he describes are themselves the mechanisms of language. The emphasis on language should remind us of the technical as well as the thematic continuity of psychoanalysis and literature: They share the same medium. They also share the same history of determination in Romanticism, and in the Enlightenment philosophy that prepared the way for Romanticism in the long eighteenth century.

Freud's affinities with Romanticism in its naturalistic mode are what first swept him to popularity. D.H. Lawrence is Freud's most persuasive spokesman in this vein. Lawrence's enthusiasm both spearheads and formalizes Freud's dissemination through the Jazz Age demimondes of London, Paris, and New York. Bohemia gives psychoanalysis its naughty and glamorous legitimacy on a wide scale in both Europe and the United States. The nature of the continuity between psychoanalysis and Romantic thinking soon shifts, however—Freud himself has changed his theories—to a new focus on Freud's linguistic rather than vitalistic side, a change that begins with Thomas Mann's more dialectical estimate of Freud in the decade before World War II. The psychoanalysis of Jacques Lacan in France has played a large part in the accommodation of Freud to this point of view in the last twenty-five years, accenting as it does the discursive complexion of both the analytic session and the Freudian unconscious. But literary history is surprisingly clear about one fact: The linguistic insights attributed to Freud by the French are well anticipated—and far more plainly articulated—in the analysis of Freud by principal American critics such as Kenneth Burke and Lionel Trilling working only a few years after Mann in the decade before World War II. Despite Lacan's contretemps with American psychoanalysis in the 1950s and 1960s, this long American reception is conceptually continuous with the more familiar French one, and predates it.

What follows in this chapter is a narrative history that charts the unfolding of literature's incremental understanding of Freud's work as literary, too, as it moves, step by step, from Lawrence's and Mann's very different early attempts to understand Freud's affinities with Romanticism to Burke's and Trilling's more elaborate ones. The change that Mann represents in Freud's literary reception is the kind of change that will define the history of modern criticism as a whole. Jacques Derrida and Harold Bloom only complete what Mann begins, aided by Burke and Trilling: a wholesale denaturalization of psychoanalysis, and a revision of Lawrence's vitalism, and our own. This denaturing proceeds by means of a closer attentiveness to the material in which Freud works as writer and analyst

alike, language itself. If there is a central preoccupation that organizes this critical history and gives it a particular shape, it is to be found in literature's increasing understanding of why Freud's characteristic trope or figure, the unconscious,
is itself a literary rather than a thaumaturgic, scientific, or even a philosophical
achievement. The movement that begins with Lawrence's notion of the Freudian unconscious as a reservoir of instinctual energy is corrected and reversed by
Mann, Burke, and Trilling—they will have some help from W.H. Auden—as
they prepare us for the rereading of the Freudian unconscious in Derrida and
Bloom that transforms Freud's theory of the psyche into a theory of language,
literary language in particular, and that transforms Freud's own rhetoric into a
demonstrably poetic one.

The artistic tradition

Behind this very systematic reception is the wider history of Freud's recep-
tion by writers and artists. It is one caught in well-known testaments—H.D.'s
Tribute to Freud (1956) or Lou Andreas-Salomé's *Freud Journal* (1958) are good
examples—and in remarks made by the way. "I consider you the culmination of
Austrian literature," wrote Arnold Zweig to Freud in 1934 (E. Freud 1970, 16).
As early as 1896, the reviewer of *Studies on Hysteria* for the Vienna *Neue Freie
Presse*, the poet Alfred von Berger, had prophetically concluded that Freud's
work is "nothing but the kind of psychology used by poets" (quoted in Jones
1:253; see also Sulloway 1979, 522). Even Arnold Schnitzler had reviewed one of
Freud's early papers, in 1895 (Ellenberger 1970, 471). Freud himself had strategically apologized for the extent to which the case histories in *Studies on Hysteria*
(1895) sounded like tales of the imagination—"it strikes me myself as strange
that the case histories I write should read like short stories and that, as one
might say, they lack the serious stamp of science"—even though it is finally to
literature that Freud appeals without embarrassment as the passage concludes:
"Local diagnosis and electrical reaction lead nowhere in the study of hysteria,
whereas a detailed description of mental processes such as we are accustomed
to find in the works of imaginative writers enables me, with the use of a few
psychological formulas, to obtain at least some kind of insight into the course of
that affection" (2:160–61).

"It was, of course, Freud's remarkable literary ability," wrote Alfred Kazin in 1961,
"that gave currency to his once difficult and 'bestial' ideas; it was the insight
he showed into the concrete human problems, the discoveries whose force is
revealed to us in a language as supple, dramatic, and charged with the excitement
of Freud's mission as a 'conquistador' into realms hitherto closed to scientific
inquiry, that excited and persuaded so many readers of his books" (382–83). In

the hands of Freud's immediate disciples, however, or as practiced by subsequent generations of intellectuals, or by the culture at large, the Freudian method of explanation becomes, as Kazin puts it, sheer punditry. Freud's own writing, by contrast, enlists the devil's party as well as the dogmatist's, and so dramatizes not just a doctrinal clash between consciousness and the unconscious that Freudian pundits simply ventriloquize, but also the struggle within Freud himself between an empirical and an imaginative rationale for the psychoanalytic project as a whole. Certain tendencies in literature such as the spontaneous aesthetic of the Beats may even by explained, according to Kazin, as literal or reductive responses to Freud that share with the pundits a failure to distinguish literature from dogma, whether in Freud himself or in their own work.

No wonder literary and artistic enthusiasm for Freud changes when Freud begins to change in the decade following 1910. He is no longer a simple champion of instinct and sexuality; the psychoanalytic movement as a whole has become a rather more complex affair. Freud is revising his own assumptions; Jung, chief among the disciples, will soon defect. Like his critical reception, Freud's reception among creative writers accordingly shifts, leaving some, like Lawrence, moored to Freud's early work, and requiring others, like T.S. Eliot and even Joyce and Virginia Woolf, to grow more defensive. Such responses remind us that Freud early on inspired the greatest tribute of all, the tribute of anxiety on the part of his literary generation's first rank. Woolf had already identified Freudian punditry in 1920 among practitioners of what she called "Freudian fiction," writers who treat psychoanalysis as though it were, in Woolf's words, "a patent key that opens every door" (1965, 154); those who mistake, to borrow Trilling's terms, the instrument of Freud's thought—his language—for its transparent vehicle. Clive Bell (1914) and Roger Fry (1924) lambasted Freud when the opportunities arose, despite the fact that Leonard Woolf had decided to become Freud's English publisher in 1922, and Lytton Strachey's younger brother, James, his chief translator.

In Paris, backlash also accompanied the enthusiasm. Freud was an excuse for Surrealism. He was also a source of creative stress. "As for psychoanalysis," quipped Joyce to Djuna Barnes in 1922, breaking his customary silence on the subject of Freud, "it's neither more nor less than blackmail" (quoted in Read 1967, 214). By 1931, Gide was declaring Freud simply superfluous, and for undeniably self-protective reasons: "How embarrassing Freud is. And how readily we should have discovered his America without him" (1931, 304). Freud himself claims not to have read Nietzsche or Schopenhauer until late in life in order to keep from being influenced by their anticipations of psychoanalysis. Surely it is the same kind of anxiety that disturbs Woolf, Joyce, and Gide in their relation to Freud himself. "Had I not known Dostoevsky or Nietzsche or Freud," says a disingenuous Gide, "I should have thought just as I did" (1931, 306). The defensiveness was contagious. "It is shrewd and yet stupid," wrote an overtly scornful Eliot of Freud's *Future of an Illusion* in 1928, complaining in particular of Freud's "inability to reason" (1928, 350). In kindred outrage, Aldous Huxley found the "dangerous and disgusting mythology" of "psychoanalytic theory" so full of "inexact" and "unsupported" claims that reading about the unconscious is, as he put it, "like reading a fairy story" (1925, 313–20). Huxley echoed the sexologist Krafft-Ebing, one of Freud's teachers, who had greeted an early paper by his former student in 1896 with the celebrated remark, "It sounds like a scientific fairy tale" (quoted in Jones 1:263).

The cooler heads, however, balance the picture. Leonard Woolf had found psychoanalysis full chiefly of literary value, this despite his wife's epistemological reservations. It was Freud's writing that made the difference. Reviewing Freud's *Psychopathology of Everyday Life* in 1914 for *The New English Weekly* (Freud's 1901 two-part monograph had only just been translated by A.A. Brill, his first English translator), Woolf thought even this largely expository work "eminently readable," and for a particular reason. Although Freud is "a most difficult and elusive writer and thinker," says Woolf, what saves the day—indeed, what makes it—is that "whether one believes in his theories or not, one is forced to admit that he writes with great subtlety of mind," and, what is more, with "a broad and sweeping imagination more characteristic of the poet than the scientist or the medical practitioner."

For John Crowe Ransom in America ten years later, in 1924, Freud's work crosses over into poetry because of its understanding of the symbolic practices that unify life and fill it with meaning. Ransom's is a wide view of psychoanalysis. It predicts the course of the reading of Freud to come, particularly the more complex reception afforded Freud by Mann. Ransom's response to Freud is neither rote enthusiasm nor mythic reduction. Knowledge of the "biological" is really, says Ransom, a knowledge of the "ghosts that haunt within us" (1924, 161). These "ghosts" are for Freud myth, custom, and religion. Such symbolic practices represent the "biological" because they protect us against it. We deduce the passions from them. The bonds of particular communities are what count. They make our psychical worlds. Ransom's stance is agrarian, but it is different from the kind of agrarian conservatism with which it is customarily allied, particularly T.S. Eliot's. Ransom's pastoral is less Edenic than Virgilian. Labor is involved. The customs and beliefs that make up a community and its unconscious express themselves for Ransom not in universal myths but in specific mythologies of a national or regional kind. Like Cather's, this is a secular rather than a theological agrarianism, local and historical in its purposes rather than global and transcendental. It shares with psychoanalysis an emphasis on the poetry of the mind as it goes about its daily tasks.

Freud's distinction as a stylist was formally recognized in 1930 with the award of the annual Goethe Prize by the city of Frankfurt, a literary prize founded in 1927, prior recipients of which had included Stefan George and Albert Schweitzer. Freud called it "the climax of my life as a citizen" (20:73). It was in fact to Goethe (himself a scientist-poet) that Freud ascribes his decision, fortunate for posterity, to become a doctor rather than a lawyer. "It was hearing Goethe's beautiful essay on Nature read aloud," writes Freud in his *Autobiographical Study* (1925), "that decided me to become a medical student" (20:8). Here Freud reminds us to value that strand of literary allusion that furnishes his prose with tropes and concepts assembled at will from Greek tragedy, German Romanticism, and Shakespeare, and that situates his work from the start within a nexus of overtly literary traditions that rival the scientific ones, and eventually overpower them, in their relative contribution to the texture of his writing.

Freud himself offers the best and clearest caution about the status of the scientific language that is, of course, a central feature of his prose. Freud's apparent biologism is more evident in English than in the original German or in French, since Freud's *Trieb* is customarily rendered as "instinct" rather than "drive," unlike the French version, *pulsion,* which maintains the oscillation or ambiguity in *Trieb* between natural and cultural determinations. James Strachey, Freud's chief English translator and architect of the *Standard Edition* of Freud's writings (1953–74), gives his reasons for choosing "instinct" in the "General Preface" to the *Standard Edition.* I will take these up later on, in my chapter on Strachey. Freud himself, reflecting in the 1920 *Beyond the Pleasure Principle* on the "bewildering and obscure processes" of instinct invoked by his habitual biological vocabulary (18:60), meditates overtly on the problem of representation in language, and, in so doing, throws the focus of his enterprise away from its apparent objects in nature and onto the irreducibly literary or figurative medium in which his career as both practicing analyst and working writer really proceeds. We are "obliged," he says, "to operate with the scientific terms, that is to say with the figurative language, peculiar to psychology. ... We could not otherwise describe the processes in question at all, and indeed we could not have become aware of them." And though "the deficiencies in our description would probably vanish," says the empiricist in Freud, "if we were already in a position to replace the psychological terms by physiological or chemical ones, ... it is," concludes the literary Freud, nonetheless "true that they too are only a part of a figurative language" (18:60). Here Freud is referring to his early and persistent, but now abandoned, ideal of a quantitative, physical language for libido, the seething underbrush of the "topography" of the psyche whose mapping and measurement were the original goals of his vision of the psyche, the first of the two formal angles of vision—the second is the "structural"—that organize his description of the mind, and that are themselves subject to revision over the course of his career (see Jones 1:367–79; 2:282–83, 290–91).

Indeed, what had transformed Freud from a creature of the physiology laboratory into a psychoanalyst whose sole materials were those of language was his growing realization, in the late summer of 1897, that his patients' endless stories of infantile seduction at the hands of servants and relatives were not, as a rule, factually true, but were usually retrospective fantasies installed by memory and desire after the fact. Within the history of Freud's own career, this is the moment at which psychoanalysis itself becomes a literary rather than a scientific affair. There is even a text. It is preceded by a sequence of events well known to all Freudians. In 1896, Freud had given a lecture to the Society of Neurology and Psychiatry in Vienna that announced his belief in the seduction theory—his belief that repressed sexual traumas in childhood were responsible for most neurotic afflictions. He had concluded then that the various forms of nervous disease he encountered among his patients (hysterics, obsessional neurotics, and melancholics) were the result of actual events that had been driven out of consciousness because the memories were too hard to bear.

By 1897, however, he had concluded that the seduction theory was an error. "What I had taken for an epitome of exact observations," he wrote in his *Autobiographical Study*, "was merely the construction of phantasy" (20:16). He explained his reasoning to his friend Wilhelm Fliess in a letter dated September 21, 1897, the text that fully inaugurates psychoanalysis as such:

> I will confide in you at once the great secret that has been slowly dawning on me in the last few months. I no longer believe in my *neurotica* [theory of the neuroses]. This is probably not intelligible without an explanation; after all, you yourself found what I could tell you credible. ... So I will begin historically from the question of the origin of my reasons for disbelief. ... [My] surprise [was] at the fact that in every case the father, not excluding my own, had to be blamed as a pervert—the realization of the unexpected frequency of hysteria, in which the same determinant is invariably established, though such a widespread extent of perversity towards children is, after all, not very probable. ... [T]here are no indications of reality in the unconscious, so that one cannot distinguish between the truth and fiction that is cathected with affect. (1:259–60)

Memory, Freud now thought, was not a mere reflector of what had happened in the past; it was also a refractor. There was something else, some other dimension of the human mind that no one had conceived of before—not just an occluded part, a *condition seconde*, as nineteenth-century medical usage called it—but an entire hidden world of wishes, desires, demands, expectations. Why had Freud been so willing to maintain the trauma or seduction theory despite its implausibility? Because it allowed him to block an insight even more unacceptable, and perhaps even more implausible despite its logical inevitability—the discovery of infantile sexuality. The seduction theory had at least allowed Freud to preserve childhood as innocent. Now that paradise, too, was lost. In their love—and in their hate—children also, Freud concluded, found themselves in a world of symbols that mixed reality with desire.

It was at this moment, as Trilling suggests (1955, 81–82), that Freud may be said to have crossed the line that divides empiricism from fiction, at least if by fiction we mean that which proceeds entirely within language and without regard for the exigencies of fact. It was, says Trilling, nothing less than a "willing suspension of disbelief" (81) that finally allowed Freud access to the unconscious mental life of his patients, and that established the terrain of psychoanalysis as a world of language and fantasy—free, by definition, from the domain of objective verification. So when Freud claimed, as he did again and again, that the poets, not the scientists, had been the real pioneers in the exploration of the unconscious, there was not only the presumption of a common shop between psychoanalysis and literature, but also a genuine invitation to treat psychoanalysis itself as a poetic achievement.

Myth or language?

There are, of course, abundant reasons for calling Freud's achievement literary in a strict thematic sense, as Mann and Trilling would show. They help to plot the immediate resonances that arise from Freud's manifest alliances with Romanticism, chief among them, says Trilling, a shared devotion to "a research into the self" (1940, 33). Freud emerges from, and revises, virtually every principal line of literary history deriving from the tradition of Rousseau and of the *Bildungsroman*, the latter "fathered" (35), says a psychoanalytic Trilling, by *Wilhelm Meister.* The central tradition of the Romantic quest in both the prose and poetry of the nineteenth and early twentieth century is filiated, of course, to the tradition of quest-narrative as a whole, and so roots Freud's project equally well in the wider mythic traditions within which another pioneering American critic, Stanley Edgar Hyman, places Freud in his reading of *The Interpretation of Dreams* in *The Tangled Bank* (1962). More formalist than thematic in its handling of myth as both a notion and as a category of analysis, *The Tangled Bank* reflects the influence of Northrop Frye's *Anatomy of Criticism* (1957), the single principal influence on American criticism after the New Criticism until the advent of the structural criticism that began to emerge in the next decade. *The Tangled Bank* also reflects, behind Frye, the tradition within psychoanalytic criticism that begins, among Freud's disciples, with Otto Rank's *The Myth of the*

Birth of the Hero (1909), and that has its afflatus, in a different direction, in the work of Jung.

For Hyman, Freud's Romanticism is recursive; it is the local expression of his wider interest in myth as a grammar or high conceit. Hyman points to the structuring metaphor of the hike or climb through a wooded and "cavernous" landscape in *The Interpretation of Dreams* as the book's concrete emblem for its own quest for a solution to the legendary enigma of dreaming. It is also its principal style of imaginative organization. "Planned" as it is, says Hyman, Freud's orchestration of his guiding imagery functions as figurative theme and variation at crucial moments in the text (especially at or near the start of the third, fifth, and seventh chapters) as it proceeds from the thicket of past authorities on dreams through a "narrow defile" that leads Freud to a view of "the finest prospects" that the book as hike or "imaginary walk" will subsequently explore and colonize (1962, 332). The privileged figure of the journey in *The Interpretation of Dreams* joins the typology of the Romantic quest-poem as we know it in *The Prelude* or in Keats's *Hyperion* fragments to its earlier roots in the mythic quests of classical and Christian romance. Hyman's reading casts Freud's questing consciousness in the role of "the primeval" (337) or "mythic hero" (336) and so leads Hyman to the myth of Freud himself as the discoverer, the overcomer of his own resistances, the hero of an autobiographical as well as an analytic odyssey. This is formalist myth criticism with a historicist payoff. It is in *The Interpretation of Dreams* that Freud reports his discovery of the Oedipus complex, the result of his own monumental self-analysis that began in the wake of the death of his father, Jakob Freud, in 1896. Here it is Freud himself who is the proper referent of that citation from the *Aeneid* that he belatedly affixed to *The Interpretation of Dreams* ("If I cannot bend the Higher Powers, I will move the Infernal Regions"). The mythical Freud, the Freud of the classic quest, says Hyman, is not only the Sophoclean Freud, the internal hero of *The Interpretation of Dreams* who discovers Oedipus in himself in the tragic agon that functions as the play within Freud's play. He is also the epic Freud, Freud as Odysseus or Virgil, surviving the trials of the underworld or the unconscious and returning home, to consciousness, to narrate them in retrospect. Hence Hyman's reading of Freud's successful quest for the grail-object of unconscious laws suggests that psychoanalysis obeys the moral shape of epic romance as it rehearses a return to domesticity and culture after trial, after subduing libido.

While it does not cross into sanctimonious or reductive myth criticism—Hyman's influence is the Jungian Frye, not Jung himself—Hyman's handling of Freud still needs a foil or corrective. Its approach is supple, but its objective is too narrow. One corrective is Bloom's "The Internalization of Quest Romance" (1968), in which Bloom shows how the quests of classical and medieval romance become allegories of inwardness under the pressures of the Protestant inwardness that

leads to British Romanticism. Hyman does not calculate the effect of heteroge-
neous generic assumptions coming to blows in given texts—Pope's are a good
example—creating historical admixtures of genres rather than the sustained
polemics such texts presumably are. Freud's are the best example. They are not,
of course, polemics, but neither are they really mythic. They are a play of genres.
Frye will have to give way to Mikhail Bakhtin for us to understand such texts as
Pope's or Freud's. It is in these mediated ways that quest-romance leads to Freud,
rather than by the simpler path of Hyman's Viconian synchrony that has Freud
till the selfsame fields as Virgil and Dante. He does not.

If Hyman wishes to dramatize a pre-Romantic Freud in *The Interpretation of
Dreams*, Steven Marcus's "Freud and Dora" (1974) finds a late Romantic or modernist Freud at the helm in Freud's case history, the "Fragment of an Analysis of
a Case of Hysteria" (1905), the case of Dora. It offers a wholly different perspective on how to situate Freud generically, and a much more familiar one in its
manifest interests. If Hyman recalls Frye and Rank, Marcus's essay anticipates
the close readings of Freud by French criticism. Here, like Conrad or Borges or
Nabokov, Freud is a questing consciousness who keeps coming up against insu-
perable resistance. The resistance is secular and domestic, however, rather than
mythic. It has to do with growing up and living in a house, not with fighting
battles, at least not with fighting battles anywhere but in one's head. In this case,
it is his patient's unwillingness to pursue the analysis far enough to reveal to
Freud what Freud knows she desires but must repress—an incestuous identification with the wife of a friend of her father's with whom her father is having an
affair. The resistance throws the focus of the project away from its manifest goal
and onto the latent one of analytic and narrative procedure itself. As in *Lord Jim*
(1900), the scaffolding of the tale is as much an object of study as is the patient
at its center. And as in *Lolita* (1955), the quest and the problem of the quest are
the same, with the narrative desire for the clarity and closure of explanation
analogous, at least in structure, with desire as such.

What is most interesting about Marcus's essay, though, is the ease with which it
makes clear that Freud's world is a thoroughgoing world of language. Again and
again, the preoccupation persists, and it is the one that most troubles a "mythic"
reading of Freud like Hyman's. Above all, says Marcus, the analytic scene enacts
the same processes as its narration, subject and method becoming virtual doubles since, both as practice and as product, the very element of being in psychoanalysis is language and symbolization. Difficult as it is to achieve coherence
amid the fragments of Dora's story that Freud receives at different times and in
no particular order, coherent narrative is not only a metaphor for mental health
or stable selfhood. It is, within Freud's already metaphoric universe, health itself.
"Everything," says Marcus, "is transformed into literature, into reading and writing" (1974, 71). Freud's notion of the world as a text becomes the tenor rather

than the vehicle in both the analytic scenario and its narrative representation. "The patient does not merely provide the text; she also *is* the text, the writing to read, the language to be interpreted" (71). The psyche itself is a structure of language, a grid or honeycomb of representations, chief among them the pathways of memory which it is Freud's task to negotiate and map. Hence Freud's texts insist on their place in modernist fiction by collapsing the distinction (as do those of Borges, Blanchot, or Barthelme) between fiction and criticism, art and interpretation, taking as the center of their own action the representation of representation, the criticism of criticism, the interpretation of interpretation. The 1909 case history of Freud's Rat Man ("Notes Upon a Case of Obsessional Neurosis") suggests just how definitive the linguistic metaphor is, since the case organizes itself around a precise verbal puzzle—a multiple pun on the German word *Ratten*—whose overdeterminations must be unraveled in order for Freud to discover the lines of association by which repressed ideas are joined together. Like *The Interpretation of Dreams*, Freud's case histories, too, are, to use Hyman's words, "full of voices, struggles, soliloquies and colloquies, and stage movement" (1962, 312).

The models of Freud's texts presented by Hyman and Marcus, then, are both literary in exact ways, even though they differ in the traditions and assumptions to which they appeal in their attempts to situate Freud's achievement as a writer. For Hyman, it is myth that characterizes Freud's imagination; every present psychoanalytic quest is a repetition of earlier romance cycles whose archetypal scenes, especially those mediated by overtly symbolic myth, represent psychoanalysis as a truth about nature and universals. For Marcus, on the other hand, Freud's world is characterized above all by language as such, and by the letter of the law of language, which Freud follows like an exegete or detective as he elucidates the radiating puns of *Ratten* or the uncanny chemical formula in the dream of Irma's injection in *The Interpretation of Dreams*. Here even desire is to be represented as a linguistic conundrum in its unconscious structure, a text rather than a natural fact. This is the difference that separates Lawrence from Mann, and that prepares us for the rereading of Freud in Burke, Trilling, Derrida, and Bloom. What organizes the history of Freud's accommodation to letters is a movement from libido to language, from instinct to representation. It is the same movement that organizes the history of Freud's own texts.

"Prior to any mentality"

Well before Mann announces the first "official" encounter between Freud and modern literature in "Freud and the Future" (1936, 412), Lawrence acts out the enthusiastic one in *Psychoanalysis and the Unconscious* in 1921. It is tendentious, and very reductive. To the extent that it is neither, it is only because Freud has not gone far enough in Lawrence's own direction. Lawrence's enthusiasm drives him to a prose rhapsody rivaled in his nonfiction only by *Studies in Classic American Literature* (1923). Its value lies in showing the limits—and the danger—of such a reading of Freud, and the need for a more cautious one. Knowing this sharpens Lawrence's nerve rather than diminishes it:

> We must discover, if we can, the true unconscious, where our life bubbles up in us, prior to any mentality. The first bubbling life in us, which is innocent of any mental alteration, this is the unconscious. It is pristine, not in any way ideal. It is the spontaneous origin from which it behooves us to live. (1921b, 13)

"Prior to any mentality"—no matter the simple categorical clarity of Lawrence's descriptions of Freud, he refuses to acknowledge the category of representation as anything more than a foil for ground or "origin," which is "pristine." "Impulse" or "idea" (10)—that is the choice for Lawrence, and the choice that Freud, too, presumably requires.

Caution has a role, however, in Lawrence's account—Lawrence is too astonishing a writer for this not to happen—but it comes as a strategy, not as a surrender. Lawrence's reductionism has its uses, not only inspirationally, but in an unexpected critical quarter. Lawrence has, like Freud himself—especially after 1915—identified the dangers of idealism with the dangers of becoming, as he puts it, "mechanical." Such oppositions are, in Freud, and even in Lawrence, on the way out:

> This motivizing of the passional sphere from the ideal is the final peril of human consciousness. It is the death of all spontaneous, creative life, and the substituting of the mechanical principle. (11)

"Fixed" principles (12) are—as they are in Freud—a problem no matter the sphere. "Idealism" is "mechanical," too; Lawrence has, in a simple point of argument, dismantled some basic presuppositions of thought. Lawrence may look like he is bound to the early Freud, and to sexuality and its discontents, but here he sees the arguments of Freud's metapsychology very clearly. Idealism is a machine. Culture is an idealizing apparatus designed to throttle spontaneity and impulsiveness by inhabiting the mind. This is how we mistake culture's control of our bodies for idealism. It is only identification talking. That is what Freud teaches.

Is this physicalism? "Innocent of mental alteration," the "pristine" must fall on the physical side of things. Where else would it fall? If it is "not in any way ideal," then it must be material, or real. I will situate Lawrence in a wider and more classical historical context in Chapter 4, where he will indeed occupy a place in the history of physicalism that culminates with Max Nordau's influential theories of race and physiognomical psychiatry in *Degeneration* (1892). But cultural and literary history are not the same thing. As a writer, Lawrence also disrupts the instinctivism of which he is a part from the point of view of the history of thought, particularly the history of popular thought. Lawrence's language undoes his use of Nordavian categories; it challenges the integrity of the differences that make up their assumptions. It is not that the performative dimension of Lawrence's prose undoes a referential polemic. The polemic is also performative. As with its handling of notional oppositions, Lawrence's prose does not rest in stable locutional pairs. This kind of tension or irregularity is characteristic of Lawrence's prose, fiction and nonfiction alike. It is what gives it its peculiar unity, a trait it shares, as we will see later on, with his poems. The danger of reading Lawrence as a pure enthusiast lies here. It reduces his prose, just as his prose, as it were, reduces his ideas. It makes them too complex. This is Lawrence's Freudianism at its best—not a hayride of instinct but a play of systems. It is a mischievous strategy, even in the reading of Freud.

Mythic identification

It is also a split or double reading of Freud that Mann presents in his two extraordinary essays on psychoanalysis, "Freud's Position in the History of Modern Thought," first published in 1929, and, of course, "Freud and the Future," Mann's address at the celebration of Freud's eightieth birthday in Vienna in 1936. Unlike Lawrence, however, Mann presents Freud's doubleness in a sober light, casting a suspicious eye on the kind of vitalism that Lawrence himself historically represents. No reading of Freud, especially in a literary context, is as capacious. One side honors a reading like Lawrence's, at least Lawrence's popular reading of Freud. The other side does not. There is something to fear in such a naturalism. Mann's strategy in both essays is that of a novelist with great evocative powers who turns, imperceptibly, into a literary critic with great analytic ones. Mann lures us into the dangers of reading Freud as a champion of the daemonic underworld before curing us of the fevers that come from doing so. In the process, he sees the way Freud thinks more fully than do any of Freud's contemporaries.

In "Freud's Position in the History of Modern Thought," Mann's descriptions of Freud are at first glance so dramatic that it is easy to confuse them with what Mann will show is only one side of the psychoanalytic enterprise. Psychoanalysis does indeed summon "the night side of nature in the soul" (1929, 172), the "chthonic" (188), and the "irrational" (182). But, Mann reminds us, psychoanalysis is not a "cult of the instinctive." It has, unlike Lawrence, say, no "animosity," as he puts it, "towards mind" (176). This distinction is, of course, crucial. The Freudian project, like German Romanticism as a whole, summons the depths, not to revel in them, but, rather, to gain an "understanding" of them (180). "Instinct," says Mann, may well be "chthonic," but it is not, as it is for "the storming party" (189)—National Socialism—"sacred" (188). The Freudian dialectic conjures the depths not to celebrate them but to subdue them. Psycho-analysis is "revolutionary" (180), not "reactionary" (179). It brings "enlighten-ment" to "the night side" (191), not torches:

> Freud's interest as a scientist in the affective does not degenerate into a glorification of its object at the expense of the intellectual sphere. His anti-rationalism consists in seeing the actual superiority of the impulse over the mind, power for power; not at all in lying down and groveling before that superiority, or in contempt for mind. (193)

Mann's equipoise is as stunning as Freud's own. So is his frankness. The "impulse" is "superior" for a purely agonistic reason; it is no match for "mind," "power for power."

In Mann's birthday lecture seven years later, the grandest accents appear to be reserved once again for that Freud who, like Schopenhauer and Ibsen, asserts "the primacy of the instinct over mind and reason" (1936, 415). Duly acknowl-edging the present political implications in Germany of a "worship of the uncon-scious" and the "moral devastation" it may imply in the world of action (by 1936, of course, Hitler has been in power for three years), Mann nonetheless identi-fies the Freudian unconscious with the "primitive and irrational," with "pure dynamic" (416). Now comes the psychoanalytic wager that he has described before. The ego is at the id's mercy; "its situation is pathetic" (417). Territory won by culture from the "seething excitations" of the id (416), the ego in Mann's view fears and opposes the super-ego far less than it fears and resists those biological forces that make up the id's more rugged dangers.

It is the turn to myth that gives the ego help. Unlike Jung—"an able," says a humorous Mann, "but somewhat ungrateful scion of the Freudian school" (418)—Mann is, like Freud himself, careful about what he means by myth. Myth is a form of representation that Freud handles very differently from Jung, as I will show in Chapter 4. Here Mann shows, as Ransom has, that it is no simple matter of transcendent symbols. Unlike Jung—and unlike Eliot—Mann is thoroughly secular. Freud's brutal picture of the fiery instinctual depths is in fact "familiar" (421), communal, downright pacifying. How is this possible if myth does not offer a transcendental perspective? Because the mythic for Mann is not—as it is not for Ransom—the universal, and certainly not, as it is for Lawrence, the primeval. The universal and the mythic are simply the traditional, which is dif-ferent from community to community. Here the mechanism of myth is carefully demystified so that the dangers of an "instinctual" and a universalist reading of psychoanalysis can both be avoided. Mann's understanding of the mythic is exact. It is not, as one might expect, an example of the emancipation of the id, but, like psychoanalysis itself, a way of controlling it. The rescue work of psycho-analysis is once again central, but in a new way. It has a job like the ego's to do, but on a wider scale. In order not to succumb, says Mann, "it is the ego's task to represent the world to the id" (417). The key term is "represent." This is the royal road to the mythic, but it comes not from whatever gods may be, but from the representations made available by history. Myth in Mann is a form of historical continuity, not of transcendence. It is a way of living, as he puts it, "through reference to the past" (424). "Life in the myth" is "life, so to speak, in quotation," a matter of style, as it were, "a making present of the past" (425).

The modality of myth is "formula and repetition" (422). Much as the ego handles the id—it is one and the same process—the "primitive foundations of the human soul" (422) have somehow to be "represented" (423). What is its mechanism? It is, says Mann, a "moving in others' steps" (421–22); it is—the Freudian term is inevitable—"identification" (422). For Mann, myth means what in less Romantic hands might be called, as Ransom calls it, the customary. Mann's is a more worldly and dynamic sense of myth than Ransom's, and certainly more worldly and dynamic than Jung's or Eliot's. Mann's myths are mythologies, his-torical practices iterating a presumably prior truth by reiterating it, true or not, in the flesh and blood of the future.

Mythic and historicist at once, Mann's understanding of myth apprehends what is universal in it by apprehending what is particular to it. Myths are particular to particular cultures; it is their similar use by all cultures that is universal, a praxis not a pulpit. Mann's is an extraordinarily cautious handling of Freud. It grasps myth and history alike in their interrelation rather than as distinct. Each animates the other in a surprising structure that accounts for one by virtue of its production by the other. Instinct has been banished from the proceedings. So has a real mythical past. Whatever past we have is available to us only by means of its repetition in—and as—myth. Identification with myth sustains both cul-ture and the individual. It is also what sustains myth. Mythic identification is, from the point of view of a transcendental myth criticism, an oxymoron; myth puts its stamp on the individual. From Mann's historicist point of view, mythic identification is a chiasmus, an active process in which myth and individual cross over into one another. Mann offers his *Joseph* novels as an example, par-ticularly the covenant there between God and Abraham. Abraham, says Mann, "is in a sense the father of God" (420), although, because of it, the customary wisdom that the reverse is true also prevails. The reasoning is the same. Abra-ham is God's father because Abraham recognizes God as his father.

This kind of Hegelian moment is everywhere in Freud (see, for example, in Eng-lish, Sussman 1982). Mann does not say so, nor, as a rule, does Freud himself. As my reading of narcissism will show, however, recognition is everything in psychoanalysis, and recognition is a two-way street. Mann's tone is both heroic and hilarious:

> The bond, it is stated, is made in the interest of both, to the end of their common sanctification. Need human and need divine here entwine until it is hard to say whether it was the human or the divine that took the initiative. In any case the arrangement shows that the holiness of man and the holiness of God constituted a two-fold process, one part being most intimately bound up with the other. Wherefore else, one asks, should there be a bond at all? (1936, 420)

Mann's double reading of Freud and his apprehension of Freud's very particular dialectic of survival through representation serve as both a challenge and a warning to the "future" of Freud in his essay's title. Neither a purveyor of the depths nor an unironic rationalist, Freud endlessly calculates the differences between the two stances. As with the psyche, this is Freud's own labor. He is always in both places at the same time.

"The mechanism of the trap"

Mann's perspicacity is almost too subtle, a science of reading rather than a religious or philosophical enthusiasm. The paradoxes of mythic identification are easily misread. Mann is not alone, of course, in recognizing their dangers, even if he is the first to be so clear about what they are. W. H. Auden's "Psychology and Art To-day," published in 1935, just a year before Mann's birthday lecture, offers a similar caution, although more modestly. The time is also right in Anglophone letters to begin the adjustment in how to celebrate Freud. Like Mann, Auden returns us to the path that will lead us back to Freud's insistence on language and time rather than on myth and transcendence. Like Mann, Auden reminds us of the difference rather than the similarity between the symbolic labor of the neurotic and that of the poet. Although Auden mentions in passing the use by criticism of certain Freudian notions and the use by the Surrealists of an associational writing "resembling the procedure in the analyst's consulting-room," he is interested in a commonsense version of what interests Mann: "To understand the mechanism of the trap: The scientist and the artist" (1935, 335). This is the "trap" that is Mann's subject, although on a far grander scale. Auden's tone fluctuates between a moving appreciation of Freud and a parody of the reductive side of Freud that promotes the kinship of lunatic, lover, and poet. By 1935, this latter kind of Freudianism has, it appears, already been popularized beyond seriousness. Auden's reservations about the ease with which art and neurosis, poetry and untrammeled spontaneity, have been joined in the public imagination anticipate, as do Mann's, Trilling's definitive account of the problem in "Art and Neurosis" (1945).

Auden is willing, however, to accept Freud's notion of the artist as someone immersed in fantasy, as his citation from the *Introductory Lectures* attests (1935, 333–34). But with Freud, says Auden, what separates the artist from the neurotic is that the artist, as Freud himself puts it, "finds a way back to reality," thanks above all to his "mysterious ability to mould his particular material" (333–34). Even in dreams, there is already a touch of poetry beyond the simple exercise of wish-fulfillment, since in the dream there is "something which resembles art much more closely": it is "constructive, and, if you like, moral" (336). It is a "picture," says Auden of his sample dream—that of a potential morphine addict whose dreaming suggests a flirtation with addiction rather than a capitulation to it—"of the balance of interest" (336). Insisting as he does on the workmanlike or "constructive" side of dream and art alike, Auden takes "the automatic element" of fantasy and its link to a notion of poetry as "inspiration" as only part of the process, as what is simply "given" (336). Against it he counterposes both the rhetorical exactitudes of the dream and the conscious technical labor of poetry. "Misappropriated" as Freud has been "by irrationalists eager to escape their conscience" (341)—Lawrence and Gide are his prime examples—Auden insists that the artist, like the individual, must fashion and transform what is simply "given": "instinct" on the level of life, the "racial property" of myth and symbol on the level of "artistic medium" (337). The neurotic, like the poor artist, succumbs to fantasy in a parody of the late Romantic notion of inspiration, while the successful artist, like the healthy person, recognizes the obligation to shape, with craft and consciousness, what has been bequeathed by history and instinct. Reversing, as has Mann, the enthusiasm for surrender to primary process, Auden accents the secondary-process prerogatives of craft and reason instead. Auden veers toward the ego psychologists in his notion that conscious craftmanship informs both poetry and personality, and so disavows a dependence on daemonization or even inspiration. Like Mann, Auden rights the balance in the history of Freud's reception, and adumbrates in the process, as Hyman and Marcus have, the antithetical and schismatic traditions that structure both psychoanalytic tradition and the traditions of modern literature and criticism.

Auden's paramount insistence on "words" rather than symbols (337) as the poet's fundamental materials translates into an assertion that art and psychoanalysis are not mythical reenactments of eternal instinctual patterns, but are "particular stories of particular people and experiences" (341). What separates Auden from the classical modernism of Eliot, Pound, or, presumably, Joyce is obvious. Representation is a matter of place and history, not of myth and transcendence. Auden's notion of psychoanalysis as a discourse about language and particularity aligns him instead with that strand of Anglophone modernism in Katherine Mansfield, Willa Cather, and Virginia Woolf that celebrates and sanctifies the quotidian. I will describe this kind of modernism at some length in Chapter 4, along with the equally different modernisms of Lawrence and Eliot.

Symbolic action

Kenneth Burke's "Freud—and the Analysis of Poetry" makes clear what is at stake in Mann and Auden alike. Published in 1939, the year of Freud's death, it shows how Freud's reception history switches overtly from myth to symbol, from libido to language. Indeed, this same shift also marks the shift that Burke himself represents in the history of modern criticism. His notion of "symbolic action" prefigures both semiotics and performance theory, including a notion of the materiality of the signifier. Like Mann and Auden, Burke wishes to consider "the analogous features" in psychoanalysis and aesthetics, and the "margin of overlap" between them: "The acts of the neurotic," says Burke, using his own terms to make a wonderfully efficient summary of earlier opinion, "are symbolic acts" (1939, 261). Noting Freud's work to be "full," as it is, "of paradoxes" (260), Burke goes to the heart of the interpretative rift we have traced in the reading of Freud. It abides within Freud himself. It is, he says, "a distinction between what I should call an essentializing mode of interpretation and a mode that stresses proportion of ingredients" (261). At the start of his argument, Burke assigns Freud, as a scientist, to the first of these positions:

> If one found a complex of, let us say, seven ingredients in a man's motiva-tion, the Freudian tendency would be to take one of these as the essence of the motivation and to consider the other six as sublimated variants. We could imagine, for instance, manifestations of sexual incompetence accompanying a conflict in one's relations with his familiars and one's relations at the office. The proportional strategy would involve the study of these three as a cluster. The motivation would be synonymous with the interrelationships among them. But the essentializing strategy would, in Freud's case, place the emphasis upon the sexual manifestation, as a causal ancestry of the other two.
>
> This essentializing strategy is linked with a normal ideal of science: to "explain the complex in terms of the simple." This ideal almost vows one to select one or another motive from a cluster and interpret the others in terms of it. (261–62)

And in Freud, says Burke, "the sexual wish, or libido, is the basic category" (263), the motive that psychoanalysis selects from the cluster and endows with exclu-sive explanatory power. Or does it?

Now comes the decisive addition that Burke brings to the history of Freud's literary reception. It arrives as a critical anecdote. An impromptu examina-tion of "bodily posture," says Burke, makes it clear that the same posture in two individuals may express two entirely different experiences of "dejection." "The details of experience behind A's dejection may be vastly different from the details of experience behind B's dejection, yet both A and B may fall into the same bodily posture in expressing their dejection" (264). The same "posture" or symbol, in other words, may have vastly different determinations, hence vastly different meanings, depending on the context in which each emerges. And psychoanalysis, implies Burke, can hardly be immune to this critique.

But how can that be? This very critique is its own central activity. As it turns out, of course, this is precisely, says Burke, Freud's own argument against symbolism or "absolute content" (265) in *The Interpretation of Dreams*, even though it coexists uneasily there with his use of the symbolic method and its system of fixed meanings (4:105, 5:353). Hence when Burke turns to this crucial interpretative topos in Freud himself, he finds that Freud is no longer simply the reductive, essentializing scientist, but also a proportionalist:

> Freud explicitly resisted the study of motivation by way of symbols. He distinguished his own mode of analysis from the symbolic by laying stress upon free association. That is, he would begin the analysis of a neurosis without any preconceived notion as to the absolute meaning of any image that the patient might reveal in the account of a dream. His procedure involved the breaking-down of the dream into a set of fragments, with the analyst then inducing the patient to improvise associations on each of these fragments in turn. And afterward, by charting recurrent themes, he would arrive at the crux of the patient's conflict.
>
> Others (particularly Stekel), however, proposed a great short cut here. They offered an absolute content for various items of imagery. (265)

Freud himself, Burke concludes, "fluctuates in his search for essence" (266). And to situate this fluctuation in relation to literature, Burke shows us exactly why the proportional mode of interpretation—nonscientific and non-mythic as it is—is crucial to both psychoanalysis (recall *Ratten*) and to the distinguishing feature of poetic or literary language when it is compared to other modes of language, particularly the language of science:

> The examination of a poetic work's internal organization would bring us nearer to a variant of the typically Freudian free-association method than to the purely symbolic method toward which he subsequently gravitated.
>
> The critic should adopt a variant of the free-association method. One obviously cannot invite an author, especially a dead author, to oblige him by telling what the author thinks of when the critic isolates some detail or other for improvisation. But what he can do is to note the context of imagery and ideas in which an image takes its place. He can also note, by such analysis, the kinds of evaluations surrounding the image of a crossing; for instance, is it an escape from or a return to an evil or a good, etc.? Until finally, by noting the ways in which this crossing behaves, what subsidiary imagery accompanies it, what kind of event it grows out

of, what kind of event grows out of it ... one grasps its significance as motivation. And there is no essential motive offered here. The motive of the work is equated with the structure of interrelationships within the work itself. (267)

So it is at the "dream level," says Burke, that the "Freudian coordinates come closest to the charting of the logic of poetic structure" (273). This is not the imprecise world of myth or symbol, even the world of what Auden calls "words," but the no-nonsense world of technique. In a startling anticipation of the most prophetic accents of Trilling's "Freud and Literature" (Trilling's essay appeared in its original form only a year after Burke's), Burke finds the rhetoric of mind and poetry to be not just similar but virtually identical. Predominant in both are the two functions in the dream-work that Freud calls "condensation" and "displacement," functions that are, as Trilling will tell us, no less than the rhetorical tropes metaphor and metonymy. Roman Jakobson's description of this identity in 1956, and its influence on Lacan, is, one can see, well anticipated by American criticism:

Condensation ... deals with the respects in which house in a dream may be more than house, or house plus. And displacement deals with the way in which house may be other than house, or house minus. ... One can understand the resistance to both of the emphases. It leaves no opportunity for a house to be purely and simply a house—and whatever we may feel about it as regards dreams, it is a very disturbing state of affairs when transferred to the realm of art. (277)

Here, of course, the poem as dream is the same as the poem as chart, to use Burke's word, since dream and poem alike are plotted within a common network or system—a chart or table of combinations—whose resources are deployed according to Freud's two ruling tropes, and whose structures, both psychical and semantic, are those of language itself. Moreover, the linguistic rather than grossly symbolic character of the analogous systems of psyche and text or poem precludes from the start anything but a proportional or variable notion of psychical and poetic meaning alike: "The Freudian emphasis on the pun," says Burke, "brings it about that something can only be in so far as it is something else" (282). This "something else" is not, of course, a fixed and final end to interpretation, like an "essentializing" notion of either myth or science. Rather, it is a notion of motive or cause as a "cluster" (278) of "structural interrelationships" (279). Each term gains its meaning from its relation to other terms in the cluster rather than from its relation to a direct and self-sufficient ground of truth or nature outside it. "Even the scientific essay," Burke concludes of Freud, "would have its measure of choreography" (283).

"A science of tropes"

If Burke is the conceptual centerpiece in the American reception of Freud as literature, then Trilling is its dramatic one. Like no other writer save Freud himself, Trilling's sympathies are so wide that they can admit both sides of the Freud that Mann has described. Trilling does, however, choose between them, celebrating one side of the opposition in 1940 and the other fifteen years later. It is to Trilling's later essay, the 1955 "Freud: Within and Beyond Culture," that we should turn first. This is the essay originally published earlier that year as a separate volume under the title *Freud and the Crisis of Our Culture*, and included in the 1965 collection *Beyond Culture*. It stands in the line of Lawrence just as surely as the 1940 "Freud and Literature" stands in the line of Mann. Moreover, each essay dramatizes within itself the historical split in the interpretation of Freud that they also represent as an opposed pair.

Although Trilling parts with Mann, in "Art and Neurosis" especially, on the question of a link between knowledge and disease, he is at the same time sympathetic to Mann's fascination with the night side of Freud's thought, and to the notion that it contains a secret affirmation. As it turns out, Trilling is indeed preparing an affirmation instead of a caution. But it has a remarkable irony, and one that shows that what Mann fears has a built-in safety device. For Trilling, Freud's biological notion of the id embodies the Freudian insistence that the Cartesian profile of man that identifies being with consciousness is a wishful myth. But even though this deepest layer of Freud's thought sees consciousness as the object of forces greater than itself and outside its control, the fact that Freud imagines these forces as natural or biological—as outside or beyond culture—is the pathway to the discovery of a genuinely reassuring idea. For the abyss, with its horrors, says Trilling, is the site of man's moral salvation even if it also provides the ground of his suffering. To explain why, Trilling presents what is probably the most eloquent defense of Freud as Romantic modernist in the English language: "He needed to believe that there was some point at which it was possible to stand beyond the reach of culture. ... It is our way of coming close to the idea of Providence" (1955, 93, 94). Reacting in advance to the inevitable response (especially in the days of neo-Freudianism and its sociological reductions of sexuality), Trilling adds: "It is so far from being a reactionary idea that it is actually a liberating idea. It proposes to us that culture is not all-powerful. It suggests that there is a residue of human quality, beyond the reach of cultural control, and that this residue of human quality, elemental as it may be, serves to bring culture itself under criticism and keeps it from being absolute" (98). The primacy of the biological abyss in Freud's thinking means that man does not belong to culture alone. If culture represses, denies man his freedom, the biological or instinctual core of being that it represses still springs forward to speak for man even when man can no longer speak for himself.

Trilling's Romantic valorization of the abyss is in the service of a notion of self or personality that exists apart from culture, that retains an essence of being that culture can never compromise. If "there is a hard, irreducible, stubborn core of biological urgency, and biological necessity, and biological *reason*, that culture cannot reach and that reserves the right, which sooner or later it will exercise, to judge the culture and resist and revise it" (99), then "there is," says Trilling, "a sanction beyond the culture" (101). The great peroration follows: "This intense conviction of the existence of a self apart from culture is, as culture well knows, its noblest and most generous achievement" (102). Trilling gives the game away, however, in that famous sentence. For the notion of a self beyond culture is, alas, itself an achievement of culture, albeit its "noblest" one, and, therefore, like any cultural product, a trope or fiction. This is the irony, and this, ironically, is the salvation. We get to have it both ways, by necessity.

In the earlier "Freud and Literature," the question, put simply, is whether there is indeed a self, a "core" of being beyond culture. Is Freud's theory of the drive a biological theory of instinct, or is it a cultural theory of merely human indoctrination into the order of things? For the Trilling of "Freud and Literature," a Lawrentian assertion of the instinctual basis of psychoanalysis is not only too close to the false popular notion of "art and neurosis"; it also tries to limit Freud's double vision to a single one. Lawrence's instinctualism, like Trilling's own saving belief in biology fifteen years later on, is in fact to be identified with the "naïve" positivism of the early Freud: "of claiming for his theories a perfect correspondence with an external reality" (1940, 39). Instinctivism and scientism alike presume a way out of language and history by an appeal to an unchanging biology. Whether or not this is Freud's own view of science we shall have to wait to see in Chapters 2 and 3. Here, although Trilling distinguishes between the "practical reality" the working analyst must discern with "a certain firm crudeness," and a notion of "reality" evolved under conditions of "theoretical refinement" (41), he places both kinds of reality, finally, in the service of what should be called a poetic and social rather than a scientific and universal real. For the reality to which Freud appeals—even at times despite himself, says Trilling—is "the reality of social life and of value, conceived and maintained by the human mind and will. Love, morality, honor, esteem—these are the components of a created reality. If we are to call art an illusion then we must call most of the activities and satisfactions of the ego illusions; Freud, of course, has no desire to call them that" (42). What has occurred here, of course, is an implicit redefinition of the contents and mechanism of the Freudian unconscious. We have moved from Lawrence to Mann, from Hyman to Marcus, in the blink of an eye. Although Trilling will, at the close of the essay, attempt a compromise vision in which man is "an inextricable tangle of culture and biology" (54), here, at the heart of the essay's genuinely radical moments, it is culture alone that is the decisive if silent term.

What follows is a Burkean corrective to the notion of a fixed, symbolically apprehended meaning, on the level of motive, in the psychoanalysis of a work of art like *Hamlet*: "We must rather object to the conclusions of Freud and Dr. Jones on the ground that their proponents do not have an adequate conception of what an artistic meaning is." Trilling is adamant about it. "There is no single meaning to any work of art; this is true not merely because it is better that it should be true, that is, because it makes art a richer thing, but because historical and personal experience show it to be true" (46). Rejecting the notion that the truth of psychoanalysis, the truth of the unconscious, resides in an indwelling "reality" to which Shakespeare's play "stands in the relation that a dream stands to the wish that generates it and from which it is separable," Trilling suggests, along the lines of Burke's argument, that both mind and poem acquire their meanings in some other way. Like the dream in relation to the dreamer, *Hamlet*, says Trilling, "is not merely the product of Shakespeare's thought, it is the very instrument of his thought" (49). This is Trilling's notion of the unconscious as the repository, not so much of an instinctual payload of raw nature—a "reality" or essence like that which motivates *Hamlet* in Jones's celebrated reduction (1910, 1949)—as of the fictions, the "created reality" of the social order and of culture. Of course, when Trilling makes the famous claim that "of all mental systems, the Freudian psychology is the one which makes poetry indigenous to the very constitution of the mind," makes the mind "a poetry-making organ" (1940, 49), he is less concerned with the factor of poetic craft than he is with something else: the identification of both the object of Freudian analysis—the unconscious mind—and the Freudian text with the necessary fiction of language. Even "science," says Trilling in his later essay on Freud, "is organized improbability, or organized fantasy" (1955, 81).

It is at this point that Trilling can build to the boldest and most precise of interpretative announcements, the prophetic words that Bloom will celebrate in "Freud and the Poetic Sublime" (1978), and that Burke, in his attentiveness to condensation and displacement, has brought us to the brink of just a year before:

> Freud has not merely naturalized poetry; he has discovered its status as a pioneer settler, and he sees it as a method of thought. Often enough he tries to show how, as a method of thought, it is unreliable and ineffective for his own science, as when he speaks of the topography of the mind and tells us with a kind of defiant apology that the metaphors of space relationship which he is using are really most inexact since the mind is not a thing of space at all, but that there is no other way of conceiving the difficult idea except by metaphor. In the eighteenth century Vico spoke of the metaphorical imagistic language of the early stages of culture; it was

left to Freud to discover how, in a scientific age, we still feel and think
in figurative formulations, and to create, what psychoanalysis is, a science of tropes, of metaphor and its variants, synecdoche and metonymy.
(1940, 50)

"We still feel and think in figurative formations," says Trilling, because we
still feel and think through "those mechanisms by which art makes its effects,
particularly the mechanisms of language" (50–51). For Trilling, as for Lacan,
presumably unknown to him as to other American Freudians this early, the
unconscious is not structured like a language; it *is* language, in the particular
arrangement with it that each of us makes. "The unconscious of society," writes
Trilling, "may be said to have been imagined before the unconscious of the individual." Freud shows us—the words are memorable—"how entirely implicated
in culture we all are ... how the culture suffuses the remotest parts of the individual mind, being taken in almost literally," the argument concludes, "with the
mother's milk" (1955, 90, 91).

Deconstructing the drive

Despite preconceptions, it is hardly a jump, then, from Trilling's "Freud and
Literature" to the world of French Freud, premised as both are on the decisive
function of culture and language in the very constitution of subjectivity, and on
a notion of the unconscious as a web of ideological determinations that fashions
the self from the ground up (see Althusser 1964). Jacques Derrida, however, is
not to be identified with the work of Lacan (for their presumable differences, see
Derrida 1975), even though a sympathy for the notion of the Freudian unconscious as language is Derrida's starting point. In "Freud and the Scene of Writing" (1967), Derrida wishes to distinguish writing from language at large, and, in
the process, formulate a precise definition of literary language as Freud himself
conceives it, and as Freud also practices it. Derrida summarizes our reception
history and brings it to a head by criticizing what, in Burke's vocabulary, we
might call an "essentializing" notion of Freud—a notion of the unconscious in
particular as what Burke himself might call a "God term" (1939, 263), or what
Ransom refers to as a "gospel truth" (1924, 161). Instead, claims Derrida, Freud's
real achievement lies precisely in the rupture or break his work enacts with all
such metaphysical quests for essence or natural "core." What Freud discovers,
says Derrida, is just the reverse of a notion of the unconscious like Lawrence's
as a plentitude of instinct represented by myth or symbol, and which is directly
translatable, as a dream element may seem to be, back into its fixed natural or
sexual meaning in a world beyond language. This view of things is, of course,
what Derrida calls "logocentrism"—a notion of meaning as a full measure or
transcript of a truth in nature and in objects that language merely apprehends

and conveys. Rather, says Derrida, neither language nor the unconscious signify in that way. For Derrida, the same is also true for spoken speech despite its misleading and only apparently privileged connection with voice and breath. It is Freud's particular achievement to have made such a discovery even before Saussure, and to show the way language and the psyche really work.

To call the unconscious language is to make a precise but occluded claim, says Derrida. By turning to Freud's earliest attempt at representing mental functioning in the 1895 *Project*, Derrida shows that Freud's linguistic metaphors are not only present in his work from the start and that they will eventually overthrow all naïvely biologistic, instinctual, even neurological metaphors in his later work. He also suggests that the metaphors Freud draws from language, both here and in *The Interpretation of Dreams* five years later, are drawn not so much from language generally as from one special—or apparently special—subdivision of it: writing, "nonphonetic writing" in particular, such as ideograms or hieroglyphs.

What is especially powerful about writing as a metaphor for representing the unconscious—for representing, if you will, the way it is inscribed by culture—is that it represents even Freud's primary process as a writing that is cut off, from the start, from any connection to the kind of plenitude of instinct with which Freudian primary process is customarily associated. Here Derrida argues against both Lawrence's notion of the unconscious as raw, and Freud's own neurological metaphors in the *Project* that function as his version of an ideal language capable of grasping the "living, full speech" of psychical energy in the mimetic discourse of a positivist science (1967, 199).

Instead, Derrida argues, Freud gives us a second notion of the unconscious along with the quantitative or neurological one. It is a notion of the unconscious as a field of memory traces, constituted by a kind of psychical writing. In the *Project*, Freud describes the origin or emergence of these memory traces or writings not as tokens of experience that are added to or engraved on a self-sufficient natural "core" of unconscious instinct that grows progressively conscious over time. Rather, the origin of the first memory traces can only be accounted for by the hypothesis of a sudden catastrophic moment or jolt that sets the whole psyche into play at once. "Life is already threatened," says Derrida, "by the origin of the memory which constitutes it" (202). The psyche originates, in other words, at the moment it begins to resist stimuli (here Freud's allegory of the birth of the ego in *Beyond the Pleasure Principle* is Derrida's implicit allusion), at which point a difference emerges between such force or stimulation and the organism's resistance to it. This difference separates self and world while constituting each in relation to the other. It is this difference that opens up what Freud calls, in Alan Bass's translation, a "breaching" (*Bahnung*, a pathway, or what Strachey calls "facilitation"), a fracturing that lays down paths or traces on the psyche's surface. The psyche comes into being only at the moment that it begins the process of resistance (202n2).

The *Project*, however, has no satisfactory model with which to go on to represent how the psyche stores these traces or pathways as memory. Storage is, after all, the central problem. The psyche must stay open to new stimulation. Where are these memory traces to be housed? It is at this point that the essay's real trajectory comes into focus. Derrida's aim here is to trace Freud's thirty-year search (from the *Project* to the brief but, for Derrida, crucial essay of 1925, the "Note upon the 'Mystic Writing-Pad'") for a model or metaphor that can account for and represent the functioning of the mental apparatus in the two separate but linked registers of unconscious memory and conscious perception. The problem, as the *Project* lays it out, is to find a figure capable of representing both processes in a single stroke: the constant ability of consciousness to receive fresh impressions and the equal and constant ability of the unconscious to store the traces they leave. No single system can do both jobs at once, since a glut or saturation point is inevitable. Hence the search for a metaphor.

The metaphor, however, cannot be found until Freud clarifies his notion of that psychical writing known as memory. Memory is not a thing or a substance, says Derrida, but the difference between one pathway or "breaching" and another, an apparently simple difference of intensity that distinguishes one trace from another, and so elaborates a field of memory even as it differentiates one memory from another. This vision of memory as a set of differences or traces is precisely what Burke means by a proportional rather than an essentialist view of how both language and the psyche operate—by means of the relations, the differences as well as the similarities, among the elements in a given cluster of language or (what amounts in certain ways to the same thing) of memory proper. Derrida simply draws out the epistemological implications of the proportional view of the "writing" that is the common medium of both literature and the psyche.

Finding a suitable representation for the double and simultaneous psychical systems of memory and fresh reception will also, says Derrida, solve the problem of the psyche's origin, of the origin of primary process or unconscious thought that the *Project* can imagine only as having happened in a single moment. The notion of an origin requires, of course, such a notion of a single, originating moment, and yet the origin Freud describes in the *Project* is, as we have seen, a function of the relation "between *two* forces," as Derrida points out (202). Derrida has already found the solution in the structure of his own double reading of the early Freud—past and present are reciprocal, in both reading and psychical life. "Resistance itself is possible only if the opposition of forces"—of stimulation and resistance—"lasts and is repeated at the beginning" (202). But how can "the beginning" be a repetition? This, alas, is a key Derridean paradox, the paradox that Derrida calls "originary repetition," a notion that disallows, on Freud's own authority, the primariness of the primary process itself, and so disallows any notion of the unconscious as one somehow representing the primacy of nature, whether neurological or mythic in its vocabulary. "Primariness," says Derrida, becomes for Freud a "theoretical fiction" (203). It is—as it is in Mann—the function of its own repetition.

As he moves from the *Project* to *The Interpretation of Dreams*, Derrida shifts his attention to Freud's predominant metaphors for the dream-work. Chief among them are metaphors of "non-linguistic writing," of "a model of writing irreducible to speech" whose figures include "hieroglyphics, pictographic, ideogrammatic, and phonetic elements" (209). These figures are important because they distinguish the genuinely Freudian method of interpretation—Burke has alerted us to this—from the method borrowed from Stekel that simply decodes dream elements as though they were fixed universal symbols rather than the tokens of particular lives. Derrida calls on Freud himself to make this clear: "My procedure," says Freud, "is not so convenient as the popular decoding which translates any given piece of a dream's content by a fixed key. I, on the contrary, am prepared to find that the same piece of content may conceal a different meaning when it occurs in various people or in various contexts" (4:105). Freud even calls on "Chinese script," notes Derrida—ideogrammatic script, which has no bond with the mythology of natural speech that accompanies the spoken word—to illustrate and insure the connection between proportional or contextual interpretation and a notion of writing that is not linked to oral speech: Dream symbols, says Freud, "frequently have more than one or even several meanings, and, as with Chinese script, the correct interpretation can only be arrived at on each occasion from the context" (5:353). The reason universal symbol-translation will not do, as Burke has already suggested, is that it "presupposes," in Derrida's words, "a text which would be already there, immobile" (1967, 211)—a text of truth behind the dream symbols to which they would univocally refer, rather than meanings that are apprehended "on each occasion from the context," from their relationships with other elements in it.

Hence by the celebrated route of dream interpretation—"the royal road to the unconscious," as Freud himself describes it in *The Interpretation of Dreams*—Derrida radically criticizes a notion of the unconscious as a cauldron of seething natural energies or even as a locus of impulses that can be apprehended, measured, quantified by science as though they were really there: "There is then no unconscious truth to be discovered by virtue of [its] having been written elsewhere," says Derrida, whether by nature or any other determinable source. "The unconscious text is already a weave of pure traces ... a text nowhere present consisting of archives"—of memory traces—"which are *always already* transcriptions. ... Everything begins with reproduction" (211). Here, of course, Derrida alludes to his notion of the origin of the psyche itself as a repetition, although what is crucial in both dream interpretation and any meditation on origins, says Derrida, is that in both cases the object of the interpretative quest is always deferred. For if writing, whether psychical or literary, functions as a proportional system of differences—as a system of comparisons and contrasts among the elements of language that alone sets those elements apart from one another—then neither can writing refer to anything more than what is produced by such operations. Both the meaning of dreams, then, and the origin of the psyche must be deferred, if by "meaning" and "origin" one means the grasp of an immanent, eternal, or authentic essence in instinct, say, or sexuality, whether in Lawrence's version or in that of Freud the neurological quantifier.

Derrida's notion of deferral is linked not only to his Saussurean notion of language as a system of writing or differences, but also—he says so directly—to *Nachträglichkeit*, or deferred action. Deferred action, like *différance*, means, as we have seen, that the past or, indeed, any object of memory or language, comes into being only after the fact, as a function of the place language or memory requires it to hold. And not only is the past or the linguistic object always reconstituted belatedly by the operations of memory and reading. The present, too, is always an effect of repetition, since the moment can be grasped, understood as such, only in relation to something else as well. Deferred action has even structured Derrida's own double reading of the *Project*. It is why Derrida's developmental allegory of a Freud who "finds" a model suitable to his needs only in 1925 is a bit suspicious. Too much of this later Freud is already in place in the *Project*. Does Freud develop, one wants to know, or are his ideas already worked out early in his career? Is the "neurological" Freud the positivist Freud that the later, poetic Freud leaves behind? Or is the neurological Freud a Freud who already has the theory of Derridean *différance* he needs to represent the psyche as a site of storage and delay? This is a good instance of the structure of Derrida's own wit as well as of Freud's own. Only a knowledge of the later Freud allows Derrida to get this much out of the early *Project*. Deferred action will much preoccupy us in the following pages. It is what allows Derrida to read Freud both diachronically and synchronically. Derrida's topical reading is actually put in place by the developmental allegory that it deconstructs. But this is no misreading of Freud. It is the very mirror of psychoanalytic process: The early is put in place by the late. The specifically literary nature of deferred action will emerge in the elaborate discussion of it that comes in the 1918 case of the Wolf Man ("From the History of an Infantile Neurosis"). Freud's patient, as I will show in Chapter 2, "remembers" the primal scene in his parents' bedroom only by means of the knowledge about sex that his subsequent experience bestows on him. Whether the primal scene of parental coitus really took place remains for Freud an open and finally irrelevant question.

Freud's search for a proper way of representing the double system of the psyche, then, is also a search for a proper way of representing reference in language itself. Language, like the psyche, functions on two levels simultaneously—the level of perpetually fresh speech or writing and the level of memory, each one dependent on the other. This epistemological play has as its counterpart not only *récit* and *histoire* in narratology, but also the "mutative" play, as Strachey calls it (1934, 369), at work in the transferential symbolizations between patient and analyst in the analytic session.

For Derrida, Freud's search for a model to represent the psychical apparatus remains waylaid until he can find one that will not simply use the metaphor of writing, but one that will also *be*, as he puts it, a "writing machine" (1967, 221)—until, that is, Freud can describe his notion of writing in a way that also demonstrates it. Whether or not this is already the case with the *Project*, Derrida insists on his developmental allegory. The mystic writing-pad is just such a "writing machine"—a literary machine—the self-erasing pad with two surfaces that is still a children's toy today. Here the "contradictory requirement" of the *Project* is at last met: "a double system contained," says Derrida, "in a single differentiated apparatus: a perpetually available innocence and an infinite reserve of traces have at last been reconciled" (223).

Once again, too, the strains of *Beyond the Pleasure Principle* are implicit as Derrida suggests the precision of the writing-pad as a metaphor for the psyche in its full Freudian profile: "There is no writing which does not devise some means of protection, *to protect against itself*, against the writing by which the 'subject' is himself threatened as he lets himself be written: *as he exposes himself*" (224). This is a remarkable description and placement, or displacement, of the Cartesian subject in its new and peculiar relation to the unconscious, the latter always closing up—by definition—in order to produce its more familiar counterpart negatively.

This is also, of course, a description of writing itself, especially literary language as it distinguishes itself from the language of a positivist science. Here, in fact, Freud requires the supposedly literal language of science to acknowledge something surprisingly frank: its own status as metaphor, as literary language in its own right. The whole field of psychoanalytic inquiry is a field of writing, *récit* and *histoire* alike. Freud does not just describe the scene of writing as a phenomenon of the psyche. "Freud's language is *caught up* in it," says Derrida. "Freud performs for us the scene of writing," reduplicates the structure of the psyche in the structure of his own text (229). Why? Because his writing, like the psychical text that it describes, can only try, endlessly and without success, to designate a genuine beginning, an authentic externality or real immediacy—nature, instinct, biology—just as the psyche itself is always unable to recover its own beginnings before repression. This is not a problem for Freud. This is the point.

Here Derrida introduces a late Freudian concept that links this structure with that of "originary repetition." In the beginning, he says, there can only have been repression itself, even before the emergence of the drive. This Freud calls "primal repression." "Primal repression" is the only concept that can account for the birth of writing, whether psychical or literary. For we can only presume or deduce, without verification, a first barrage of stimuli from the outside world as the event that sets repression or protection from stimuli into motion in the first place, and that, in the difference between them, begins the process of path-breaking known alternately as memory or writing. What we do know for certain, however, is that there cannot be one without the other—no force without resistance, no stimulation without repression—because each term requires the other in order to be coherent, each notion coming into being, rhetorically at any rate, by means of its difference from the other. It is only repression that can, in the final analysis, account for drive or even stimulation, since the tokens of repression are the only evidence we have for what is unconscious.

Repression, then, comes first, before drive or instinct, much as the Wolf Man's later knowledge of sex actually precedes his earlier knowledge of parental coitus. For Derrida, what Freud the scientist dramatizes is not something that is also literary, but something that is literary from the start. Indeed, says Derrida, it dramatizes Freud's notion of literary language and his presumable object as one and the same thing: "A *becoming-literary of the literal*" (230).

Past and present in poems and in persons

Published a decade after Derrida's essay, in 1978, Harold Bloom's "Freud and the Poetic Sublime" brings the definition of Freud as literary to an exact focus. If, as Derrida claims, Freud's language is itself implicated in the kind of psychical writing it describes, Bloom shows how writing as a whole, especially literary writing, is likewise a ratio of forces in contention. Its dramas of influence redouble those of the psyche. Despite the "antithetical modes" of science and poetry (1978, 188), says Bloom (Trilling's "Freud and Literature," he adds, is still the classic demonstration of the problem), Freud is, finally, a poet regardless of his scientific intentions, since "he cannot invoke the trope of the Unconscious"—for the unconscious is, as Freud himself never fails to remind us, a hypothesis, a fiction, a trope—"as though he were doing more (or less) than the poet or critic does by invoking the trope of the Imagination, or than the theologian does by invoking the trope of the Divine" (189–90). And for Freud, the "most vital trope or fiction in his theory of the mind" is "the primary process," the original seat of the unconscious which, in Freud's later terminology, will be called the id (190).

But "to quarry" the poetic Freud for "theories of creativity," says Bloom, we need to study him, not in his reductive profile as psychoanalyst of art in the sense that Trilling deplores, but "where he himself is most imaginative" (192). For Bloom, this is principally the late phase of Freud's career that begins with *Beyond the Pleasure Principle*, moves to the 1925 essay "Negation" and the 1926 *Inhibitions, Symptoms and Anxiety*, and whose "climax," as Bloom puts it, is "Analysis Terminable and Interminable" in 1937. The centrality of *Beyond the Pleasure Principle* (Derrida's essay has begun to sketch it out) lies in its formulation, decisive for this entire late phase of Freud's career, says Bloom, of "the priority of anxiety over its stimuli" (192). The problem of repetition-compulsion that Freud interrogates at the start of the book stymies him because it is a factor in dreams, fantasy, and neurotic symptoms that does not accord with the wish-fulfillment theory that otherwise explains all three phenomena. Why one repeats a painful or fearful event troubles Freud because it may require a shift in assumption. His principal example of repetition-compulsion here is his portrait of his grandson playing a game with a spool, which he makes disappear behind his bed only to make it reappear again by pulling it back out. This, says Freud, is a repetition in fantasy of the daily comings and goings of the child's mother. Her departures can only be distressing to the child, and yet it is these moments of loss which the child, despite his distinct lack of pleasure, willfully repeats in his symbolic play. Trilling points out in "Freud and Literature" that the episode represents a deliberate attempt to promote "fear" so as to gain "active mastery" (1940, 52, 53) over it. Bloom takes this perspective further still by remarking that such behavior, especially on the part of children, is an attempt "to master a stimulus retroactively by first developing the anxiety." What is shocking is that this is "the *creation of anxiety*, and so cannot be considered a sublimation of any kind" (1978, 193). This intentional development of fear or anxiety, in other words, is not a reaction or resistance to an actual threat (in the case of Freud's grandson, the game proceeds even when the mother is at home, when the real threat of departure is absent), but an anxiety that precedes all threats. In the biological allegory of the birth of the ego that follows Freud's portrait of the child, this originary anxiety motivates what Freud has already named "primal repression," the "theoretical fiction" that sets the primary process in motion from the start.

What the portraits of Freud's grandson and the hypothetical birth of the ego share, then, is the exercise of repression—a primal repression—before there is anything to repress. If originary anxiety creates primal repression, primal repression, as Derrida has already suggested, creates the force that any repression requires so as to be what it is, a resistance to force. For Bloom, this force is the drive itself, which anxiety and primal repression install retroactively, belatedly (Bloom's way of translating *nachträglich*). It is a scenario of origins by which consciousness can imagine its beginnings as jolt or catastrophe, as the moment at which drive surprised it. The drive, that is, is propped on or against the repression that brings it into being after the fact, the fiction the psyche invents in order to account for and represent its own birth or origin. Or, to put it in the terms of Freud's "Negation," it is by means of its negation that drive as such emerges, as the resistance to its erasure that the notion of resistance itself requires in order to be what it is. This rhetoric of the psyche is a rhetoric of "contamination" or "crossing over," a graphic suggestion of the way drive and repression, drive and negation, each come into being by means of crossing or contaminating one another. As we read through Freud's career closely in the next chapter, we will see how the notion of primal repression unfolds, especially in "On Narcissism" (1914), where its prehistory lies.

There is, then, ample reason for Bloom to assent to Trilling's contention—and Lacan's—that psychoanalysis is a "science of tropes," and that the rhetoric it studies is the rhetoric of the defense mechanisms by means of which the ego establishes and sustains itself. Indeed, in Bloom's reading, the rhetoric of psychical defense is a rhetoric precisely because, in its attempt to turn away from stimuli or influence—to "trope" them, for the root meaning of "trope" is "turn"—the psyche in fact fashions the very thing it turns away from, creating drive, for example, by fleeing from it as though it were there. For Bloom, then, "drives *are* fictions," fictions on the level of both the psyche Freud describes and the Freudian rhetoric that describes it. Just as the drives are the psyche's originating fictions, they are also, says Bloom, Freud's own "enabling fictions" (1978, 210) as a writer. Hence the first of a series of formulations of the literary status of Freud's texts to emerge from Bloom's argument: The structure of the psyche and the structure of Freud's language match each other exactly. They are, in fact, one and the same. Freud's description of the psyche is really a description of his own writing. Like the belated and inferred emergence of the drive in the rhetoric—the defensive "troping"—of psychical action proper, what Freud calls "the unconscious" also emerges as a deferred effect of his own rhetoric, "a purely inferred division of the psyche," as Bloom reminds us, "an inference necessarily based only upon the supposed effects the unconscious has upon the way we think and act that can be *known*, that are available to consciousness" (194). Primal repression, then, is Freud's most literary trope, says Bloom, since it is the model, as Derrida has already implied, for the structure of literary reference itself: the retroactive installation of a referent which language situates, through rhetoric, outside of language, much as the defense or trope known as primal repression installs the drive retroactively, as a catastrophic beginning to the individual's life.

If the psychical text and the literary text are, for Freud, one and the same, then the psyche as Freud represents it should also provide us with some account of what Bloom calls the will-to-creativity in poetry. Hence a second literary mapping of the late Freud. If, in *Beyond the Pleasure Principle*, the purpose of the repetition-compulsion is "to master a stimulus retroactively by first developing the anxiety," the will-to-creativity in poetry, says Bloom, is also conditioned by the threat of "anteriority" (198), an earlier force that looms as a rearguard catastrophe for the poet, much as the drive does for the psyche. Bloom links this psychical structure in Freud to the literary notion of the Sublime, which Bloom defines as follows:

> As a literary idea, the Sublime originally meant a style of "loftiness," that is, of verbal power, of greatness or strength conceived agonistically, which is to say against all possible competition. But in the European Enlightenment, this literary idea was strangely transformed into a vision of the terror that could be perceived both in nature and in art, a terror uneasily allied with pleasurable sensations of augmented power, and even of narcissistic freedom, freedom in the shape of that wildness Freud dubbed "the omnipotence of thoughts," the greatest of all narcissistic illusions. (197)

Hence the Sublime, at least in post-Enlightenment poetry, is a "negative" moment, and rises out of an encounter with someone else's prior moment of negation.

How does Bloom manage to equate the catastrophic emergence of drive for psyche with the fear of a literary precursor in Freud's own writing? By identifying the notion of drive as Freud's own earlier achievement. This is a stunning moment of argument. Drive is an achievement that rises behind Freud now as a threat (especially if we regard *Trieb* as "instinct"), a threat Freud must defend against by revising his whole theory of the drives late in his career. Here the structure of Freud's mechanisms of mind matches the structure of his own texts in another, more elaborate way. If, in *Beyond the Pleasure Principle*, the force of drive threatens the very emergence of the psyche at its origin, then drive itself must be associated with death. And yet how is such a situation possible if drive is also Eros, the drive in its customary, pleasure-seeking role of instinct or libido? In order to free himself from this impasse, Freud invents the death drive. Here is a realm of mental functioning "beyond the pleasure principle." It solves the clinical problem of repetition-compulsion by turning it into a literary problem that can be surmounted with a new invention. The result is the surprising alliance of Eros with repression in a common struggle against the death instinct. The sexuality that culture represses is, as it turns out, bound to culture and repression for its very existence, since drive itself is only the effect of its contamination by a repression that presumes its force.

Bloom is therefore led to make two crucial identifications: The death instinct equals literal meaning and the life instinct equals figurative meaning. Why? Because the bond of Eros and repression that signifies their complicity in producing one another represents the mature Freud's "Sublime" moment of self-conscious achievement as a poet who knows unabashedly that his drives are fictions, rhetorical products of his own figurative language. Eros, then, stands for the notion of drive as fiction, as figure, bound to culture because it is a literary invention. The earlier Freud, by contrast, understands drive in a literal sense, in the sense that it is a real biological energy that science can hope to measure. This is also, argues Bloom, Freud's reading of himself. Thanatos or the death drive, then, stands in turn for Freud's notion of drive as a literally available store of libidinal energy or biological essence, the ideal of the early empiricist Freud that the later, poetic Freud wants to "wound" (211), as Bloom puts it, to "un-name" or disavow (212). He does so, says Bloom, by making his own earlier notion of drive as instinct "uncanny" or unfamiliar to himself, and so enters the Sublime in Bloom's precise, and "negative," sense: "that mode in which the poet, while expressing a previously repressed thought, desire, or emotion, is able to continue to defend himself against his own created image by disowning it" (204).

If the later Freud revises the early Freud by exchanging a notion of drive as quantifiable libido for a notion of drive as immeasurable fiction or trope, the process also includes a theory of literary language as distinct from the language of science, and one that justifies and sustains Freud's status as poet of the Sublime. This is the third focus to emerge in Bloom's essay, and it centers on the revision of the "economic" metaphor for psychical functioning that in the early Freud stands for the attempt to measure or quantify libido that the late Freud rejects. The late Freud, says Bloom, explicitly modifies his notion of the "*economic*" (208) functioning of the psyche from one that presumes an energy available in nature that can actually be measured or fixed to one that presumes no more than a set of relationships among forces that can be measured only proportionally, only in the relation of force to force, or, to use Mann's phrase, of "power for power." If Freud's late notion of economy is what Burke means by the proportional, Freud's early notion of economy is what Burke means by the "essentializing" mode of inquiry he has labeled scientific in the customary sense. Thus the late Freud becomes a poet by criticizing his earlier assumptions about language as a scientist. By abandoning the literal or essentializing language of empiricism—or, as Bloom puts it, by "wounding" (202) it by calling instinct death—Freud embraces instead the proportional or figurative language of literature, a style of language that presumes no stable referent in nature by which its figures may be verified or judged.

This new notion of the economic, says Bloom, allies Freud once again with the Sublime, this time through an exact link with Milton, Freud's favorite poet:

> To estimate the magnitude of such excitation is to ask the classical, agonistic question that is the Sublime, because the Sublime is always a comparison of two forces or beings, in which the agon turns on the answer to three queries: more? equal to? or less than? Satan confronting hell, the abyss, the new world, is still seeking to answer the questions that he set

for himself in heaven, all of which turn upon comparing God's force and his own. (208)

Thus, *Paradise Lost* is "the most Freudian text ever written" (207), says Bloom, not only because in it "temporality fully becomes identified with anxiety," but also because Freud's language shares with Milton's the same "economic" mechanism of signification, a purely relational one that relies only on the contrasts and comparisons among the elements of its own language to specify a world. Milton's poem measures *only* by proportion, never by recourse to fixed "symbolic" codes that can translate the size, for example, of Satan's spear. The reasons, of course, are the same for Milton as they are for Freud. Not only must prehistory, whether instinctual or creationist, be narrated by the fallen language of consciousness or of history proper; what is being described are, in both cases, also "enabling fictions" to begin with, things, quite literally, out of this world.

Beyond formalism

The dazzling use to which Freud has been put in recent years on the subjects of ideology (Žižek 1989), gender (Butler 1990), and race (Bhabha 1994) is testimony to the deeply social impulses in psychoanalysis to which Althusser's reading of Lacan was the first to testify. Less impressive than the use dialectically of Marx and Freud—it was structuralism that bridged the one-time gap between them—is that it is a very particular element in Freud that generates the insights of all three varieties of such a political criticism: identification. Identification is key to any social psychoanalysis after structuralism. And key to identification is its modality: representation. Social structures, in other words, are literary structures. At the very heart of the political is the aesthetic. However political Žižek, Butler, and Bhabha are, they also remain literary because their arguments require them to discuss how identification—a mode of representation—functions.

Representation is at the center not only of psychical life, but of social life. It is what joins the two, in an exact and common modality. Representation structures our biases and molds our hearts. Specifying its nature will preoccupy us throughout this study. If representation is the key to identification, then identification, as we will see, is also the key to understanding Freudian representation. It is its precondition, as it were, what requires and enables it. Our reading of both Freud's career and his sources will show how central it is to any estimation of a distinctly literary Freud. Studying narcissism will unpack its structure early; studying pornography will situate it more globally later on. Pornography will require us to ask questions about identification that will return us to both its distinctly social and its distinctly literary qualities. They have a common home in language, and in discourse at large. Freudian identification in particular, and

Freudian representation in general, are discursive formations that are continuous with, rather than distinct from, the language with which Freud describes them. It is only fitting that we turn at the close of this study to a critic whose usefulness now rivals Derrida's, Bakhtin—he will have been of help throughout—to forge a new and unlikely alliance that will expand our view of Freud and Bakhtin alike. Most important, it will expand our notion of representation in Freud. It will also allow us to see that Freud is literary and social for the same reasons.

Literary readings of Freud are harder to come by than they used to be. Mikkel Borch-Jacobsen's *Remembering Anna O.* (1996) is the moment at which the close reading of psychoanalytic texts went sourly historicist. Borch-Jacobsen, an exquisite reader of Lacan, rejected psychoanalysis for the same reason he rejected close reading: Both presumed the object, psyche or text, to be porous and unstable. This used to be a literary virtue. Now it was a vice. Primal scenes had to be real. In both psychoanalysis and criticism at large, undecidability in interpretation could be relieved by history as such. No dialectic need be found between them. History and interpretation, in a bold rejection of Freud, were severed.

Whether or not this is a legitimate representation of New Historicist approaches in either psychoanalysis or in literary criticism is itself undecidable. What is New Historicism, and what are its objects? As usual, the historiographical and epistemological difficulties become psychoanalytic ones. Is the "return" to history a repression of semiotics and deconstruction, or an elaboration of them? It is, of course, both, a magnificent instance of ambivalence, and of the splitting characteristic of ambivalence when the ego—here, the ego of criticism as an institution—is faced with stress. The cross-cultural accents of political criticism remain vivid, however, simply by asking these psychoanalytic questions. Even Patrick J. Mahony's highly wrought demonstrations of Freud's "polyvalent verbal usage" (1989, 72) are in the service of an expanded sense of what is cross-cultural about our reading of Freud, especially when we read him in English instead of German. Mahony's attentiveness to Freud's language and to the ways in which there is a "fit," as he puts it (1986, xiii), between textual and psychical activity also joins him with the more classical tradition of reading Freud as literature that begins with Burke and Trilling. Mahony recalls Trilling's old contention that psychoanalysis, like literature, is "a science of tropes," and that the mind itself is "a poetry-making organ." This, of course, is also what links psychoanalysis with the social: that the mind thinks in representations, and that the poet, as Shelley reminds us, is for that reason the unacknowledged legislator of the world.

A discursive reading of Freud, then, has the particular advantage of showing how presumably formal literary structures—those of rhetoric, for example—are also phenomenological and even neural structures. Psychical defense and writing are in fact the same, converging as they do in the figure of trope or rhetoric itself, the turning away that is also a figure or structure of language. Freud's revised notion of economy describes rhetoric as a defense and defense as a rhetoric by showing how the very trope of defense produces what it defends against by presuming it, just as repression turns away from the drive in order to spark it into life. Economy is in this sense the master figure of Freud's combined theory of language and of the psyche, since it is both the structure of literary language and of forces in contention in an almost quantitative way. The social resonance of even these formal structures in both Freud's textuality and his medicine is obvious. So are its more classically literary ones. Freud's particular power lies in his ability to persuade us of the pressure of the unconscious at the very horizon of life as we know it. Freud devalues consciousness as a category in order to make the unconscious loom even more powerfully against it, just as the fiction of a lack of conscious precedent for psychoanalysis assures Freud himself the role of hero and discoverer.

The daunting overdeterminations that threaten the originality of Freud's achievement from the point of view of literary influence have as their counterpart, of course, the equally populous overdeterminations that assail Freud from the point of view of the history of science (see Ellenberger 1970; Sulloway 1979). Freud defends himself against this double vortex of literary and scientific precedent in economic terms, too, since the radically double characteristics that make his language at once literary and scientific are also the ones that free him in turn from the determinations of either tradition. Though Freud's language swerves, often wildly, from the regularities of literary and scientific discourse alike, each swerve is nonetheless lawful from the point of view of the other—what is literary is precisely that which cannot be vouchsafed in the name of science, and vice versa. The trope of biology, for example, in a late visionary work like *Beyond the Pleasure Principle*, stands out as a poetic figure only at the moment that it transgresses what biology as a science is privileged to say, that among the instincts there is one that wishes for death. The boundaries of poetry and science, in other words, are in each case an effect of the violation of one by the other. Freud's double language of science and vision, then, is an apparatus or machine, to use Derrida's vocabulary, that allows Freud to employ the rhetoric of each tradition even as it simultaneously releases him from the obligation to stay bound by either one. Freud's language is rhetoric and defense at once—they are the same thing—a language that situates itself simultaneously within the contexts of science and poetry, and that in the same gesture insures its independence from both traditions alike. Nor should we forget that the same literary economy also sustains the early Freud as he invokes the traditions of dream interpretation, for example, only to deny them, placing himself among the authorities even as he frees himself from them. Nor should we forget either that Freud's early masterpiece, like the work of his late phase, also brings the unconscious into being as an effect of resistance to it, in the staged repression that Freud exercises over his dream-associations when he hesitates, or in his bashful regret that he is expecting too much from his reader.

Whether in relation to his own discoveries, then, or in relation to tradition, Freud establishes his priority as a writer by situating both his texts and the objects of his science in a realm of imagination that benefits from a wealth of influences while paying taxes to none. The imaginative priority to be had through economy is perhaps best represented by the mystic writing-pad, that compensatory machine whose surface remains fresh and original because it constantly erases influence or stimulation even as it absorbs and represses it as a series of traces inscribed on the layers beneath. Like the fiction of consciousness, the original poet like Freud shields himself from influence by admitting and forgetting it, and so becomes a site of influences which he manages to erase despite the impossibility of doing so. Just as Shakespeare uses traditions at will in a mingled discourse that appeals to countless regimens while submitting, in the end, to none in particular, so Freud contaminates science with literature, literature with science, to produce a prose-poetry whose only real boundaries are those of his imagination. And just as Milton chooses the most authoritative of anterior myths in a gamble to assert his priority over the past, so Freud chooses for his equivalent purposes the most authoritative of anterior nineteenth-century myths, the myth of science. Like Milton, too, Freud is poised between belief in his enabling myth and belief in himself; between the acknowledgment of his citizenship in a historical community and his desire to stand apart from it; between an inevitable belatedness and an achieved earliness; between, finally, the epic of certainty and the lyric of anxiety.

2
"Sensations" and "ideas"

Doublings

What consequences does the contention that Freud's writing is about writing have for a reading of Freud's career as a whole? Freud's work—its nature, its history, its origins, its influence—is a complex affair. Michel Foucault, in his essay "What is an Author?" (1969), describes it with extraordinary precision. Like Marx, he writes, Freud is the "initiator" of a "discursive practice":

> Freud is not simply the author of *The Interpretation of Dreams* or of *Wit and its Relation to the Unconscious* and Marx is not simply the author of the *Communist Manifesto* or *Capital*: they both established the endless possibility of discourse. ... In saying that Freud founded psychoanalysis, we do not simply mean that the concept of libido or the techniques of dream analysis reappear in the writings of Karl Abraham or Melanie Klein, but that he made possible a certain number of differences with respect to his books, concepts, and hypotheses, which all arise out of psychoanalytic discourse. (1976, 131–32)

Foucault's animosity toward Freud in the latter phase of his own career, particularly in the first volume of *The History of Sexuality* (1976), is itself an example of Freud's influence as Foucault describes it. Foucault is a Freudian because he cannot help it. Freud is part of the air we breathe; indeed, he *is* the air we breathe, whether we like it or not.

As Foucault suggests, Freud's customary stance as a narrator is really, to use a contemporary metaphor, an interactive one. He invites you to argue with him. He invites you, not to be persuaded, but to resist. It is not unlike the analytic situation. This rhetorical site is where the "truth" of psychoanalysis is, as it were, performed—in the agreement between reader and writer, patient and analyst, to disagree about something that is, presumably, already there. This is why it is not, in the first or the last instance, a question of the empirical truth or falsehood of

Freud's claims. What matters is the structure of Freudian reader-response that puts those claims into place. No wonder the perils of psychoanalytic treatment include ignoring physical causes for suffering. The nature of Freud's institutional misreading is often, to use a tired but true metaphor, religious, the result of treating the Founder's text as though it were Scripture. This is also why Freud, like the Bible, is literature. His texts are polysemous, but his interpreters, not being literary critics, do not fail simply to celebrate Freud's endless possibilities of meaning; they require Freud's texts to mean one thing rather than many. Arguments with Freud's "truth," whether from Adolf Grünbaum's perspective (1984) or from Jeffrey Masson's (1984), fail to address this simple but decisive point. In so doing, such arguments also succeed, quite against their intentions, in actually promoting Freud's continued success. Disagreements with psychoanalysis maintain, rhetorically speaking, the disputable truth to which psychoanalysis does or does not properly refer. Indeed, the more disagreements the merrier. This is the situation that Foucault describes.

It is therefore the constitutive elements of Freud's writing and the ways in which they shape the world of psychoanalytic process that deserve our primary attention. Freud's method of handling us as readers is so familiar that we tend to overlook the devices that structure it. Chief among them is his famous irony, although it is never withering or contemptuous. Indeed, Freud's tone and manner are always genuinely ironic, since they say one thing while meaning another. The narrator can engage, and even persuade, the reader by appealing to his or her presumably superior judgment when the narrator's judgment seems to be weak or foolhardy. The deliberate comparison of the case histories in *Studies on Hysteria* to "short stories," for example, makes the reader think that Freud is selling himself short. The reader responds with an involuntary sympathy. The ironic later Freud earns the reader's generosity in a similar fashion: by appealing, with extraordinary audacity, directly to the reader's unwillingness to accept his dark arguments, in *Civilization and its Discontents* (1930), for example, or in *An Outline of Psychoanalysis* (1938). The reader responds with a heightened sense of his or her own argumentative courage and fullness of heart. Such writing is, as we sometimes call it today, following Bakhtin, dialogical, rich with contending tongues and defined by their collision. Nor is such a volatile kind of writing without its startling implications.

If, as Foucault maintains, the key to Freud's texts is that they produce the endless possibility of argument with them, then, to use Bloom's term, their "misreading" becomes their only and outrageous rule. This is not just the structure of your reading of Freud or of mine; it is also, as Foucault notes, the institutional structure of psychoanalytic history as a whole, which, like our contemporary skirmishes, is defined by disagreement and debate. Transference, of course, is the clinical trope for this mode of relation, and it regulates the economy of Freud studies as well as of Freudian practice. We see this aspect of Freud at its most charming in the *Five Lectures on Psychoanalysis*, the brief series of lectures that Freud delivered at Clark University in 1909, with a marketing purpose in mind. We see this aspect of Freud at its most pugnacious in *The Question of Lay Analysis* (1926), as Freud, with a mercilessness reserved for questions that fall, properly speaking, outside the realm of psychoanalytic theory, takes his reader through a series of vertiginous confrontations that require a continuous reexamination of one's assumptions simply in order to keep one's feet. Here confrontation serves not to antagonize but to stabilize the reader in a new, wider field of reference and feeling that the presumed antagonism has actually created. Freud is a dialectician, provoking his reader to bring an entire trail of beliefs and assumptions into play—positively, negatively, or in between. Nor is transference the only mechanism that thickens the Freudian plot. There is also overdetermination. How can there be a "single" reading of a Freudian text—I emphasize the dubious status of the "single" in psychoanalysis by placing it in quotation marks—even when a "single" subject attempts one? There are too many vicissitudes at work in text and subject alike to vouchsafe it.

Rich similitudes between text and phenomenon do not just crop up in Freud. They positively structure his work. Freud's texts double the objects they describe. Freud's psychical mechanisms resemble the mechanisms of his text, and the mechanisms of his text resemble the mechanisms of the psychical apparatus. There are any number of doublings to discuss in addition to the reader's transferential relation to Freud's writing and the overdeterminations that condition it. Roman Jakobson's identification of condensation and displacement with metaphor and metonymy is perhaps the most well known (1956), although, as I noted in Chapter 1, Burke and Trilling anticipate it. More recently, Donald Spence (1982) and Peter Brooks (1984, 1994) have elaborated the details that link the narrative mechanisms of the psychical apparatus, those of the ego in particular, with those of narrative as such, giving the final touches to a long tradition of regarding Freud's writing as literary that begins, as we have seen, with Ransom and Burke. We can include among Freud's doubling effects the way in which the *Five Lectures on Psychoanalysis* of 1910 reflect Freud's early topographical or spatial model of mind by virtue of its formal organization by topic—*topos*, or place—while the later *Autobiographical Study* of 1925, describing as it must the shift to the newer, temporal model, is itself structured, quite unlike the Clark lectures, as a history. The monumentality of myth in *Totem and Taboo* (1912) certifies the findings of the doctrinal decade early in the century regarding human instinct and its various expressions in primitive and ancient culture, but the doctrinal decade is soon shattered, like the monumentality of the father in *Totem and Taboo*, by the crisis of the metapsychological phase, and the onset of Freud's own mid-career crisis as a writer. This kind of reflexivity everywhere structures the movement of Freud's work. Much as the baggy monsters of *Studies on Hysteria* and *The Interpretation of Dreams* slim down to the comparatively more compact *Psychopathology of Everyday Life* (1901), *Three Essays on the Theory of Sexuality* (1905), and *Jokes and their Relation to the Unconscious* (1905), so the hesitations of the characteristic Freudian essay in the metapsychological phase evolve into the sleek Freudian essay of the 1920s and 1930s.

Nor is allegory absent. The argumentative agons of Freud's writing often mirror their theoretical concerns. Narcissism is the central category of psychoanalysis during the intense self-scrutiny that characterizes Freud's middle period, much as Freud's concern with the authority of the new psychoanalytic model of mind in *The Ego and the Id* is bound up with a defense of the Oedipus complex. As Bloom has noted, Freud's career is structured like a poetic quest-romance, with its movements guided by the trope of deferred action. Each major text overtly revises the one before it as we move from *Studies on Hysteria* to the dream book, from the dream book to the occlusions of the metapsychological phase, and from the metapsychology to the high ground of *Beyond the Pleasure Principle*, by which time Freud's system has been well enough refined to sustain shocks of any kind.

Deferred action and the belated paradigm of the Wolf Man

This characteristic doubling between text and object in Freud is nowhere more evident than in the psychoanalytic approach to time. Time is the very condition of both writing's production and unfolding, and of the real birth and death of the subject. How does psychoanalysis solve the terrible temporal problems that the abandonment of the seduction theory raises? What are memory and its objects, including the images or representations out of which they are presumably made? Any schematic handling of Freud's account of temporality ought to begin in the middle of his career, in 1918, when he has finally clarified and formalized his approach to time, and to the related problems of memory and repression. Begun in late 1913 and finished in 1914, the famous case of the Wolf Man is really a part of the metapsychological phase. Freud waited four years to publish it, accumulating arguments in his revisions to refute Jung's biologizing notion of inherited tendencies to account for infantile sexuality. "From the History of an Infantile Neurosis" is a text of overdetermined privilege in psychoanalysis. It formalizes the structure of Freud's thought as a whole probably more efficiently than any of his other writings (even the 1925 "Negation"), and does so at an unlikely but in fact central moment in the plain chronology of his career as a psychoanalyst. Following the 1914 essay on narcissism in composition and just preceding the 1920 *Beyond the Pleasure Principle* in publication, it occupies the near-center of Freud's official middle phase. Its assessment of temporality, as Derrida and Bloom have attested, is its overweening preoccupation. It gives us the overview we need in order to begin a reading of his work.

Like the belated emergence of the Wolf Man's importance in the history of Freud's reception, the belated emergence of its key term is itself the best example of the modality it represents. Derrida has already called attention to it: *Nachträglichkeit*, or, as Strachey translates it, deferred action. And not until Laplanche and Pontalis write at some length about the case's premier notion in 1967 does it become genuinely effective, especially in Anglophone usage, and our view of Freud changed by its application. One psychoanalyst even regards deferred action as a neurological mechanism, which he calls "retranscription" (Modell 1990). The Wolf Man belatedly clarifies Freud's earlier intimations of the notion in the 1895 *Project*; in the structure of recollection adumbrated in "Screen Memories" (1899); and in the "*Fausse Reconnaissance (Déjà Raconté)*" of 1914. Deferred action means that we know origins—"the primal scene" in the case of the Wolf Man—only later on, by the distance that estranges us from them, by virtue of what seems only to screen or obstruct our memory of them.

Freud derives what will become the ineluctable modality of all discursive production from what his patient both declares and describes, thematizes and dramatizes. The Wolf Man's dream of the frosty white wolves in the tree outside his window as a four-year-old—the childhood dream around which the analysis centers, and whose interpretation is its driving desire or primitivist/positivist grail-object—is, Freud tells us, the deferred and disguised memory of an event (the primal scene proper) that the patient experienced, or could have experienced, at the age of one and a half, that of witnessing his parents in the act of copulation. But because a child of one and a half does not yet possess the knowledge of sex required to interpret, or even to register, such a scene, it cannot properly be said to exist for him at the moment of its "real" or chronological occurrence. It is only when the dreamer gains a knowledge of sex that the memory—the primal—may come into being at all. This "sexualization after the event" (17:103n), as Freud calls it, is to be accounted for as follows: "He received the impressions when he was one and a half; his understanding of them was deferred, but became possible at the time of the dream owing to his development, his sexual excitations, and his sexual researches" (17:37–38n). They are, in short, "the products of construction" (17:51).

Such a structure is a miniature of the modality of psychoanalytic knowledge at large, particularly the rhetorical means by which Freud fashions the phantasms of his imaginative universe and the categories that define it. The figure "unconscious mind," of course, is Freud's enabling oxymoron, and, like Milton's "darkness visible," Conrad's "heart of darkness," or Lévi-Strauss's *pensée sauvage*, it is an educative or pedagogic oxymoron, a symptomatic and parabolic error required of rhetoric when it is asked to do unusual or inventive things. A mixed metaphor whose own transgressions according to accepted Cartesian usage ("mind" equals "consciousness") are what produce the newish space of Freudian hyperinteriority, "unconscious mind" signals that Freud's project is in fact posited on the self-contradictory implications of such oxymora. In the *Three Essays*, for example, Freud begins with a familiar kind of psychoanalytic paradox: How can one know what happens in early childhood if one of early childhood's principal characteristics is that we regularly forget its history? Similarly, Freud assures us in *The Interpretation of Dreams* that "nothing but a wish can set our mental apparatus at work" (5:567), even though such a statement requires us to ask in turn whether psychoanalytic thought itself is therefore no more than wish-fulfillment.

By its curiously natural appeal to the reader, the deferred action of the Wolf Man assumes the presence of the primal as the metaleptically logical referent of what succeeds it. "Light is thrown," says Freud, "from the later stages of his history upon these earlier ones" (17:47). Like the goddess Psyche, Freud's psyche, too, is—like all Romantic idealities—produced after the fact, the seat of an ambiguous primacy, simultaneously deferred and present. Traces of a desire endemic to modernism at large, the unconscious and the primal scene are symptoms of Freud's own desire to reach for the warmth and immediacy of beginnings in the face of his late position in history. This is a particularly northern European desire for parity with the southerly priority of the ancients, the Hebrews, even the Renaissance, and one presumably to be fulfilled by the search for the bedrock of *Trieb*. This serves as Freud's particular version of a realm, to use Trilling's definition of the will to modernity, "beyond" or "apart from culture." In Freud's dark and ironic modernism, however, such primacy or origins emerge only belatedly, culture or symbol situating a nature preexisting it, as Keats does in the nightingale ode.

Literary examples of deferred action are overwhelming in their abundance as well as in their precision of mechanism. Every literary critic is familiar with the paradoxes that Milton exploits in *Paradise Lost*, not only for the sake of realizing the poem's grand theater of action, but also for calling attention to the ironies that both situate and assail it. In a paradigm equal to Freud's own, the early Romantic Milton rejects the truth of classical mythology (the best example is the early *Nativity Ode*) only to resurrect it with apparent unwillingness in the later poem. For without pagan representations, "erring" (1:747) as they are, no such Christian poem can speak. The price of the poem's readability: that we know origins or primal scenes only through the belated technologies that obstruct our view of them, and, in so doing, construct whatever view we have. Much as the Wolf Man's primal scene emerges as a function of his later knowledge of sex, so Milton's Christian truth can only be articulated by means of pagan error.

The primary event is known not despite but because of the distortion through which it appears afterwards. There is, properly speaking, no objective or original event as such (it is the "product" of a "construction"), only its (re)construction through the rhetoric of narrative or memory. These are more than narrational paradoxes; they are also those that structure the wager of faith. "Who himself beginning new?" (8:251), asks Milton. Subject and cosmogony have the same structure. Faith in the origin of one is faith in the origin of the other. But it is not faith that does the work. It is a temporal labor of a very clear kind. Stanley Fish (1967) has made this labor apparent in the poem's diction. Eve's "wanton ringlets" (4:306) and "coy submission" (4:310) are wholly inappropriate in the Garden of Eden. No one is, presumably, "coy" or "wanton" there. And yet the irony is just the point: Like the poet, though unlike Adam and Eve, the reader is impure, postlapsarian. Neither the reader nor Milton has any other way of imagining the situation. Even the attempt to represent Eden is not only a measure of our sinfulness; it is also an example of how sin endlessly conditions all that we think and feel.

Deferred action also constructs canons. T. S. Eliot's familiar description of canon-formation in "Tradition and the Individual Talent" (1919) is actually a description of deferred action:

> No poet, no artist of any art, has his complete meaning alone. His significance, his appreciation is the appreciation of his relation to the dead poets and artists. You cannot value him alone; you must set him, for contrast and comparison, among the dead. I mean this as a principle of aesthetic, not merely historical, criticism. The necessity that he shall conform, that he shall cohere, is not onesided; what happens when a new work of art is created is something that happens simultaneously to all the works of art which preceded it. The existing monuments form an ideal order among themselves, which is modified by the introduction of the new (the really new) work of art among them. (1919, 15)

Eliot, as a rule, represses this temporality, as we shall see with *The Waste Land* in Chapter 4. He prefers instead to dwell on those "ideal" cloudbursts of inspiration that obscure the real "aesthetic" and "historical" dynamic of canon-formation. In linguistics after Saussure—and in a realm of frankness well beyond Eliot's own—it is hard to hide from deferred action, even if the precise temporal basis of signification in deferral remains obscure until Derrida. From a linguistic or semiotic point of view, deferred action is a fine example of the temporality of the signifier. It is what requires the famous aporia between signifier and signified. It is a constitutive gap, not a gap to be overcome. This is what makes Eliot sad. One recognizes something because one has seen it—somehow—before. There is no present, and no presence. Everything unfolds in time, leaving a space, as it were, between what is known and the knower. This is Derrida's deferral, or *différance*. As in deferred action, the referent is both present and absent simultaneously, full and lacking.

Nor should one forget that Freud's notions are redoubled by his writing. If the privilege of the Wolf Man case comes from its representation of psychoanalytic knowledge and its objects of putative inquiry as equivalent, it is because by 1918 Freud's narrational skill has reached a kind of technical perfection which silently recapitulates the structure of the patient's memory in its own operations as a text. Rather than simply assert what conclusions about deferred action his evidence may allow and then document them in a linear argument doubtless more convincing than the sinuous one he gives us instead ("I am afraid," says Freud at one point, that "the reader's belief will abandon me" [17:36]), Freud actually simulates the movement of the analysis itself as it produces explanations for fresh memories that in turn require fresh explanations, producing in turn fresh memories, and so on. Much as Freud's patient will lead him to momentary certainty only to disappoint it, so, too, will Freud lead his reader to high ground only to return him to the muddle. Freud sequentially revises his conclusions much as his patient's narratives habitually revise their evidences. Indeed, in the supplementary sections inserted between 1914 and 1918, the text becomes a patently deferred elaboration of itself, allowing the implicit doubling to become explicitly reflexive. Freud's narration and his patient's memory may appear to be different, but their structures are homologous and their production of one another interdependent. Narration and story coincide precisely but metaphorically, analogously rather than literally. They are adequated even as they remain different. The ability to compare them is also what makes them incomparable. Rhetorical and representational planes, *récit* and *histoire*, are doubles rather than twins. Hence the novel of manners, for example, may be said to narrate the forms of life as a life of forms, and so find in its subject a reflexive counterpart for its own manipulation of literary manners. If the two planes coincide literally, as in Robbe-Grillet or Blanchot, the result is instead purely reflexive art, narration narrating itself exactly by making its readability its overt problematic. Novelistic realism, by contrast—like Freud's own writing—is a doubling that is also a splitting. By virtue of accenting the figurative rather than literal status of the two planes' identity (an irony to which even "pure" reflexivity such as Robbe-Grillet's or Barthelme's is ultimately subject), such a mixed mode actually avows the linguistic or semiotic scaffolding that sustains its illusionism in the separation that seems only to conceal it.

It is this silent but pervasive redoubling that is the hinge of Freud's triumph in the Wolf Man case. As we shall see later on, Strachey extends the reach of this redoubling to include the translation of Freud itself, using the transference—another such redoubling—as his model. Such redoubling tells us that our knowledge and the mode of its reception are the same, that there is no genuine subject/object relation between a past or *histoire* and a present or *récit* that may be said simply to transcribe or remember it. Freud's realism is always under the jeopardy of Freud's reflexivity. This jeopardy, however, is precisely—and ironically—what insures the psychoanalytic project: Freud's psychical object and the action of his texts are the same thing. This is why the incoherence that will jeopardize the entire psychoanalytic project in Freud's middle phase becomes another instance of its functioning. It brings Freud to a vivid redefinition of things. Freud's career, despite its suspicion of mythic paradigms, is also a romance. To chart its principal movements means to watch the calm of the dreambook deteriorate in "On Narcissism," and to see it restored in the triumphant Romanticism of *Beyond the Pleasure Principle* and *The Ego and the Id*. Final testimony to the power of psychoanalysis, self-revision will allow Freud to exploit as well as to exemplify deferred action in his late, magisterial phase.

Bergson and the *Project*

Rather than solve problems about representation, however, deferred action raises them all over again. Like religions, psychoanalysis prompts one question above all others. Where, one asks, is its realm of action? What is the epistemological status of its objects, particularly the unconscious? Not a religious man, Freud asks himself the same questions. If deferred action is the modality of representation, what kind of representation, whether psychical or discursive, does it produce? This question is already a question being adduced as early as the *Project*, and in far more self-consciously theoretical terms than those regarding representation that Freud gains from Breuer in *Studies on Hysteria*. In *Studies on Hysteria*, the signifier is arbitrary—Anna O.'s inability to drink is a good example—motivated only by contingency and association. In the *Project*, the nature of signification is explained more fully. Here Freud has intervened in an implicit debate in philosophical psychology between Henri Bergson and William James. The debate involves the difference between "sensations" and "ideas." Emerging from a medical vocabulary that circulated in the middle ages, this difference organizes the associationist philosophy of Locke and the Enlightenment associationism of Hume and David Hartley that follows it. This movement of thought is prelude not only to brain science, as I will show in Chapter 4; it is also the distinct environment of assumption passed along to James and Bergson alike. Coming late in this tradition in his *Principles of Psychology* (1890), James is full of meditations on where the link between sensations and ideas is, and where, most of the time, it is not. Bergson's dissertation, the *Essay on Time and Consciousness* (1889), which brought him early fame and respect, comes very close to locating this link, but falls short. It is Freud's key source for the *Project*, a deeply buried influence whose exact—or almost exact—Freudian formulations are astonishing. So are Freud's repressions of them. Only Bergson's book on humor (1900) is listed in the *Standard Edition*'s bibliography.

Although Bergson's *Essay* is the decisive text on "sensations" and "ideas" before the *Project*, it is important to note that the distinction between "sensations" and "ideas" is everywhere in the nineteenth century. It appears in discourses seemingly remote from philosophical psychology, particularly in literary criticism. Victorian critics of the novel distinguished between the novel of "sensation" and the novel of "ideas," and had specific aesthetic-response patterns in mind for each of them (Kendrick 1977). Novelists themselves did the same. Hardy's first two published novels, *Desperate Remedies* (1871) and *Under the Greenwood Tree* (1872), are a fine example of the formulaic distinction between novels of "sensation" and novels of "character" in the Victorian literary marketplace. Novels of "sensation" were potboilers, like *Desperate Remedies;* novels of "character" were novels of ideas, focusing instead on theme and setting rather than on action, as Hardy does in his second book. As their titles suggest, George Eliot's *Adam Bede* (1859) or Mrs. Humphry Ward's *Robert Elsmere* (1888) are novels of "character," or, as the Victorians also called them, "portraits." Wilkie Collins's *The Woman in White* (1860) or *The Moonstone* (1868) are, by constrast, novels of "sensation," whose high-jinks plots earned them the metaphor of the "chain" to describe their highly deliberate manipulation of the reader. The subtitle of Pater's *Marius the Epicurean* (1885) announces both the familiarity and the authority of the distinction in its selfsame terms: *His Sensations and Ideas.*

In the *Project*, "sensations" and "ideas" are called "quantity" and "quality." Freud simply substitutes the language of the laboratory for the language of poetics. Only in the passage from "quantity" to "quality" does an organism achieve the quality of being "psychological," of having what we call personality—the quality, as it were, of having "ideas" as well as "sensations." But what is the nature of the link between the two? How does it come to pass? Freud's transformation of the period's philosophical vocabulary into physicalist terms is a way of translating a philosophical language into a scientific one, and back again. That is the very kind of thing that the model itself represents—the translation back and forth of "sensations" and "ideas." It is an attempt, not to mediate "body" and "mind," but to find the equation that makes them continuous.

Fundamental as the difference between sensations and ideas is to the late nineteenth century, William James reminds us how easy it is to resist the happy solution to which it leads, and that even Bergson, as we will see, exploits to great advantage. "Imagination and sensation," says a punctilious James, "are not quite as distinct as one at first is tempted to suppose" (1890, 2:72). Here James wishes to repress the very continuities that Bergson and Freud elaborate. Bergson will make it halfway—and further—to Freud's own later solution. What James calls "imagination" and "sensation"—"ideas" and "sensations"—are linked in Bergson and in Freud, not kept apart, as they are in the idealism repressed beneath James's pragmatism. James admits that "conceived or imagined objects"—"ideas"—"hang … to the sensations" (2:311), but he has no idea how they do so. It is because he will not relinquish his faith in either a *vraie vérité* or the fair-mindedness of the democratic animal:

> Some will interpret these facts by calling them all cases in which certain images, by laws of association, awaken others so very rapidly that we think afterwards we felt the very tendencies of the nascent images to arise, before they were actually there. For this school the only possible materials of consciousness are images of a perfectly definite nature. Tendencies exist, but they are facts for the outside psychologist rather than for the subject of the observation. The tendency is thus a psychical zero; only its results are felt. (1:254)

James will not admit that deferred action is the mechanism of perception ("images … arise, before they were actually there"). "Results" do not lead him back to "*psychical*" cause, but to "a *psychical* zero." "Thought," simply, is "cognitive of an outer reality" (1:272). All is a matter of "consciousness" and "attention" (1:288).

For Bergson, however, the distinction between "sensations" and "ideas" is decisive, as it was for the young Freud, who had apparently read the *Essay* very carefully. Bergson had clarified the difficulties that the distinction presented, but he had not really solved them. Part of the solution involved seeing the distinction as one that a physiologist like the young, neurological Freud would regard as a distinction between quantity and quality. Bergson, however, is a little uncomfortable with the language of science. He stays on the philosophical side of the fence, although with a fine rigor that has him invent, before the fact, an almost psychoanalytic distinction between what he calls the "affective" and the "representative" (1889, 42), or, in a Freudian vocabulary, "affect" and "idea." The *Essay*'s formulation of the relation between "sensations" and "ideas" is virtually Freud's own, even the nod to physiology with the use of the term "quantity" as a cognate for "sensation":

> I do not see how … differences of sensation would be interpreted by our consciousness as differences of quantity unless we connected them with the reactions which usually accompany them, and which are more or less extended and more or less important. (37–38)

This is an indirect response to James's inability to explain why "images … arise, before they were actually there." Bergson has already established Freud's equivalence between "sensations" and "quantity." But, like James, he also requires "consciousness" to validate the link between "quantity" and our "reactions" to it in order to know that the link has occurred. This is to put the cart before the horse. As with James, it is a repression of deferred action. It is "differences of quantity" linked somehow with "the reactions which usually accompany them" that are the point. How does this occur? The assumption of consciousness to vouchsafe the link between sensations and ideas is not just problematic; it is insurmountable. That can happen only after the fact. "The reactions which usually accompany" sensations are not "usual" until the accompaniment has been made. In Bergson's schema, only consciousness can do that. But, alas, there can be no consciousness until this "usual" accompaniment has already been accomplished and a subject is in place to experience it. Although Bergson cites an experiment by Hermann Helmholtz in which the "interpretation" (51) of quantity into quality has already miraculously occurred in the perception of physical stimulation, the theoretical problem remains. "Quantity" cannot be in place, according to Bergson, without a consciousness to "accompany" its reception. We can estimate quantity as quality only after the link between them exists.

Bergson sees the problem, but the solution is not clear to him because of his philosophy of consciousness:

> It cannot be said that you have compared two sensations with one another: you have made use of a single sensation in order to compare two different luminous sources with each other. (55)

Helmholtz and his followers have indeed only "compared two sensations with one another." They have not, as Bergson suggests they should, found the mechanism that links sensations with ideas. What is missing, in other words, is not only the question of mechanism. What is missing is also a way to account for the link in terms other than those of the awareness presumably characteristic of consciousness.

Bergson is not unaware of the solution, but the presuppositions it requires disquiet him. They force him to use the terms of the physiologists, including the distinction between "quantity" and "quality." He is clearly not happy about it:

> It is no use trying to measure this quality Q by some physical quantity Q' which lies beneath it: for it would be necessary to have previously shown that Q is a function of Q', and this would not be possible unless the quality Q had first been measured with some fraction of itself. Thus nothing prevents us from measuring the sensation of heat by the degree of temperature; but this is only a convention, and the whole point of psychophysics lies in rejecting this convention and seeking how the sensation of heat varies when you change the temperature. In a word, it seems, on the one hand, that two different sensations cannot be said to be equal unless some identical residuum remains after the elimination of their qualitative difference; but, on the other hand, this qualitative difference being all that we perceive, it does not appear what could remain once it was eliminated. (63–64)

"What could remain" is the "convention" of meaning in relation to a sensation. That the idea that is linked to a sensation is somehow arbitrary because it is conventional is what disturbs Bergson more than his pretense that it is the other way around. Indeed, the later, more familiar Bergson is the one who believes that conventionality stifles the *élan vital* and inhibits our ability to see directly into the "luminous sources" of life. The notion that such a conventional link between quantity and quality is necessary for consciousness to be in place returns Bergson to what he dislikes most of all: the assumption of mental activity beyond or before "consciousness," a proposition which, in his mind, unlike Freud's, narrows life rather than expands it.

What is the solution? Bergson has it, but it is at odds with his philosophy of consciousness. It is a simple solution. It is the requirement of memory or, as Bergson puts it, borrowing a term from Helmholtz's contemporary, Gustav Fechner, a "residuum" —a network, as Freud would put it, of memory traces. But Bergson does not want to account for the link between sensations and ideas in any terms but those of consciousness. Despite all of his elegant but unintended invocations of unconscious mental functioning in the *Essay*—and despite his public support of Pierre Janet (Ellenberger 1970, 321, 343)—Bergson will not relinquish his voluntarism, even if it will cost him the battle that he is fighting. "What could remain" after a given stimulation is "eliminated" is precisely this "residuum," or capacity for memory. Otherwise, neither the stimulation nor its cessation could be experienced—could be "conscious"—at all. Even late in the *Essay*, Bergson complains about the "shadow" of memory—it is a "ghost" that makes us "live outside ourselves" (231). This is a prefiguration of Freud's "Mourning and Melancholia" (1917), but one that resists its brand of insight rather than welcomes it. For Bergson, to be determined is the problem, even if that is what is needed for memory to occur, whether at an originary level that links sensations and ideas, or, for the adult, for whom the life of "social representation" (231), which for Bergson is artificial, is in fact neither good nor bad, but simply inevitable and enabling. Most extraordinary of all, Bergson, despite his insistence that "free will" or "consciousness" is "a fact" (173), presents late in the *Essay* a figure for the psyche so presciently Freudian that it repeats before it occurs the famous metaphor of the "crust" (169) that surrounds the infant ego in *Beyond the Pleasure Principle*. There, Freud will show that this "crust" produces just such a "residuum" from the very beginnings of life. This "residuum" will have become the Freudian unconscious.

Here Bergson's direct influence on the *Project* is most readily apparent. That the movement from sensations to ideas needed a mechanism was finally clear. Memory had a role; it was the field of comparison against which sensations and ideas could both emerge. It required the assumption of a "residuum," or an unconscious. For Bergson, however, this "residuum" must still be identified with consciousness because, to exist, it must be available to it. Stubborn, like James, but for different reasons, Bergson cannot surrender his belief in free will, even if it backs him into unforeseen Lacanian assumptions about the subject's having to regard himself as an object. The early Deleuze (1957, 1966) remained ambivalent about Bergson's enthusiasm for presence and his belief in it as a defense against the realities of time and memory. Kristeva has not (1995). As with James, consciousness must for Bergson remain transparent to itself. This voluntarism leaves the mechanism that links sensations and ideas shrouded in James and Bergson alike. Not so Freud.

How does the shift from "quantity" to "quality" occur in the *Project*? Paul Ricoeur's belief that the *Project* belongs only to Freud's "period of scientific thought" (1970, 73) is a belief that even Derrida seems to hold. Here, however, Freud has already begun to solve the problem in "the correlation between energetics and hermeneutics" (69) that Ricoeur's own reading of Freud says comes later, and only in a tentative fashion. Ricoeur's terms mask their historical source as "sensations" and "ideas," although, even for Ricoeur, it is still a question of finding the link or "correlation" between the two. Freud is able to describe this mechanism in the *Project*, with Bergson's help. Two later elaborations of the argument, however, will be required, one in "On Narcissism" (1914) and one in "Instincts and their Vicissitudes" (1915). But the foundations are securely in place here in 1895, and they proceed, as Freud's vocabulary suggests, from Bergson himself:

> A main characteristic of nervous tissue is memory; that is, quite generally, a capacity for being permanently altered by single occurrences—which offers such a striking contrast to the behavior of a material that permits the passage of a wave-movement and thereafter returns to its former condition. A psychological theory deserving any consideration must furnish an explanation of "memory." Now any such explanation comes up against the difficulty that it must assume on the one hand that neurones are permanently different after an excitation from what they were before, while nevertheless it cannot be disputed that, in general, fresh excitations meet with the same conditions of reception as did the earlier ones. It would seem, therefore, that neurones must be both influenced and also unaltered, unprejudiced. We cannot off-hand imagine an apparatus capable of such complicated functioning; the situation is accordingly saved by attributing the characteristic of being permanently influenced by excitation to one class of neurones, and, on the other hand, the unalterability—that characteristic of being fresh for new excitations—to another class. Thus has arisen the current distinction between "perceptual cells" and "mnemic cells"'—a distinction, however, which fits into no other context and cannot itself appeal to anything in its support. (1:299)

The saving addition, of course, is the language of physiology. Though Bergson works hard to integrate Helmholtz, Fechner, and other experimentalists into the *Essay*, as a rule he is less enthusiastic about the mincing language of the positivists than he is about the figural richness of French philosophical argument. This includes its own literary "residuum," the host of prior French thought and literature that includes Bergson's real anxiety-producing influence, Montaigne, although it is Pascal who takes over in the second half of Bergson's career. It is always the unconscious and what is past that Bergson cannot tolerate.

Unlike Bergson, Freud combines the language of philosophy and the language of physiology, with immediate results. The question in Bergson was the same as the one Derrida poses for Freud: how can one conceive of an apparatus capable of both fresh stimulation and of memory at one and the same time. Only an unconscious "residuum" together with consciousness can meet this dual requirement. Bergson rejects it. Freud does not. Here are two systems, one "influenced," one "unaltered, unprejudiced." They belong to two classes of mental functioning—consciousness and the unconscious, as Freud will call them—and they will meet the dual demands of selfhood that Bergson's account cannot.

How does this system of memory and consciousness get put in place? Here is the mechanism, at last, for the link between sensations and ideas. The mechanism is that of "contact-barriers" (1:298), at once a histological trope (neural science calls these "barriers" the brain's receptor sites) and a psychological one (classical psychoanalysis calls them defense mechanisms). They provide buffers up and down the line. Their logic is also an uncanny prediction of the logic of *Beyond the Pleasure Principle* and testimony to the continuity of Freud's career early and late. First, the histological question: How does the "undifferentiated protoplasm" of originary life become "differentiated" (1:298)? Even "differentiation" is a function of "conduction" (1:298). The reception of stimulation produces the "contact-barriers" by a process that simultaneously breaches the organism and creates an interior into which the organism may flee for safety. The "contact-barriers," in other words, produce the very difference between inside and outside that they appear only to serve. Jolt or catastrophe, to use Bloom's terms, is this kind of originary event. Now the condition is set for the development of an unconscious or a "residuum." "Conduction … will create a differentiation in the protoplasm and consequently an improved conductive capacity for subsequent conduction" (1:299). Once the contact-barriers have put the two systems in place, the link between sensations and ideas, quantity and quality, is mechanically possible. The two systems of conduction have neurones that are, on the one hand, "permeable" (1:299), and, on the other, "loaded with resistance" (1:300). In the memorial differences these latter begin to store emerges the field, first, of a cognitive unconscious, and then, propped on it, a psychological one. These latter "afford," says Freud, very clearly, "a *possibility of representing memory*" (1:299).

But this is not quite enough. To fill out his design, Freud will also turn around and supplement science, too:

> For whereas science has set about the task of tracing all the qualities of
> our sensations back to external quantities, it is to be expected from the
> structure of the nervous system that it consists of contrivances for trans-
> forming external quantity into quality. (1:309)

What are these "contrivances"? They are a strategy that links the activity of the
first system of "permeable" neurones with the second system of resistant ones.
What is the dynamic of this strategy, and what exactly does it link? "Where
do qualities originate?" asks Freud. "Not in the external world. For, out there,
according to the view of our natural science, to which psychology too must be
subjected here. ... , there are only masses in motion and nothing else" (1:308). A
new calculation is required. The impermeable or resistant neurones of the second residual or unconscious system are of necessity—now it is clear—no more
than what they can be: memories, traces, images. They are secondary, derived.
They are representations. The conclusion to which Freud is already led—and
unlike Bergson it does not disturb him—is that our world of inward sensations
is never pure. We experience it in the belated terms of the representations that
allow us to match one thing up with another by means of what we already know.
We recognize events because they repeat things from the past. Freud is quite
clear about this.

> While one is perceiving the perception, one copies the movement one-
> self—that is, one innervates so strongly the motor image of one's own
> which is aroused towards coinciding [with the perception], that the move-
> ment is carried out. Hence one can speak of a perception having an
> *imitation-value*. Or the perception may arouse the mnemic image of a sen-
> sation of pain of one's own, so that one feels the corresponding unplea-
> sure and repeats the appropriate defensive movement. Here we have the
> *sympathy-value* of a perception. (1:333)

This is precisely what James refuses to see, and what Bergson cannot. "Perception" itself has—or must have—"an *imitation-value*" to come about in the first
place. This is not an "imitation" of the world or the self, as imitation presumably
is in art or life, but of memories. Does, Freud asks, a present event or perception "imitate" a prior memory of it? This is very Wildean indeed. These are
heightened memories of a presumably paradigmatic kind, whether in the use
of the body, or in social interaction. All "perception," says an ironic Freud, has
a "*sympathy-value*"—a sympathy with the self who remembers, and wishes to
remain comfortable among its memories. The subject is, from the ground up,
a link between sensations and ideas, first, to differentiate itself from the inani-
mate world, and, second, to differentiate itself from itself in order to produce a
coherent psychological world. This world is based on an unconscious as well as
a presumable consciousness, and makes its judgments on the basis of the "sympathy-value" its perceptions can find in its "residuum" of unconsciously remem-
bered ideas.

Freud's writing, as it always does, also doubles what it describes. The birth of the unconscious emerges as a conceptual necessity in the *Project* as a reflection of the unconscious presence there of Bergson's *Essay*. Consciousness can only know its objects if it has already seen them, out of the past. This is simply deferred action, but Bergson rejects it. For Freud, by contrast, deferred action is the very structure of influence, both in life and in texts. It is how he has added to Bergson's philosophy the physiologist's trope of two systems of neurones and solved Bergson's problem for him. Freud's dialectical use of Bergson and science serves as an example of deferred action historiographically. What distinguishes Freud from such parent discourses as philosophical psychology on the one hand and the language of physiology on the other is his constant exchange of them that makes each chase down the other in a battle of priorities that mimics the ascendancy and decline of "values" in the subject's life. This strategy is writ large in the full title of the *Project*. The *Project* is for a "scientific psychology," not a philosophical one. Here is Freud's difference from, and similarity to, both Bergson and the laboratory alike. Freud's is the combination of the project of a philosophical psychology—Bergson's, and, behind him, James's—with that of neurology.

The Freudian handling of influence, both for the psychological subject and for the writer, is precisely that of playing off one influence against another. We have seen it at work in Derrida's and Bloom's description of primal repression as something that not only protects but that also produces what it protects against. Freud solves his anxieties of influence by using each one to supplement what is lacking in the other. Freud slays one determination by raiding its foil or counterpart. What looks like the solution to a physiological problem turns out to be the solution to a philosophical problem recast in the language of physiology. Deferred action structures Freud's double stance, too: If he leaves science behind, he is a poet; if he leaves poetry behind, he is a scientist. Catch him if you can. This is a Shakespearean use of influence, although Freud does it, not with commedia dell'arte and courtly love, but with laboratory research and the vocabulary of Bergson. Even Freud's literary structures are examples of the structure of the psychical apparatus that he invents on top of Bergson's own.

The doubly defensive use of overdetermining influences to fight off one another reflects the activity of the psychical apparatus in a particularly vivid way. Survival—the subject's and Freud's own—is at stake. With deferred action as one's only guide, reading Freud, being a Freudian subject, and even writing about Freud all become paradigmatic instances of the necessity to organize and store overdetermination. It is the necessity that is Freud's ultimate concern as both a writer and as a psychologist. Once again *récit* and *histoire* match. The Freudian text, like the psychical apparatus, must protect itself against overstimulation and loss of coherence. It does so by the endless "retranscriptions" of deferred action. Not only does Freud use literature and science dialectically to protect the coherence of his writing; psyche and world use each other to protect the newness of the subject that their dialectical interaction has likewise formed.

What links science and literature rather than distinguishes them is now clear: the need to control overdetermination. There is no way around this simple conclusion. How are science and literature continuous in Freud rather than distinct? What project do they share? Thomas Kuhn (1962) made this procedural identity plain to a wide audience many years ago. To produce a site for testing something is to produce a site in which one can focus the question of why something behaves as it does. One does so by asking what its dynamic relation is to any series of variables in the relations to be tested. Controlling variables is controlling overdetermination. Each test isolates a narrower concatenation of possible combinations, then isolates a narrower field still. Such an interpretative chain is one in which only a single relationship is left standing. Overdetermination is the source of variability; it points to more than one cause, or system of causes, operating at the same time. But this is not true of science alone. Control is what science, literature, and psychoanalysis all share in common. Controlling variables is controlling overdetermination. This is true of both the object and, ideally, as it were, of the scientific method. The clinician seeks to control variables, the methodologist overdetermination. The scientist and the poet share the same practice, particularly in relation to what we can call tradition in both cases—the institutional "residuum" that makes up the echoing fields of their respective labors in a history of forms and conclusions. Psychoanalysis plays the two traditions off against each other in a simulation of both the psyche it represents and its own double action as a form of writing. Much as the Freudian subject builds up a "residuum" for the purposes of protection, so Freud's texts build up a residue against which they are to be read as the means of their own protection. This buffer is, as Bloom points out, Freud's own prior texts. Freud has freed himself from all traditions, to this extent. The only past that concerns him is his own. The doubling is allegorical as well as reflexive. The temporality of Freud's reader is like the temporality of Freud's subject. Both are running for their lives to keep things coherent. And, of course, because what is always at issue are relationships, answers are never forthcoming. The question of cause has to wait, endlessly, on the prior question of temporality. Deferred action is what structures the relationship between sensations and ideas, quantity and quality. The agency of time is its mechanism.

We have already seen a literary counterpart to science from the point of view of time. It is the way Eliot constructs canons through deferred action. Now even the question of canons can be asked in a neurological context. Why canons? To organize semiotic porousness, the condition of the tissues as well as of texts. The anxiety of the nervous system to survive overstimulation is not unlike that of the writer's anxious dialectic with tradition. The poet, too, sifts through influences in order to survive, the variables dwindling down, as we will see in the discussion of biography and literary history in Chapter 8, to a chosen few. Nor is this structure of anxiety altogether different from the reader's anxiety in trying to survive the overstimulation that reading by definition is. We shall see why this is so in the description of reading in Chapter 7.

Tissues, texts, and trauma: *Studies on Hysteria* and *The Interpretation of Dreams*

Freud's dream-work, of course, is the most familiar site of the doublings with which we are concerned. It bears an uncanny resemblance to the narration that appears only to report it. The dreambook shows us Freud, after all, reading the readings the dream-work performs on its raw but absent materials; or, to put it another way, Freud's writing redoubles the writing of the dream-work insofar as the dream-work is a gloss or commentary on a latent content deduced—like the purported objects of Freud's texts—from the vestiges of the repression that defines it. Its own devices correspond, as one might expect, to the chief devices of the dream-work as Freud will describe them in Chapter 6. The fourth of these devices—"considerations of representability"—is the condition for the other three. These first three—condensation, displacement, and secondary revision—play out their strategic mechanisms in Freud's narration of them as well as in their own inner workings. They are, as I will show, the principal motifs in their own description.

First, though, what is "representability," and what "considerations" are at work in its possibility? This question will preoccupy us for the remainder of this study. We already know what representation's "condition" is. It is deferred action. We also know that deferred action sutures the relation between "sensations" and "ideas," between the "affective," in Bergson's vocabulary, and its "representative." Hence, "representability" is the "condition" *of* representation, and, though it is not quite the same thing, *for* representation. *Studies on Hysteria* is the text that supervenes between the *Project* and *The Interpretation of Dreams*. What can *Studies on Hysteria* tell us about representation? We know that representation here is unmotivated in relation to what it signifies—unmotivated, that is, from an "essentializing" point of view, to use Burke's term. There is plenty of motivation between symptom and its unconscious sources, but it is entirely associational and historical. That is the point. Why is Emmy von N.'s "clacking" (2:49) inappropriate? *Studies on Hysteria* explains how by presenting a rather strict form of semiology, recognizable from Barthes (1959). Hysteria is a second-order semiological system, a mythology to the patient, a metalanguage to the analyst. It demotivates the sign by remotivating it within another field of reference in the patient's unconscious. "What provokes the symptom," say Freud and Breuer in the "Preliminary Communication," "is the accident" of the "connection" (2:4). This is true not only of Anna O.'s inability to drink, but of Elisabeth von R.'s physical pains, which are punitive conversions of her love for her sister's husband. Even here, deferred action rules: The pains, says Freud, came "only after the event" (2:169). This is the sole basis of "the symbolic relation between the precipitating cause and the pathological phenomenon" (2:5). The myth of hysteria makes the sign a signifier in a new, second-order system. This new system or field of reference is the patient's unconscious. It emerges by narratological, not empirical, necessity. But to the extent that the overstimulating world is structured like a narrative to the subject, the two necessities are really the same.

Nor is Freud's own preoccupation with representation merely a function of his literary agon with Bergson, or even of his scientific agon with Helmholtz and Brücke. It, too, repeats, in another key, the doubling between Freudian datum and Freudian text that identifies neurological toxicity with literary anxiety of influence. The influence is not confined to science and philosophical psychology when the context is hysteria. In the overdetermined cultural history that leads to psychoanalysis, one very specific element targets this problem in an extraordinarily concrete way. It is the history of trauma. Trauma is an extreme form of overstimulation whose memory traces are so deep that even the effects of such experience cannot be erased. As we will see, the difference between endogenous and exogenous trauma is an exaggerated one. Both the American Civil War and the Crimean War produced new kinds of violent, machine-inflicted injuries on soldiers that in contemporary domestic life in Europe and America had their counterpart in shocks and injuries to passengers on the newly invented railways (Schivelbusch 1977). With "railway spine," as such injuries were called, doctors had to decide whether a complaint stemmed from a brain injury or was the psychological effect of having had a bad experience and retaining a memory of it. Here Freud's attendance at the French neurologist Charcot's hypnosis demonstrations in Paris from October 1885 to February 1886 takes on a particularly sharp focus (Chertok and Saussure 1973, 71). While it is true that Charcot helped Freud to believe that there was, in Charcot's phrase, a *conscience seconde*—another Parisian "source" for Freud's unconscious—Charcot also placed psychoanalysis in the middle of the railway spine debate, and therefore in a history of concern about trauma and its status wider than is generally assumed. Here the early psychoanalytic preoccupation with questions of trauma recapitulates the questions asked by John Erichsen and others in the 1860s regarding train accidents: Did a physical injury actually take place, or was the trauma psychological?

The question, of course, is misconceived. If mind and body, inside and outside, are, as we have seen, already continuous in psychoanalysis, the difference between physical and psychical trauma must be one of degree rather than one of kind. Masson and Borch-Jacobsen are both too quick on the trigger in wishing to execute Freud for repressing the "reality" of trauma, whatever that may mean. Trauma is always quite real. The difference is one of, well, quantity, rather than one of quality. In rejecting the seduction theory, Freud does not simply leave neurology and enter literature. He reimagines the very relation between ideal and real, inside and outside, mind and the material. Here the birth of psychoanalysis is not at odds with the history of neurology, but a refinement of it. As a form of shock, railway trauma is of a piece with the question of stimulation and protection in both science and philosophical psychology. Like hysteria in a psychological key, railway spine is, in a physical key, an instance of stimulation and protection at its most extreme. Like epileptiform illnesses, such events in the sphere of stimulation and defense are pathological, whether the damage is histological or psychological. Is a convulsive seizure in a patient with head trauma a suitable analogue in the physical sphere for a hysterical patient whose convulsions emerge from a different—a psychological—kind of trauma? Is a painful memory in any sense also physical? Why does a psychopharmaceutical like clonazepam treat both epileptic convulsions and panic attacks, and nothing else? What relation is implicitly drawn between them? The memory of verbal abuse is also material, though to a variably reduced degree. Nor—and this is where we presumably began—is physical abuse obviously without its psychological consequences. The railway spine debate, in other words, actually raises questions in poetics: Is signification iconic? What is being represented, to whom, and in what ways? The abandonment of the seduction theory does not "move" psychoanalysis from science to literature. It shifts the concern of psychology and science alike to the status of the image or representation. We have not "moved" from science to literature at all. We have, surprisingly, moved instead closer to the question common to them both: What is representation and how does it function, whether in the mind, or in the presumably distinct world of biology? Science and literature, body and mind are, from this point of view, no longer distinct. What they share is the desire, first and foremost, to survive, whether as cultural projects or as animate ones.

Freud's reader is never immune from these conditions. Freud's way of structuring the literature on dreams in Chapter 1 is an excellent example of it. Here the reader is treated to the very condition of the Freudian psyche by being set out to sea amid waves of reference and allusion to which the layperson can only react with horror and amaze. Overdetermination does not just play a role in psychical determination; it also plays a role in the bibliographical traditions that burden Freud's writing. While this is always true of Freud, its grandest site is the dreambook's oneirohistoriography. The trends of dream interpretation throughout history give Chapter 1 whatever form it has. Freud's attempt to mimic their vicissitudes, however, leads him into a defensive posture in order to protect himself against the apparent chaos of his subject matter and the danger it poses to coherence. Whether or not the history of literature on dreams really falls into the trends Freud invents for it or whether this is simply Freud's defensive response to its overwhelmingness is not irrelevant. It allows us to see that these two things are necessarily one and the same. The history of the literature can only be represented by categories that reduce and delimit it. This is the generous way of putting it. It protects one against the toxicity of overload.

The result is a canny introduction to dreams that bears a closer resemblance to the dream-work itself than to a placid review of the scientific literature. This is not only doubling. This is also Freud's way of navigating, with a strong executive confidence, the overdeterminations that assail him as a writer. Freud sees the ironic advantages to be had from pouring an avalanche of dream commentary on himself, from the very beginning of Western time. But compared to the history of Freud's real precursors—the poets, acknowledged and unacknowledged, as well as nineteenth-century scientists and philosophical psychologists—the history of dream literature is altogether more pliable. It is strong enough to sustain him, but also weak enough to do his taxonomic bidding. Freud will secure his release from this plastic tradition even as he inscribes his work within it. But to what particular purpose? The reader's silent preparation for what is to come only later in the book. There is probably no clearer way to see Freud's rather high-handed methods—and even more high-handed, if largely unconscious, motivation—this early in his career. The history of dreams presented in Chapter 1 is not only not the history it purports to be. The synchronic structure Freud supposedly finds in his tradition turns out to be no less than the structure of the unconscious itself as it will emerge in Chapters 6 and 7. Chapter 1, not surprisingly, was composed after the rest of the manuscript had been completed.

Though there are innumerable ways of anatomizing the literature on dreams from antiquity down to the nineteenth century, the special way in which Freud arranges his evidence is symptomatic. It is a species of condensation, the first element of the dream-work's three proper elements, and the first of Freud's devices in Chapter 1. Freud begins with *chronos*—with a historical and, as a nineteenth-century reader might be led to assume, a developmental perspective on past theories of dreaming. But Freud soon abandons *chronos* in favor of *topos*, in favor of an attention to the recurrent sites—"the two opposing currents" of opinion "at every period" since "before … Aristotle" (4:3)—to which this history that is no history at all habitually returns. Reducing his tradition by freeing it from the constraints of narrative time itself, Freud puts in its place a nonhistory of conflicting opinion or enduring "contradiction" (4:9) which is nearly the same from antiquity to the nineteenth century. Freud diffidently removes all that is historical from his history, change and contingency alike, in keeping with a strategic intent, that of condensing history itself into a virtually synchronic state of "contradiction" or difference. What emerges instead is a state of simultaneous and necessarily interdependent tensions—dreaming as prophecy or remembrance, as daemonic inspiration, as self-engendered illusion. The literature, in other words, reflects its subject exactly. The history of the literature on dreams is structured like dreams. Dreams themselves admit of no contingency, no past, no present, only a miraculous synchronicity in which anything and everything is possible at once, particularly "contradiction," which, in the absence of other rules, itself becomes the rule.

Freud also uses a more familiar rhetorical technique for securing the existence of the unconscious, although its very familiarity is what tends to obscure its function as a device. It is the book's second borrowing from, or doubling of, the dream-work. Consider, for example, the following apology in Chapter 6 for Freud's reticence in reporting fully to the reader the associations to one of his own dreams:

> I am forbidden to do so for reasons connected with the nature of the psychical material involved—reasons which are of many kinds and which will be accepted as valid by any reasonable person. (4:310)

Freud's famous reserve about disclosing the full implications of associations to which certain dream-thoughts lead him has been taken not so much as hypocritical repression or even as stinging self-irony, although even these charges are not unreasonable. Instead, such hesitation is traditionally read as further testimony to Freud's Romantic heroism in revealing to us as much of himself as he has. We can only presume at such moments that darker thoughts must lie still deeper. It is, however, a decided strategy, Freud's second distinguishable one in the text. It is a familiar trope—displacement, or metonymy, the second of the dream-work's elements that Freud's narration both doubles and parodies. It claims the dream to be nearby by pointing to a piece of it, and it claims the unconscious to be nearby in turn by pointing to a fragment of dream. What we construe as the pressure of such repression causing Freud to halt, often a little too ostentatiously, ambivalent about his chain of evidences, is a sign not so much of Freud's hypocrisy as of a calculated feint. For the effect of what seems to be a denial or a retreat from the game—the emergence of repression in the midst of an argument intended to undo its thrall—in fact pushes the game further along, giving it an inner tension or difference from itself constitutive of narrative desire in the usual ways, and redoubled in the text's explicit project of desiring the satiety of a psychoanalytic explanation. The result: the constitution of the unconscious negatively, its emergence as something against or on which Freud's hesitation can be propped. This is how Freud's reader produces the unconscious as a category necessary for Freud's text to cohere whenever Freud the dreamer blanches with shame. Like Freud, and like the Freudian subject, the reader must also make sense of it all. The reader's is also a constitutive defense, a necessary and unconscious practice in the reading of Freud. Perhaps the very nucleus of Freud's inventive referentiality lies in this metonymic or, more exactly, synecdochic procedure, a procedure common in Freud. Philip Rieff noted it in 1959. It requires the reader of the dreambook to reason by displacement in order to keep things whole.

Such metonymic displacement brings us to the third of Freud's devices, and the third of the master tropes in the dream-work, secondary revision. It is the device laid out as the telos of Chapter 6, on the dream-work proper, and a device that may be said to subsume all the others. It is the central logical contention that Freud himself holds throughout the text—that the presence of dreams is known by the tokens of their absence. It is the condition, as it were, of the condition of representability. Secondary revision is a form of deferred action. It is the inevitable first interpretation that comes simply as the result of reporting or even remembering a dream. Secondary revision is an almost privileged model for the very existence of dreams and, by extension, the unconscious. Like God, dreams and the unconscious that produces them are known only by the tokens of their disguise or departure. If the dream's difference from itself is what defines it as such—if its parts require a whole so as to be parts of it—then the report or memory of the dream is all-important, indeed decisive, in its constitution as a referent. Secondary revision is the first step in the dream's interpretation because its interpretation and its report are the same thing. In Freud's words in Chapter 6, secondary revision "subjects" the dream—the implications of the pun are also provocative—"to a first interpretation" and a consequent "misunderstanding" (5:500). Both interpretation and misunderstanding require there to be or to have been something present which has already been inadvertently or silently interpreted, and which has properties discernible enough to be understood—to be produced—with varying degrees of analytic sufficiency. Such a structure is reminiscent of Lacan's injunction to return to Freud, as though Freud's text were already there, in an original state, like the unconscious; with no influences on it to shape our view of it. In Lacan's own case, the shaping power is American ego psychology, against which he reacts as his enabling polemic. Even to call secondary revision "secondary" is to presume a primary revision beforehand despite Freud's assurance that secondary revision is among the dream-work's founding operations.

So it is from the *récit* of the dream's narration, belated by definition in relation to itself, that its *histoire*—its preexistence, its quiddity—can alone be construed. Never discovered, since to call the report a distortion is already to require something more primary to have been there first. Distortion and repression are the very evidence of the dream-work that they are assigned to hide or dissimulate. The dream-work is no more and no less than the conditions of its own production. We might even say that it is no more and no less than the conditions of its own representability. Its mechanisms are its readers' responses to it: condensation, displacement, secondary revision, all guided by the master trope of the "considerations of representability," which they both anatomize and subtend. This is not only how the dream-work acts but also what the dream-work is. There is no difference between them. Nor is there an identity. The relation between manifest and latent content is not one of difference or identity at all, but of a ratio that comes into being only after the dream's remembrance and interpretation. If the dream reflexively signifies the activity of the dream-work, it is the interpretation that retroactively signifies the activity of the dream. But this is no homology either. The dream is, to use Derrida's term, structured like a supplement, present and absent at the same time. The dream is at once full enough to be interpreted, but lacking enough to require interpretation. The dream, in other words, is structured by—as—deferred action.

The lack of homology or identity between meaning and interpretation is the very gap that structures the Freudian subject and the Freudian text, and that accounts for the sadness of both. *The Interpretation of Dreams* makes this shocking inevitability extraordinarily clear in what is perhaps its boldest moment:

> But before starting off along this new path, it will be well to pause and look around, to see whether in the course of our journey up to this point we have overlooked anything of importance. For it must be clearly understood that the easy and agreeable portion of our journey lies behind us. Hitherto, unless I am greatly mistaken, all the paths along which we have traveled have led us towards the light—towards elucidation and fuller understanding. But as soon as we endeavor to penetrate more deeply into the mental process involved in dreaming, every path will end in darkness. There is no possibility of explaining dreams as a psychical process, since to explain a thing means to trace it back to something already known, and there is at the present time no established psychological knowledge under which we could subsume what the psychological examination of dreams enables us to infer as a basis for their explanation. On the contrary, we shall be obliged to set up a number of fresh hypotheses which touch tentatively upon the structure of the apparatus of the mind and upon the play of forces operating in it. (5:511)

Compare this passage from Chapter 7 to one at the start of Chapter 2, where Freud makes clear, with an irony we can see only now, precisely what is amiss about dream interpretation before psychoanalysis:

> "Interpreting" a dream implies assigning a "meaning" to it—that is, replacing it by something which fits into the chain of our mental acts as a link having a validity and importance equal to the rest. (4:96)

The passage from Chapter 7, especially in its correction of the passage from Chapter 2, assures us of two things: First, Freud's invention is new. It cannot, as dreams cannot, be inserted into a prior code of meanings and turned into a recapitulation of someone else's—someone's prior—meaning. Specificity is crucial. Second—and this is the basis for Freud's specificity and originality—psychoanalysis is not a mimetic project. It does not give us a representation of the psychical apparatus. It gives us, in Freud's texts and in his way of thinking, an extended example of it. Freud rethinks and rejects the classical notion of mimesis itself. What we really mean by mimesis, as Freud's metaphors show, is no more than the insertion of one's own impressions into a chain of other impressions with which one has become identified. This is the description of "imitation" in the *Project*. Mimesis, in other words, is only a consensus of impressions, a commonly agreed-on state of mind between one set of impressions and others. The psychical apparatus does not record what it sees. It stores and processes it, or, rather, it processes it by storing it. It does so through the variety of defense mechanisms that it has available to it, many of them social in nature, to guard against stimulation. In this fashion does the unconscious become historical in more than a personal way. Cultural mythologies are often handed down as the warp and woof of family relationships.

Psychoanalysis and its vicissitudes

If secondary revision is the decisive trope of the dreambook, then revision as such, as Bloom reminds us, tends to become the master activity of Freud's enterprise in the years following 1910. The metapsychological phase includes the five "surviving" papers of 1915–17, although a more garrulous estimate begins the metapsychology with "On Narcissism" (1914), and focuses special attention on "Instincts and their Vicissitudes" (1915). These two texts of Freud's middle phase contain its key changes. Let me use them to frame a discussion of the metapsychological phase as a whole.

"On Narcissism" revises "Formulations on the Two Principles of Mental Functioning" (1911). There, in the earlier essay, where the first phase of psychoanalysis really comes to an end, pleasure and reality, libido and consciousness, still battle it out. Then, in 1914, Freud takes an irreparable step that follows from the discovery of narcissism, the metapsychological equivalent of the rejection of the seduction theory: the rejection of the notion of a libido prior to any of its manifestations or emanations. Ego does not exist apart from the energies by which it is constituted, nor do the energies. The ego itself is libidinally cathected. Ego and libido intermix, but in a new way. They are no longer rivals; they are consorts. How this occurs, however, is unclear. To make it clear, Freud's enterprise requires, like the infant child, the supplement of a theory of images. More precisely, it still requires a theory of image-acquisition. It already has one; it is called "identification." It is how "sensations" and "ideas" are linked, or connected. Now that its mechanism is clear and in place, identification suddenly—belatedly—gains a wider role as a psychoanalytic category, and finds its precise contexts of emergence. Identification is not, of course, the only form of representation in Freud, but it is the occasion here for Freud to work out his theory of images with particular sharpness. In narcissism, what will end up as desire, for others as well as for oneself, begins in need, the simple need to protect against sensations. This is how the mind becomes the mind—by producing defensive representations. This is when desire surprises it, and distinguishes itself from need. With *Group Psychology and the Analysis of the Ego* (1921), the notion of identification will fully coordinate this movement of "ideas" in the individual, including, of course, the structuration of desire. The ego is given its determinations there by the images produced by social interaction, beginning with the infant's first moments of life.

In "On Narcissism," the earliest relation to self turns out to proceed with the help—if you can call it that—of others. Not only do symbolization and primary process—"idea" and "sensation"—begin their work together. They ironically do so—who would have expected it?—with the help of the family. It is not a solitary process at all. "On Narcissism" is concerned not only with the birth of the subject, but with the subject's relation to the family romance. The passage from the "sensations" of auto-erotism to the "idea" of a self requires Freud to see that the child must find an image to connect to auto-erotism in order to enter the human order. This is how the child constructs a relation between "sensations" and "ideas." A retroactive or deferred relation between body and mind is produced which is not there at the start of life. The temporality of this relation is precisely what Bergson cannot imagine in the *Essay* and is the reason he cannot solve the problem of the advent of "ideas" as Freud can. This deferred or dissonant structure for selfhood is the very hallmark of the Freudian subject, and the reason for its difference from Bergson's and James's alike.

"On Narcissism" solves the relation between "quantity" and "quality," "sensations" and "ideas," with an ease that is surprising. The relation between "sensations" and "ideas" becomes the very fulcrum for infantile ideation, and the first instance of it. It also shows us the link between representation and psychical defense. In order to defend itself against an uncertain environment, the infant symbolizes—represents—its environment. It projects its response to it onto it. This is its way of representing both it and itself. The hazards of this kind of identity are well known to us all. It already includes the backdrop of the still more inward drama of self-formation through repression, particularly primal repression. Defense and representation, sensations and ideas, even aim and object—these are all homologies, versions of one another. The relation between each pair produces the God-term each one is designed to generate: self, psyche, instinct. Their rhythm is also a chiasmatic one. The structures they produce are all characterized by the fissure, or, really, the lag instituted into the very conception of the psychical apparatus by the conditions of time. The subject, we must always remember, is structured by deferred action.

How does the child connect, to adopt Wordsworth's phrase, the landscape with the quiet of the sky? The child connects the "sensation" of auto-erotism—wholly autonomic in its urgent origins—with an "idea." "Masturbation," says Freud in the *New Introductory Lectures* (1933), "is the executive agent of infantile sexuality" (22:127). Despite the child's presumable solitariness, the child masturbates in a relation to those around him, a topic I will take up in my chapter on pornography. Freud's later distinction between primary and secondary narcissism is unnecessary. Narcissism is always both primary and secondary at the same time. Its attempt to make the self special and separate is based on relationships with others. In order to be primary, it must be secondary. Its anxiety is always that of influence. In narcissism, the autoerotic "idea" actually predates its later variants by already being based in either object-choice or identification. What the difference is between projection and identification grows fuzzy—we noted this peril a moment ago—as does the line between identification and object-choice itself. "Ideas" develop from infantile masturbation to or for significant others. These ideas are therefore always doubly displaced from what they signify, adjunct not only to the sensations to which they attach themselves, but also adjunct to the ideas that presumably satisfy them. By virtue of the constitutive deferral of the "object," they can never be satisfying. We have already stressed the temporality of this structure and its consequences for the epistemological status of the subject. The self to which this annex of sensations and ideas refers is a belated one. It comes into being only after the link between sensations and ideas has been made.

The retroactive constitution of the subject in narcissism, in other words, is also structured by deferred action. This produces amusing ironies not only in the reading of Freud, but in the reading of contemporary historiography, especially that of the New Historicism. To prove the conclusions of "On Narcissism" historically is the burden of Thomas Laqueur's *Solitary Sex* (2003), although with an unintentional and non-Freudian irony. Laqueur maintains that Freud's discovery of narcissism is simply the end of a long history of studying self-abuse. This fact elicits Stephen Greenblatt's specific praise (2004), since it reduces Freudian narcissism to a redundant proof of the truth of Laqueur's proposition that growing prohibitions regarding masturbation in the nineteenth century elicited a refinement of the very behavior they were designed to eliminate. In the process, a more complex web of subjectivity was spun. Greenblatt and Laqueur alike miss the point. Their own enablement as historians, especially Laqueur's, is based on the Freudian insight that they can now dismiss as typical. It is because of the Freudian notion of narcissism that we can now see, as

Laqueur does, that masturbation plays a constitutive role in the development of the self. Thanks to the historiographical deferred action that it enables, the notion of narcissism allows a whole history to come into view retroactively. For Laqueur or Greenblatt to claim that Freud is only a latecomer to the history he allows them to discover is to repress the Freudian mechanism that allows them to see it. This mode of strategic enablement in relation to Freud derives from the work of Foucault, to which I shall turn in a later chapter. As with Laqueur and Greenblatt, the repression and appropriation of Freud is key to Foucault's own achievement.

More to the point here is the child. Recall that the infant's self-representation does not come alone. In the dyad with the mother, more is available to it than chiasmus, which is the exclusive modality of narcissism. There is also condensation and displacement, metaphor and metonymy. The mother serves the child as both good and bad breast; she is, in other words, both with the child and apart from the child. She switches, in an alimentary rhythm that is already symbolic, between metaphorical oneness and metonymic distance. The mother is, in her own presumable originality, also structured by displacement. She gives satisfaction and frustration, pleasure and pain. The mother/child dyad is not undifferentiated in its origin. The difference at its heart is precisely what spurs the desire to close it. The mother is this difference, and thereby already the bearer of the Oedipus complex, as we will see. As both condensation and displacement, metaphor and metonymy, the mother is both present and absent, reflector of the child's secure self and cruel purveyor of its indifferent punishment and deprivation.

Although we are accustomed to giving all credit for narcissism to the mirror stage, auto-erotism precedes it, developmentally. Auto-erotism already inscribes the infant into the socially Symbolic. The infant's future encounter with the mirror will inscribe it, belatedly, into an Imaginary modality with which it can learn to mystify and mollify the Symbolic that already overwhelms it in its sharp encounters with the mother. With autoeroticism, the Imaginary emerges well before the mirror stage, and the Symbolic well before the child's presumably later entrance into the Oedipal situation. They emerge together, in primary narcissism. The Imaginary and the Symbolic do not follow one another sequentially in a developmental schema; they are codependent from the beginning. Most important, the Imaginary gives personality its first line of psychical defense, a way of dealing with the anxieties of presence and absence associated with the mother, who already embodies the Symbolic in her comings and goings. The Imaginary is a misreading of the Symbolic.

Let me call this dyad with the mother a supplement to narcissism. Here, the mother provides the infant with an object that is actually no more than an aim. No wonder she reflects the child's face in her own. The child is the reconstituted object of the mother's own narcissism. The object itself—the child—can only be an aim in the mother's eyes. But all is well from the point of view of the law of culture. The aim is to discover, not her, of course—the child is, and will be, prohibited from actually doing that—but the child's own self. That this self is already a gauze of other people's responses to it is fine with the child. That is all he is to himself anyway—his own response to his circumstances. Other of Freud's ironies are less severe. Although "On Narcissism" tells us that this self is an "object" for itself, in point of fact this "object" is endlessly evanescent, the perpetually unfulfilled grail-quest of the internalization of quest-romance.

The social bond with the mother also has ramifications for Freud's language. Freud calls the self that emerges in narcissism the *Ichideal*, the "ideal ego." This is when the context is narcissism. Here the subject forms a conception or "idea" of itself. What, then, is, by contrast, the "ego-ideal," or the *Idealich*? Žižek's assumption that the ideal ego does the "constituting" while the ego-ideal is "constituted" (1989, 216) not only represses the temporality that structures their relation, but also their reciprocal origin. *Idealich* and *Ichideal* are themselves an example of how the psychical apparatus functions, particularly under duress. It splits. Each of the terms produces the other. Even before the mirror stage, the enabling difference between "ideal ego" and "ego-ideal" is already in place. It is not "present," but reciprocal. It shows just how social even primary narcissism is. The parents are involved. It also shows just how solitary social interaction is. It is all projection. No wonder. How do one's "ideal conception of one's self," to use Conrad's phrase, and one's ego-ideal emerge as a struggle, in both Freud's language and in experience, to stay distinct and apart? *Ichideal* and *Idealich* form a chiasmus. As the one turns over into the other, and back again, each part of the structure takes its place by turns. The temporality is odd, but familiar. It is deferred action. That which comes later—the ego-ideal—puts in place, retroactively, that which precedes it—the ideal ego. Among the most daunting of the problems at work here is that an ideal conception of one's self and of someone else are virtually indistinguishable. Narcissism is a kind of identification before the fact—an identification both with the paternal aggressor and with the mother whose presence the father fantastically abrogates for the child. In the very emergence of the self to itself, the family romance is already at work, this by virtue of the child's active fantasy world and the splitting it engenders. In Chapter 9, I will show how pornography is, both clinically and aesthetically, the concrete externalization of this paradigmatic site. "In the individual's mental life," says Freud in the first paragraph of *Group Psychology*, "someone else is invariably involved, as a model, as an object, as a helper, as an opponent; and so from the very first individual psychology, in this extended but entirely justifiable sense of the words, is at the same time social psychology as well" (18:69). "Model" and "opponent" are the father; "object" and "helper" the mother. Oedipus—and splitting, of identification and object-choice alike—already reside at the very heart of self-discovery. "On Narcissism," in other words, is already a part of Freud's third phase, or, to put it another way, the third phase is consistent with the presumable intractabilities of the metapsychology that precedes it.

So consistent is "On Narcissism" with Freud's third phase that *Group Psychology* is its best gloss. There the difference between ideal ego and ego-ideal is called a "differentiating grade" in the ego (18:129). It is the chiasmatic rhythm between them that counts—what "differentiates" them one from the other—not the choice of one position over another. The two have been intermixed since their beginnings, in primary narcissism. "Super-ego" in *The Ego and the Id* is at one and the same time a name for this perpetual internal difference, and an attempt to establish a developmental end to its otherwise endless movement back and forth. This chiasmus or "differentiating grade" joins our other familiar ones: aim and object, which produce instinct; sensations and ideas, which produce the subject. What does the chiasmatic play of ideal ego and ego-ideal produce? Why, the subject's inscription into the social order. These three structures are in fact hierarchical. Each is propped on the other—"instinct" first, followed by the subject, then the political unconscious.

Chiasmus is given its proper Freudian name—at last—in "Repression" (1915): "*primal repression*" (14:148). Freud has already used the term "primarily repressed" in the Schreber case (1911, 12:67–68), but does not fully explain it until now. "Primal repression" is the movement that the *Project* has described as one of resistance to stimulation. The breaching that is its result has the ironic effect of producing, as Bloom and Derrida have shown, the very "instinct" that is repressed. Primal repression produces the drive it defends against. In "Repression," "idea" and the "instinctual energy linked to it" (14:152) are, as terms, vestiges of the Bergsonian vocabulary of the *Project*. They are also proof that Freud is still interested in the "*transformation* into *affects*" of "*instincts*" (14:153). Now the solution to the "transformation" problem is clearer still. The transformation is accomplished in the dimension of time by chiasmus, in the associational crossing back and forth between quantity and quality, sensations and ideas. Chiasmus and deferred action are one and the same. Thus the question of what is "consciousness" in "The Unconscious" (1915) is not as shocking a question to ask as it sounds. If the subject is a function of the differentiating grade between ideal ego and ego-ideal—both identifications—then how can one speak of a "conscious" subject as opposed to an "unconscious" one? Freud's subject is dialectical and material, the function of groups, however small, or large, or both, as in family life, or in the varieties of fetishism; the distinction between "consciousness" and "the unconscious" is no longer appropriate. Because we are a play of identifications, there is no longer a difference between consciousness and the unconscious (see also Solms 1997). Freud's distinction between "thing-presentation" and "word-presentation (14:200-04)" is a good example of his nostalgia for the oppositions of the first phase when their presuppositions regarding consciousness and the unconscious are under fire. Any return to the system of first-model Freud is now impossible.

"Mourning and Melancholia" (1917) is a projection of Freud's mourning for his outmoded first model, and the reason for it. The "shadow" that falls on the ego in melancholia (14:249) is the "shadow" of identification. For Freud, it is his fallen, earlier image of himself, which is dead. Things are no longer about consciousness and what is unconscious. As "On Narcissism" has shown—Freud dreads this implication—identification is there even at the start of life because we live through others. Although depression takes an exaggerated and an especially painful form in the neuroses, it is nonetheless the central fact of all mental life from a Freudian point of view. "Narcissistic identification with the object" can become "a substitute for the erotic cathexis" (14:249) because self and other are already in both positions at once. Although Freud says that identification "*precedes* object-cathexis and is distinct from it" in "A Metapsychological Supplement to the Theory of Dreams" (1917, 14:241), this is true only from a chronological point of view, not from the point of view of the time of the subject, who changes. The "differentiating grade" between ideal ego and ego-ideal is also that between identification and object-choice. The latter is the projective version of this structure; the former is the introjective. The paradox that underwrites it is the rationale for its ironic tone. We are who we are by virtue of a relation to someone else. As Trilling has reminded us, this gives us a curious double advantage: an invigorating resistance to culture, as well as an endless participation in it.

Freud's notion of *Trieb*—"drive," or "instinct"—has also shifted accordingly. This is the particular burden of "Instincts and their Vicissitudes," to which it is only now appropriate to turn, belatedly, to get the full benefit of the deferred action that looking at it now provides. It elaborates a new theory of the drives to accompany the new theory of representation that narcissism has required. If *Group Psychology* makes narcissism's social implications clear, "Instincts and their Vicissitudes" makes clear the new epistemology of Freud's revamped poetics. The peroration of *The Interpretation of Dreams* has prepared us for it. It is Freud's attack on mimesis in its customary sense. Representation is not, as it is in Bergson, the mimesis or copy of drive or instinct, its expression, as it were, or way of showing forth what is latent in it. This assumption, too, must come to an end. It already has in Freud's new notion of the ego's relation to libido in narcissism. What new relation between drive and representation takes the place of the mimetic one there? Why is the ego libidinally cathected? Because the play of narcissism and its identifications has the same mechanism that links "sensations" and "ideas." It is the same kind of mechanism that links "drive" and "representation" in "Instincts and their Vicissitudes." This is surprising. The relation of representation to drive raises as many questions about what representation is as it does about what drive is. As with the relation between ego and libido in narcissism, the relation between drive and representation is not, as I have suggested, one between tenor and vehicle. Representation is not a copy of drive in the language of consciousness, any more than the ego is a distorted copy of what is repressed. Drive and representation make up neither an opposition nor a difference, at least not a "full" or "present" phenomenological difference or distinction among existents. No, representation and drive, says Freud—like ego and libido—are interdependent, and not only rhetorically. They are interdependent in their very nature. Here phenomenology and rhetoric behave similarly because they share a common semiotic enterprise. Freudian subject and Freudian narration are doubles not because each copies something but because each produces something. "Instinct," in the famous definition, "appears to us as a concept on the frontier between the mental and the somatic, as the psychical representative of the stimuli originating from within the organism and reaching the mind" (14:122; as Strachey notes, the same change was added to the third, revised edition of the *Three Essays*, also in 1915 [7:168, 168n1]). Strachey's translation of the German *Trieb* as "instinct" rather than "drive," a notorious point of contention in debates about the *Standard Edition*, is one to which we will turn in Chapter 5, as I have already promised. For now, let me emphasize how such debates designate precisely the kind of semiotic undecidability in the structure of "instinct" itself that the questions involved in translating it raise epistemologically.

"Instinct" or "source"—Freud is canny in not being too forthright about this identity—needs an "aim" with which to find an "object." But "instinct" or "source" also needs an "object" in order to have an "aim." "Instinct" is the putative "source" of this interaction, but, like dreams, it can only be inferred. Like the dream or the unconscious, "instinct" is, to use Burke's phrase again, a "God-term," a term outside the game that explains it. The notion of "aim" as mediate is misleading. An "aim" does not mediate. It sutures or represses what is really a site of construction on the part of the two terms that straddle and order it retroactively, producing in the process the two terms that seem already to be there. Freud is still working on an old question, from the *Project*. This is the way quantity and quality, sensations and ideas, gain a relationship. Like that of the transition from quantity to quality, it is also a site whose phenomenology is once again put in place by deferred action, by inferring, backward, from object-choices and object-relations, first to their "aim" and then to their "source" in "instinct" or drive. Each term is a vehicle, in other words, for the other, and proceeds, not by tautology, but by chiasmus.

Although the parliamentary term that Freud takes from Bergson and uses to describe "instinct," "representative" (*Repräsentant*), is not identical with the term "representation" that he uses elsewhere, the presumption of both the German and the English terms to stand *for* something is one and the same. But is mimesis the structure of either democratic or aesthetic representation? Do "representative" and "representation" both refer to something else, something to which they point transparently? A parliamentary representative is really a synecdoche, a part of the whole that it refers to, and so a trace of what has also been left behind, back home. "Representation" involves an even more complex figural operation. Representation is drive, or, to put it another way, drive is representation. But how can that be? Because, as we have just seen, each term is really a vehicle for the other, and proceeds, not by tautology, but by chiasmus. "Representation" is not a vehicle for the tenor of "instinct"—that would be mimesis. To interpret the essay in this manner would be to miss its central point. No, representation and instinct are responses to each other. Once again, this is not simply a rhetorical construction. For Freud, it is also a phenomenological construction. Let us go ahead and call it a histological one, too, remembering that tissue for Freud has the same structure as text.

The second piece of the puzzle from the *Project* is now in place. Representation—the condition of being "representable"—comes as a response to stimulation. In 1895, stimulation, or quantity, is converted into quality, or ideas, gaining associative weight or cathexis through both chance and motivated connections between idea and affect. Now, in 1915, it is clear that "idea" emerges as a defense against or resistance to "sensations" themselves, which do not come into being for the subject until this moment of protection. This point cannot be overemphasized. In this formulation, the relation between the two is not one of mimesis either. The "idea" does not "copy" the "sensation." The relation is, rather, one of stimulation and flight. In 1920, in *Beyond the Pleasure Principle*, this resistance to stimulation becomes, as we shall see in the following chapter, a fable for the very existence of animate life as a thing presumably apart from its environment.

Early and late alike, Freud's environmental metaphors—strictly speaking, they include his neurological as well as his primeval ones—apply also to Freud's reader and to Freud's texts. Like the protist or the nervous system, Freud's reader lives in an atmosphere whose very air is dominated, to some extent toxically, by the demands of psychoanalytic method and thinking. Because signifiers are material, our exchange with Freud's texts, like the protist's exchange with its surroundings, is an environmental one, too. Freud's Darwinism is obvious in the fact that it is the organism that responds to its environment rather than, as in Lamarck's scheme, being determined by it passively. The same is true of reading Freud, as Foucault has reminded us. Our arguments with Freud are like an irritation of the tissues. Once Freud is in your system, you cannot get him out. My point is to privilege neither the textual nor the histological trope, but to indicate their continuity. Science and literature are a common landscape in psychoanalysis. This is not because each component of psychoanalysis, the medical and the "humanist," has its eye on the same thing. It is because, from the materialist point of view that is Freud's own, the exchange of signifiers in the nervous system and in the mind occurs in an epistemologically continuous environment.

Like the psyche that it describes, psychoanalysis is no longer the site of war between Eros and civilization, desire and repression, nature and culture. The discovery that the ego is libidinally cathected is profoundly destabilizing for the terms of prior psychoanalytic inquiry. It requires, as in melancholia, their abandonment. The psyche is no longer a tug of wits between consciousness and the unconscious. The psyche is, like Freud's texts, a play of vicissitudes seeking balance, resolution, or constancy. Discordance in assumption is now what the system is about, and is. It is the new allegory of, and for, Freud's midcareer change. Typically, what is a formal problem gets thematized; discordance in the system translates into a new, heightened sense of the psychological subject as incoherent, as discordant in ways that exceed the simple, and now problematic, differences between consciousness and the unconscious, or between ego and libido. The history of Freud's thought reveals more and more overtly the way in which his system, as Bloom suggests it does, develops an unconscious of its own: by revising itself so as to put its newer components, in this case the "component instincts," into place. Now the first model, with its certainties about the sources of excitations, is, as it were, the new system's "residuum." It is its complex of memory-traces, its primary process, against which the system's new "realizations" are its refreshed secondary process. This discordance between systems, and between the first and second phases of Freud's career, is not just what will preoccupy Freud as a system-builder endlessly seeking coherence. The dissonance between the two systems also becomes Freud's notion of the psychical apparatus itself in the new, second model.

The structure of Freud's relation to his sources is another example of the survival psyche that "On Narcissism" and "Instincts and their Vicissitudes" alike depict. It, too, is an apparatus for deflecting influence, like the ego defending itself against stimulation or anxiety. If Freud settles the problems of sensations and ideas in the history of empiricism by overcoming Bergson in the *Project*, he settles the problems of Hegelian self-consciousness in "On Narcissism." "On Narcissism" shows the extent to which this Hegelian element in psychoanalysis remains hidden until its relation to its source can be resolved. With narcissism, being for Freud is—at last—always being for an other. To say that ideas are the function of sensations is nothing new. To say that they are libidinized is only to be frank and specific about why and how. Being for another, however, situates sensations and ideas not only in their proper rhetorical setting but also in their proper social setting. This specific social situation is sexual. It is both intimate and early. It is also quite public. Sustaining the psyche is a way of sustaining the community to which, in the early Freud, psyche, with its seething repressions, is customarily opposed. Now, identification creates a field of desire at the same time that it creates a field of self. The two are inseparable. They stir each other up. Nor is object-choice, like drive itself, a simple matter of mimesis. Being for an other is identification. Identification puts the subject in the position of desiring what its identifications desire. This is why narcissism is a social praxis. It is also why psychoanalysis can be both empiricist and Hegelian at the same time. Historiographically, the two traditions, like narcissism and identification themselves, produce each other in a play of differences. The structure of Freud's thought is an example of the psyche it describes.

The figure of the father

The losses first. The self-revisionary phase that begins with *Beyond the Pleasure Principle* in 1920 may be seen as a resolution, at the level of both metacommentary and of empiricist science, to the discordance in Freud's system engineered by the discovery of narcissism six years before. At the loss of nothing less than the organizing categories of his first phase, Freud must invent new ones with which to replace them. This is the scar that narcissism as a concept leaves on Freud's corpus. It disrupts the ease with which we can use first-model terminology, especially the distinction between consciousness and the unconscious, and, of course, the topographical metaphor of mind. The enigma of *Beyond the Pleasure Principle* becomes easier to understand when considered from the point of view of rhetorical rather than logical necessity. Without a conflict between ego and libido, Freud, "dualistic" by temperament (18:53), looks for, and appears to find, a new conflict between life and death. But, as Freud's indebtedness to Fechner there will show, the difference between life and death is not a conflict. We will see why it is difficult to regard *Beyond the Pleasure Principle* as a text about conflict in the next chapter. Freud is no longer about conflict. "On Narcissism" has seen to that. Ego and libido, even life and death—they are a continuous field. The metapsychology inaugurates Freud's preoccupation with coherence in a new kind of way, both thematically and reflexively. The central text of the third phase, *The Ego and the Id*, manages to stabilize and secure it.

The Ego and the Id returns us to a familiar Freudian concern, the precariousness of the ego and the paradoxes that constitute it. It is Freud's new reflexive allegory—he must remaster his system again. No wonder control is one of Freud's principal themes in a text whose task it is to reinvent the foundations of psychoanalytic—that is to say, Freudian—authority. Here Freud will present his new model of mind. This is the gain. It is a response to the loss. The attempt to write a genealogy of the ego is a direct function of the now-massive contingencies that sap the ego's originality. It is a classic case of defense as representation. It is the introduction of the term "super-ego" into the vocabulary of psychoanalysis in *The Ego and the Id* that promises more difficulty for the ego than does the introduction of the perennially ambiguous "id", the term (*das Es*) borrowed from Groddeck and perhaps best glossed as a combination of Lacanian "need" and the "it" of Pater's formulation, "it rusts iron and ripens corn" (1873, 59). In fact, the two terms absent from the book's title—super-ego and Oedipus—are its most prominent players. Super-ego and Oedipus both, as we shall see, are not what they seem. They are hypostases of what are in fact secondary and derivative functions. If the ego is now driven into determinations more absolute than before, it is not just because much of the ego becomes unconscious in *The Ego and the Id*. Nor is it because the super-ego is, by definition, a secondary and derivative business. It is because the super-ego is a social category. What was only implicit in "On Narcissism"—that a social dimension structures even the world of the crib—is now overt.

Chapter 3 formally introduces the notion of super-ego, a notion whose emergence in Freud's work lies, at least in one direction, as we have seen, in its earlier adumbration as the "ego-ideal" (19:28). It is one of Freud's early terms for the status of the father-*imago* in particular. This history, or false history, of the birth of the ego out of its agon with super-ego is the book's central allegory. It is reminiscent, in a theoretical key, of Freud's own fight with the history of dream interpretation. "The character of the ego," says Freud, "is a precipitate of abandoned object-cathexes" and "contains the history of those object-choices" (19:29). This is, of course, disappointing. What we have, or so it seems, is an ego composed of the history of its ego-ideals, one of which, and only one of which, is the ego-ideal of the father. There is, of course, narcissism, that first moment of identification that must, by definition, precede identification with the father, since it is an identification with oneself, and with the mother. But narcissism, as we have seen, is really the result of a reciprocity between ideal ego and ego-ideal. It is the child in the mother's eyes as well as in the mirror. The identification with the mother splits her in half, just as narcissism as a whole splits the subject in half. It does so in order to give it a whole to split. Its relation to the father now, as it will be later, too, is, as a rule, situational, and largely created. Surprisingly, Freud will insist that "the origin of the ego-ideal" (19:31) is not narcissism at all. It is the subject's "'identification' with the father in his own personal prehistory" (19:31). Freud even feels the need to reiterate this discordant assertion in a redundancy that goes too far: "It is a direct and immediate identification and takes place earlier than any object-cathexis" (19:31). Now, for the first time, Freud has gotten himself in a true fix. This is not the case. There is an "earlier" "object-cathexis" than the father: There are two of them—self and mother. But recognition by the mother comes first. The relation to the father is mediate, not immediate, because it comes as a response to the absences of the mother. All it helps to secure is the authority of the family romance, not the authority of the father, whom it believes in order to explain things.

Why should the father be privileged in this way? "Paternity," says Joyce in *Ulysses*, is "a legal fiction" (1922, 207). The priority of the father depends on the prior priority of a successful narcissism, which requires that the subject already be inscribed within a structure of law and desire within which the father plays a significant part. The presence/absence of the mother and the father's respon-sibility for it in the child's mind assure this signification. Identification with the father is identification with the aggressor, in order to keep him, and the whole social order, at bay, even at the beginning. It can only be from this reduced and ironic point of view that Freud assumes the hegemony of the Oedipus complex, whose shadow already falls on the infant (19:31). Freud does admit that, for the child, "two relationships" (19:31)—one to the mother's breast, the other with the father—"proceed side by side" (19:31–32). The Oedipus complex is both early and belated, preconditioned by the inscription of the child—and the par-ents—into the structure of the law of the father long before its official onset.

Thus, in Chapter 5 of *The Ego and the Id*, the expected problems in chronology, rise to the surface as soon as Freud begins to summarize his new theory. The ego is "formed," says Freud, "out of identifications which take the place of aban-doned cathexes by the id"; "the first of these identifications always behave as a special agency in the ego and stand apart from the ego in the form of a super-ego" (19:48). Ideal ego, having become ego-ideal in one developmental fiction, now becomes super-ego in a second. Or so Freud would have us think. Freud's conclusion, despite the indefinite article in its articulation—the father is "a fac-tor" (19:48) of special privilege—is scandalous. The super-ego is dependent not on all the "identifications," but on "one" alone, he says—"the first identification" (19:48). And that "first identification" is not narcissism, the mirror stage, or even the mother, but the father. Chronology, however, does not explain what has happened. Only deferred action does. The father, having been fantasized to be the reason for the mother's disappearance, is installed, retroactively, as respon-sible for what the child experiences as the splitting of the mother into bad and good breast. "On Narcissism" has already made this clear. Retroactivity makes it look as though the father were there first. But even if he is, he is only there challenging things. He presents nothing originary except rivalry. This, too, is recognition by the other, and doubly so. The father's presumable presence not only adds to the child's narcissism; it also insures the proximity of the mother.

How, then, do we know that the father-identification is the "first"? We do not, and cannot. The super-ego may be "the heir to the Oedipus complex" (19:48), but this is because the Oedipus complex is not really about the father, but about the family romance. The father's position in the family romance is not only partial, but secondary. Not only is he not "first"; he comes after the mother, and after the child, as a mere reason, often absent, for any suspension of their play:

> The broad general outcome of the sexual phase dominated by the Oedi-
> pus complex may, therefore, be taken to be the forming of a precipitate in
> the ego, consisting of these two identifications [one with the mother, one
> with the father] in some way united with each other. This modification of
> the ego retains its special position; it confronts the other contents of the
> ego as an ego ideal or super-ego. (19:34)

Why, then, does Freud wish to defend the priority of the father despite the fact that the Oedipus complex emerges, not from a "first" identification with him, but from a complex of family relationships? Let us keep deferred action in mind. What is really at stake? Much as dreams precede their distortion at the level of *histoire* because they succeed it at the level of *récit*, or much as the primal scene precedes its remembrance because it follows it, so the father precedes super-ego at the level of *histoire* because he succeeds it at the level of *récit*. The very emergence of the father's centrality in the Oedipus complex is, in other words, not just retroactive, but an example of secondary revision or deferred action. In fact, the father—supposedly our greatest psychical difficulty—is probably the greatest of Freud's defense mechanisms. What the father protects clinically we shall see when we turn to pornography in Chapter 9. What the father protects from a narrative point of view here is easily apparent.

Defense in psychoanalysis is also an opportunity. In *The Ego and the Id*'s companion essay, the 1924 "Dissolution of the Oedipus Complex," we can see how Oedipus works as a defense for Freud himself. In his remarks there on castration, Freud implicitly alludes to the Wolf Man by telling us that the reality of castration-anxiety occurs for little boys only after they see the vaginas of little girls. "It is not until" such "a *fresh* experience comes his way," says Freud, "that the child begins to reckon with the possibility of being castrated" (19:175). It is, in other words, only through what happens later on that we come to know what has happened before. Deferred action, in other words, structures castration-anxiety, just as it does the father in *The Ego and the Id*. Is it good for nothing?

The retroactive production of the Oedipus complex is repressed by Freud for a good reason. Its deferred action has a useful side. It can be exploited. The father becomes a function of the son, the past the property of the future. The son is father to the father. It is a costly loss in the power of the father, although it is a considerable gain to the son, however embarrassed he may be. Only such loss can provide the son, the latecomer, with any power at all. As Eliot puts it in

"Tradition and the Individual Talent," "the past" is "altered" by "the present" as much as "the present is directed by the past" (1919, 15). Freud's latecomer has this single power, the power to write (that is to say, to misread) the past. By inventing the Oedipus complex to defend against the mother's absence, the child also defends against the father's power. What we think is the granting of authority is really a mechanism of protection. Here the child engages in a classic instance of Mann's "mythic identification," on a grand scale, and in the grand style. Freud's name for this operation is an example of it. To call it Oedipus is to endow it with the gravity appropriate to it from the child's point of view. Freud's gravity as its stylizer is equally inappropriate and grandiose. Because it is a "complex," Oedipus also shows that it need not be with any of the drama's participants that the child identifies, but, rather, with a position *ab extra*, a sight of its structure based on spectatorship and exclusion. I will take this up at length in my discussion of the ontology of the pornographic image. In *The Ego and the Id*, to identify with this position of spectatorship and exclusion means—of course it does—distinguishing oneself from the father rather than being, or wishing to be, him. Being the father may involve possession of the mother, but it also involves incorporation by the father. Identification with the Oedipal situation rather than with the father himself is how this expensive outcome is customarily avoided.

Self-empowerment and literary empowerment—the Freudian system is running smoothly again—are the real if hidden themes of *The Ego and the Id*. Freud himself must dissemble it, however, since it is the very means of production of his own power as a writer. He inserts himself so strategically among the scientists, poets, and philosophers that credible historians can speak only of parallels with psychoanalysis rather than of genuine precursors or fathers of it. We have seen Freud offset his influences and slay each one in turn. The first chapter of the dreambook is the first rehearsal for Freud's final rewriting of history in *Moses and Monotheism* (1939). Freud may come late in history, but it is he who gets to tell the tale. Belatedness is at once gain and loss, loss and gain. Freud escapes determination by being overdetermined at the moment of his enablement. Locke and Hegel, Fechner and Helmholtz, Fliess and Breuer, Shakespeare and antiquity. Like Darwin and Marx, Freud's curricular transdiscursivity is the very condition that allows his inventiveness to take place. It was around 1900 that the disciplines as we know them were being distinguished, coterminously, as it turns out, with the transgressive dialogism of evolution, Marxism, and psychoanalysis, the breaking of rules aiding in the fashioning of each alike. Psychoanalysis managed to inscribe itself from the start in a myriad of systems, including that of literature. It is this multiple inscription that allows our notion of a literary Freud—among others. The expectation by which we tend to assess any discursive product as the univocal function of the determinations of a single tradition such as poetry or science is an expectation that Freud exploits even as he violates.

Silently using the priority over time granted him by secondary revision, Freud, in the ironic name of Oedipus, alone fulfills the twin and impossible wish of modern literature: to be simultaneously new and old, unique and recognizable, original and traditional. The psychical apparatus that Freud has imagined does just this; it houses the old so that it can apprehend the new. Oedipus fails; Freud succeeds. Freud's texts produce their world by provoking a mode of reception that has insured both their functional and their phenomenal reality. For psychoanalysis, these are the same thing. Perhaps it is Freud who is the real pragmatist.

3
Psychoanalysis and aestheticism

"Constancy" and chiasmus

The traditions of influence through which Freud makes his perilous way do not, of course, include science and philosophical psychology alone. They also include literature. This is to say too little and too much. Freud's literary reception has already alerted us to the many ways in which psychoanalysis was not only anticipated by the poets, but also kept pace with them. We may like to set Freud among the cloudy trophies of Shakespeare and Milton, Goethe and Wordsworth, but he must also be set among the wide range of his own contemporaries. Freud's career saw both the fullness of the Victorian climate and its decline. His relation to literature therefore falls into two parts: his relation to late nineteenth century literature, and his relation to the modernism that follows it. It also falls into two parts in another way: It parallels Victorian trends, and it influences modern ones. Let us take up the Victorian in this chapter, and modernism in the next.

How should we describe these relationships? By returning to our characteristic doublings between the formal mechanisms of Freud's texts and those of the psychical apparatus, and between these and Freud's own relation to discursive precedent. Of the chief similitudes between Freud's narration, his objects of description, and his historical relationships, we have left one unexamined. What is the psychical prototype for chiasmus? Metaphor is condensation, and metonymy is displacement; secondary revision is metalepsis. What does chiasmus double, or redouble, in the Freudian apparatus? We know that chiasmus is a dynamic and that it takes place in time. Chiasmus is the condition of possibility for both psychical activity and for writing. As deferred action, it is the first "consideration" of "representability"; as secondary revision, it is the first condition of recall. But is it more than a condition? Does it correspond to a psychical function, or does it just set the condition for psychical functioning?

We do not have far to go to find the answer. It begins with another of Freud's anxieties as a writer. The site at which these questions emerge in Freud thematically is the same site at which they emerge for Freud as a matter of influence. In both ways, this site redoubles the activity of the psychical apparatus that Freud describes. It is, as it is with Breuer or Bergson, a professional site—another crossing of science and philosophical psychology—not a literary one as such, at least not yet. This site is Freud's relation to Gustav Fechner, and to what, in 1920, in *Beyond the Pleasure Principle*, can no longer remain repressed about Freud's debt to him. Fechner, despite his almost three years of illness and inactivity from 1840 to 1843—well before the publication of the first volume of his epochal *Elements of Psychophysics* in 1860—maintained both a devoted scholarly audience and, as a pamphleteer, a devoted popular one. Predating James and Bergson alike, Fechner occupied the borderline between Romantic science and an emergent positivism; he crossed the vocabulary of Kant and Hegel with physical experimentation and quantification. In his popular work, a "spiritualist" orientation often predominated.

Freud's debt to Fechner is a simple but decisive one: "the principle of constancy" (see also Ellenberger 1956). "The principle of constancy" is the mechanism that controls overstimulation in the physical sphere, and overdetermination in the psychical. The principle of constancy is an active and conservative principle, whether in the historical process of the individual or of the group. It seeks stability for the organism, the psychical apparatus, and the social order all alike. Freud's absorption of "the principle of constancy" as a notion as his career proceeds—and, unconsciously, much earlier—is the reflexive counterpart to the function the principle of constancy performs diegetically: to keep the organism functioning smoothly. Here at last is the psychical counterpart to chiasmus. The principle of constancy is the very principle of coherence as such. Freud has found not only a metaphor for balance of mind; he has, as we shall also see, found its very movement in the structure of the tissues. The principle of constancy is what links the Freud of the *Project* with the Freud of *Beyond the Pleasure Principle*. In so doing, the principle of constancy gives psychoanalysis a wholeness over time—a constancy—that it can now describe as the goal of the psychical apparatus itself. Its process—deferred action—and its product—constancy—are one and the same.

Fechner's "principle of constancy," or "principle of stability," plays a role in Freud's attempt to imagine the psychical apparatus as early as 1895, in both *Studies on Hysteria* and the *Project*. Freud refers to it as "the theorem concerning the constancy of the sum of excitation" in a letter to Breuer in 1892 (1:147). Breuer, who admired Fechner second only to Goethe (Jones 1:223), describes the mechanism in his theoretical section of *Studies on Hysteria* three years later, giving credit to Freud for the newer, psychoanalytic variation: "Here for the first time," writes

Breuer, "we meet the fact that there exists in the organism a *'tendency to keep intracerebral excitation constant'* (Freud)" (2:197; Breuer's emphasis). In the *Project*, the principle of constancy is called "the principle of neuronal inertia: that neurones," as Freud puts it there, "tend to divest themselves of quantity" (2:296). Freud gives credit for the idea to Fechner, however, only when he quotes him directly in *Beyond the Pleasure Principle* in 1920:

> In so far as conscious impulses always have some relation to pleasure or unpleasure, pleasure and unpleasure too can be regarded as having a psycho-physical relation to conditions of stability and instability. ... Every psycho-physical motion ... approximates to complete stability, and is attended by unpleasure in proportion as, beyond a certain limit, it deviates from complete stability. (1873; quoted in Freud 1920, 18:8–9)

This solves an ancient problem in Freud, and one never fully elaborated in Freud's texts until now. Although its possibility emerges in *The Interpretation of Dreams*, its importance is not clear until it is viewed from the later point of view of *Beyond the Pleasure Principle*. The principle of constancy is really a way of explaining why "abreaction" or the "cathartic method" will not suffice in *Studies on Hysteria*. Here at last this story may emerge in its proper context and be joined to my wider argument. Its logic is not forthcoming until now, in 1920. The mind cannot simply "talk" away its losses or seek discharge from tensions in pleasure; it must learn to absorb them. Abreaction is not sufficient to obtain a state of constancy or inertia. An increased sense of the mind's ability to act as a sponge for stimulation is necessary. This is the change that *Beyond the Pleasure Principle* brings to Freud's thinking.

"Discharge," as it turns out, is always incomplete. A residue of stimulation remains behind, whether from within or without, as a material token of the self's experience, part of its "residuum." In this sense, memory has a physical dimension. "Constancy" must have more than "discharge" at its service. Otherwise, it would threaten to spill out the contents of the very self it means to protect. No wonder Anna O.'s "chimney-sweeping" with Breuer was only a partial success. Freud himself had stopped using hypnosis because it only momentarily alleviated hysterical symptoms. Without awareness of their aetiology and mechanism on the part of the patient, the attacks, Freud found, recurred. Thus the "talking cure"—psychoanalysis proper—replaced hypnosis and "chimney-sweeping" alike. Now, "discharge"—the abreaction of reliving the traumatic event and by catharsis expunging its toxicity—gave way to a new approach, in Freud's own practice, if not in Breuer's. The new approach was one based in Breuer's hero, Fechner, rather than in Freud's physicalist mentor Hermann Helmholtz. It even surpassed what Bergson had given him. It required the patient to grow so as to absorb the memory of trauma, real or imagined; to be able to tolerate the difficulties of life rather than turn away from them.

The difference between abreaction and tolerance—between catharsis and psychoanalysis proper—is precisely the difference between Helmholtz's "discharge" and Fechner's "constancy." For Helmholtz, the nervous system can be expunged, or "swept clean," to use the vocabulary of Anna O. It can blow off steam because it is conceived of in terms of mechanical physics. Here is Helmholtz, in 1861, summing up his famous experiments, published in 1847:

> The amount of energy in the whole system of the universe must remain the same, quite steady and unalterable, whatever changes may go on in the universe. (1861, 113)

But discharge is the very precondition of this "conservation of energy":

> If mechanical power is produced by heat, we always find that a certain amount of heat is lost; and this is proportional to the quantity of mechanical work produced by that heat. (112)

This is because the organism, apparently like the steam engine, must release a proportion of what it takes in to keep its own internal forces balanced in relation to the environment:

> Now if you compare the living body with a steam engine, then you have the completest analogy. The living animals take in food that consists of inflammable substances, fat and the so-called hydrocarbons, as starch and sugar, and nitrogenous substances, as albumen, flesh, cheese, and so on. Living animals take in these inflammable substances and oxygen— the oxygen of the air, by respiration. Therefore, if you take (in the place of fat, starch, and sugar) coals or woods and the oxygen of the air, you have the substances in the steam engine. The living bodies give out carbonic acid and water; and then if we neglect very small quantities of more complicated matters which are too small to be reckoned here, they give up their nitrogen in the form of urea. (116)

For Fechner, in 1860, this mechanical analogy is insufficient. The body, unlike a machine, does not simply excrete what it does not need in its fuel, nor does the mind. In neither can discharge and catharsis function transparently. But even more is at stake in Fechner's recasting of "conservation" than the change from discharge to absorption. It is the old question of mind and body itself. As a psychophysicist, Fechner wants to address both. He does so by mooting the problem of a difference between mind and body—between idealism and materialism, psyche and soma—by regarding them as continuous. How different from Helmholtz's is his view of the organism and of the psyche that emerges from it? The inner and the outer are, for Fechner, "reciprocal" (1860, 59). "Kinetic energy," Fechner says, "can be developed in a system through the mutual interaction of its parts." Its "fluid media," in a delectable phrase, are governed by structures of "mutual influence" (22). The "magnitudes" of given "stimuli are ... representative of the extent of physical activities that are related to sensations dependent on them in some manner" (19). "Psychophysics" is not an oxymoron; it is a chiasmus. "We find on closer examination that in their most general and ultimate sense," writes Fechner, "psychical measures are based on the fact that an equal number of equally strong psychical impressions are due to an equal number of equally large physical causes" (51). For a moment, Fechner's impressionism grows manifestly aesthetic, intimating Pater's cadences with uncanny accuracy: "The number of these psychical units is determined by the number of psychical impressions, where the magnitude of the cause of the single impression, or any multiple thereof, serves as a unit" (51). Even the return to a purely scientific vocabulary, however, cannot keep the deep structure of Fechner's prose from engaging in its customary shifts: "Thus, just as we can make physical measurements only on the basis of the relationship of the physical to the psychological, so we can, according to our principle, derive psychical measures on the basis of the same relationship, only applying it in reverse" (51).

Fechner's repeatedly chiasmatic figurations are in the service of a representation of organic systematicity whose structure is itself chiasmatic. It is also a structure regulated by a principle of constancy. Implicitly distinguishing his use of the term "conservation" from Helmholtz's, Fechner describes a system for which stability rather than discharge is the keyword: "The law of the conservation of kinetic energy then does not prevent the energy either of a system or of a part of the infinite system of the universe from temporarily changing, increasing, or diminishing, nor from changing permanently" (129–30). Here, Fechner's idealism ironically allows him to be more of an empiricist than Helmholtz. He plays the two traditions off of one another, as Freud will do: "Only one thing is certain: the energy is restored when after any amount of preceding impulses, the parts of the system return to their original positions under the influence of their inner forces" (27). No wonder the notion of the "threshold" becomes useful (199). As an empirical category, it is a representation of the condition for stability. As a rhetorical figure, it represents a site constituted by crossings—the vocabularies of Hegel and Helmholtz, for example—and regulated, like its empirical counterpart, by intensities of only a more or less bound kind. Fechner has solved the body/mind problem by reading each category as a function of the other.

The relation of mind to body recapitulates the relation of body to environment. Sense perception and the internal production of images in memory or in fantasy are—as they are in the tradition leading to Hartley and will be in Fechner's disciple Freud—interdependent. What is their mediator? A "residuum" (1889, 64), to recall Bergson's description of Fechner's notion of memory and assumption. It is what Freud will call the unconscious. Propped on the brain in a recapitulation of its development, the mind, says Fechner, is also a part of the body as a whole. Real or not, thought leaves a trace of itself behind. Discharge never sweeps clean because a residue, or memory, whether physical in the case of reflex, or ideational in the case of the mind, is required to give a person a history, a mode of being in the world.

For Freud, the conclusion was plain. One had to assume a residue or trace—a memory—in, or, indeed, *as* the unconscious. Only against such a force can the individual adjudge future events both material and psychical. Here, too, emerges another key but muted difference, the only gradated difference between neurology and psychology themselves, and the nature of Freud's passage, if we can even call it that, from the first to the second. Freud's own terms in the *Project* are, as we can see now, the clearest. It is the difference between a "quantity" of stimulation (by which we traditionally mean the "physical") and the emergence, propped upon it, of "qualities," or ideas (by which we traditionally mean the "psychological"). The world of private representations that they produce between them—the world of psychoanalysis—has the neural infrastructure that Fechner describes.

Thus, the central role of "constancy" in *Beyond the Pleasure Principle* and, later on, in *The Ego and the Id*. Here, we already have a good sense of the new structural model of mind that Freud formalizes in 1923, and of the way it solves problems that the earlier topographical model, relying on the discharge of stimulation to keep consciousness clean or constant, could not. It can represent the psychical apparatus as a machine designed to *store* influence and stimulation rather than discharge or expel them. This is the old problem, and it is still being processed. Consciousness can never be swept clean; its very boundaries are open to question, even in the midst of full functioning. Pleasure, the grander version of what the early Freud calls simply wish-fulfillment, is no longer the organism's chief motivation in life. Survival is, or at least appears to be. Indeed, to invoke the "organism" rather than the self or subject is to measure what else has taken place in Freud's theory: a shift away from the early focus not just on the ego, but, as "The Unconscious" has predicted, on consciousness (see also Solms 1997). Freud's concern now is less with "consciousness," and even psychical life, and more with, to use Virginia Woolf's phrase, "life itself" (1919, 107). Survival depends on the existence of an organism stable enough as such to be an entity differentiated from the rest of the world. What does one struggle against in order to survive? The desire to rest, to be at one with an otherwise antagonistic alterity. This is the death instinct. Hence, constancy is not the discharge of stimulation in the release once known as pleasure. Constancy is the endless absorption of alterity, despite the fact that being has as its premise a distinctness from what it is not.

If we look closely at Fechner's role in Freud's early thinking, it is already the possibility of a structural model of mind that interests him. Excess or discharge was even then to be regarded as symptomatic rather than as purgative. The organism is already functioning "beyond the pleasure principle" even in the early Freud. "Pleasure" cannot sweep clean. This is the point back in the 1890s at which Freud abandons the "discharge" vocabulary of his actual teachers, Helmholtz and Ernst Brücke, and exchanges it for Fechner's vocabulary. Although Fechner himself has no choice but to give credit for "the great principle of the so-called conservation of energy" to Helmholtz (1860, 29), "constancy," unlike "conservation," does not need to let out steam to function. Peter Amacher (1965) regards Freud's teacher Theodor Meynert as having mediated the influences of Brücke and Fechner by imagining reflex or discharge as implicitly in the service of a principle of stability (36, 41).

For Freud, another notion was required to give "constancy" a means of facilitation and representation. In *The Interpretation of Dreams*, "the great Fechner," as Freud calls him there (5:536), provides him with it: the concept of psychical locality. Even in the book's first chapter, the latter concept allows Freud to imagine "a *mental* apparatus built up of a number of agencies arranged in a series one behind the other" (4:49). The mental apparatus is, in other words, built for storage. It is also, as I suggested in Chapter 2, hierarchical, in a purely structural sense. This is what allows what I have called propping, in a sense different from that of Laplanche and Pontalis (1967, 29–32): the propping of psyche on brain, and of personality on psyche. Writes Oliver Sacks of the Freud of the 1880s, who had already fallen under Fechner's spell: "Freud was able to show that … it was not the cellular elements which were different in primitive organisms"—or in the human brain—"but their *organization*" (1998, 12; for the neuropsychoanalytic rendition of Freud's conclusions, see Solms and Turnbull 2002, 24–25).

This notion leads Freud in Chapter 7 of *The Interpretation of Dreams* to propose a model of mind that moves beyond the topography of consciousness and the unconscious that is presumably dominant there, and that intimates the later structural model of *Beyond the Pleasure Principle* and *The Ego and the Id*. Its metaphoricity is that of inside and outside, not of surface and depth. Its higher keys are those of storage rather than of stature. The operative term is "series," as Freud gives us a psychical "apparatus" rather than a psychical archaeology:

> I shall carefully avoid the temptation to determine psychical locality in any anatomical fashion. I shall remain upon psychological ground, and I propose simply to follow the suggestion that we should picture the instrument which carries out our mental functions as resembling a compound microscope or a photographic apparatus, or something of the kind. On that basis, psychical locality will correspond to a point inside the apparatus at which one of the preliminary stages of an image comes into being. … The components … we will give the name of "agencies," or (for the sake of greater clarity) "systems." (5:536–37)

These "agencies" or "systems" transact stimulation between the inside and the outside, preserving balance or constancy in the system as a whole—between, that is, inside and outside as such—by using psychical localities as a "series" of storehouses, some closer to the surface than others.

Freud, in other words, has already reached *Beyond the Pleasure Principle* in this dimension of *The Interpretation of Dreams* because he has already imagined the mind as a place of endless absorption. Its systems, some closer to the surface than others, are propped one upon another as a "series" of reciprocal dependencies. The path of Freud's career after 1900 is a path toward a model of the mind that will fulfill these requirements of the principle of constancy, not only as a principle of harmonious Freudian psyche, but also as a principle of coherent Freudian textuality. The psychical apparatus is a compensatory one designed to maintain the principle of constancy in relation to both past and present stimulation, just as Freud's texts, through all the phases of his career, are a compensatory apparatus designed to maintain its own power and coherence in relation to the literary and scientific influences that threaten it—Helmholtz and Brücke's, for example, or, for that matter, Fechner's own—and to the potential for incoherence in the system itself. From a reflexive or literary point of view, constancy is the principle of each text's coherence, and of Freud's career as a whole as it moves forward.

Not unlike "constancy" in its reflexive or literary implications is its rhetorical counterpart or formal double, the figure, of course, of chiasmus. It is where we started, and the site to which we inevitably return. Chiasmus is, like constancy, basic to both Freud's writing and his theory. Chiasmus is a loop or a crossing over—"the pleasure of art," for example, and "the art of pleasure." We see it often in writing, as a way of noting interdependence and, sometimes, paradox. My principal argument, for example, may be put chiasmatically: If we can read literature psychoanalytically, we can also read psychoanalysis literarily. Trilling likewise describes what he calls the "reciprocal" relation between Freud and literature through the use of chiasmus: "The effect of Freud upon literature," he writes, "has been no greater than the effect of literature upon Freud" (1940, 32). On a clinical plane, chiasmus is the structure of psychical defense. The privileged kid becomes a delinquent in order to maintain his or her sense of difference or distinction. Chiasmus is also the structure of the analytic situation. In order to proceed with life, the patient falls ill. In order to fall ill, the patient in the meantime identifies, however symptomatically, all that he or she wishes to repress by producing symptoms. Chiasmus is also key to the conversation with the reader that Freud's writing inspires. Reader and text cross over each other constantly, thereby bringing the play of psychoanalytic discourse into being. Between them, they also mimic or simulate the structure of the Freudian subject. If as a reader one is always at odds with Freud's texts, the Freudian subject is constitutively at odds with itself. According to Freud's revised, structural theory, one is also constitutively at odds with the world, as an organic precondition for hatching or nurturing the ability to be self-divided psychologically. The figure of chiasmus, in other words, structures both the phenomenology and the ontology of the Freudian subject. Chiasmus is the rhetorical structure of the principle of constancy. The efficiency of Freud's reflexivity—the doubling or similitude between the themes and structure of his writing—is almost enough to lull us into a merely aesthetic appreciation of psychoanalysis as literature.

Psychoanalysis and aestheticism

Of course, that depends on what we mean by "aesthetic." *Aesthêsis* means "perception," and the originator of "aesthetic" criticism, the Oxford don Walter Pater, took as his own focus the structure of human apprehension. Like Fechner, although beginning some twenty-five years later, Pater had a wide appeal. His *Studies in the History of the Renaissance*, published in 1873, vaulted him into instant, if controversial, fame. The book divided its readers into two camps: those who agreed with Pater's endorsement of pleasure as the chief value in art and life; and those who, like Virginia Woolf's father, Leslie Stephen (1875), found it necessary to mount a moralist counteroffensive. The rigors of Pater's presumably soft "impressionism," however, are a perpetual surprise. Like psychoanalysis, aestheticism is a discourse of and about stability, transgression, and overdetermination; like psychoanalysis, it is also a discourse that searches out the nature and the origin of the boundaries that make up subjectivity as we know it. Not only that. The similarities between psychoanalysis and aestheticism lead to an unsettling question: How new is Freud's revolutionary formulation of subjectivity? Within his own fields of reference—neurology, oneirocriticism, empirical, and philosophical psychology—Freud is, given his formidable skills as a tendentious bibliographer, without peer. Juxtaposed with Pater, however, Freud finds a surprising double or mirror image. It is also Pater's disciples, the Bloomsbury Group, who will, quite literally, translate and publish Freud in English beginning in 1922 (see Meisel and Kendrick 1985).

Freud's friendliness toward Pater is manifest in his 1910 study of Leonardo; he discusses Pater's essay on Leonardo in *The Renaissance* no fewer than four times (11:68n1, 110, 111, 115). Freud is especially impressed by the Englishman's ability to see in the Mona Lisa's smile the "sinister menace," as Freud puts it, adopting Pater's language, of the "unbounded tenderness" of Leonardo's mother (45). As with Freud, Pater's emphasis is on "brain-building" (1878, 173), or self, and the influences that shape it, particularly the deferred action that fashions the self through retrospection.

Pater's prefiguration of Freud emerges in an even wider light in his essay on Wordsworth (1874), which estimates the poet's strength by focusing on his understanding of melancholy. Like the heroes of Pater's own imaginary portraits, Wordworth's heroes suffer from reminiscences that shatter the ego and that often take on, despite the beauty of the language that renders them, an almost crudely material form. Wordsworth represents the cause of grief through apostrophe—in charged sites of mourning, real and psychological, such as the churchyard in "The White Doe of Rylstone," or, on a grander scale, in the animation of natural landscape by the poet's own eye in "Tintern Abbey" or *The Prelude*. All apostrophe has mourning at its root. The churchyard, and even one's childhood home, is an example of what Pater calls "that pitiful awe and care for the perishing human clay, of which relic-worship is but the corruption" (1874, 49–50).

But brooding on death has its uses. Like Pater's Marius, rearranging with his hands the encrypted bones of his ancestors, Wordsworth's heroes, especially the poet himself, thereby succeed in moving beyond melancholy by virtue of its exaggerated exercise. This also allows Wordsworth to redistribute the pain he represents by evoking pathos in his reader. Nor is it a "discharge" or cathartic model that informs this kind of Romantic pleasure. It is, rather, a model of "constancy," too, since this mode of reading raises and enlarges the reader's appreciation rather than asks the reader to judge. It is a magic or "religious" (49) kind of melancholy, culturally productive rather than symptomatic. It allows the reader to see more. It is also worth asking whether this is the origin, too, of the allure of the photographic image, whose "ontology," as André Bazin famously described it (1945), is based on the metaphor of embalming the human body. The photographic image measures a gap between what was once alive and is now absent or dead, a structure identical with that of Wordsworthian melancholy and the pathos that it evokes. It is also identical as a structure with deferred action, its *tableau vivant*, as it were. It accounts for the uncanniness of the filmic image, particularly its dubious immediacy.

But the most far-reaching similarity between Freud and Pater is to be found in a comparison of the "Conclusion" to *The Renaissance* and *Beyond the Pleasure Principle*. Pater's language is already Freud's, from both a rhetorical and a phenomenological point of view. Pater's "Conclusion" contains an implicitly Freudian portrait of the psyche in a state of willful undress:

> Let us begin with that which is without—our physical life. Fix upon it in one of its more exquisite intervals, the moment, for instance, of delicious recoil from the flood of water in summer heat. What is the whole physical life in that moment but a combination of natural elements to which science gives their names? But these elements, phosphorus and lime and delicate fibres, are present not in the human body alone: we detect them in places

most remote from it. Our physical life is a perpetual motion of them—the passage of the blood, the waste and repairing of the lenses of the eye, the modification of the tissues of the brain under every ray of light and sound. (1873, 233–34)

Where the line falls between self and world, inside and outside, is difficult to ascertain; it changes from moment to moment in its effort to maintain a state of constancy in subject and object alike. As in Freud, the self is also construed, first and foremost, as a physical or material self, even though, in both writers, materiality is infinitely porous: "That clear, perpetual outline of face and limb is but an image of ours, under which we group them—a design in a web, the actual threads of which pass out beyond it" (234). Nor is Pater lacking Freud's ambivalence. The self's very separation from the world is both a triumph and a defeat. "In the narrow chamber of the individual mind," says Pater, there is, for the most part, only "isolation, each mind keeping as a solitary prisoner its own dream of a world" (235). Pater's solution to such melancholy is to recognize it, like a good Freudian, for what it is—a tissue of images and illusions:

> When reflexion begins to play upon those objects they are dissipated under its influence; the cohesive force seems suspended like some trick of magic; each object is loosed into a group of impressions—colour, odour, texture—in the mind of the observer. (234–35)

To "be present always at the focus where the greatest number of vital forces unite," says Pater, is "success in life." "Our failure," he warns, is "to form habits" (236).

Pater's scientific metaphors—"lenses," "tissues"—are surprising, especially the way they break down the presumed division between the physical and the psychical, and make them reciprocal. They form a chiasmus, or a crossing over; their play, or the lack thereof, is structured by a principle of constancy. Pater, as it turns out, not only prefigures Freud; he also recalls Fechner. As far as we can tell, Pater did not read Fechner (see Inman 1981, 1990), although their similarities, like Pater's with Freud himself, are abundant. Indeed, the first volume of Fechner's *Elements of Psychophysics* presents a model for the relation of body and mind that is an aesthetic as well as a psychoanalytic one. For Pater and Fechner both, the inner and the outer are interdependent, or, in Fechner's term, "reciprocal."

Here, meanwhile, is a Paterian Freud, describing the birth of consciousness in *Beyond the Pleasure Principle*:

> What consciousness yields consists essentially of perceptions of excitations coming from the external world and of feelings of pleasure and unpleasure which can only arise from within the mental apparatus; it is therefore possible to assign the system *Pcpt.-Cs.* a position in space. It must lie on the borderline between outside and inside; it must be turned towards the external world and must envelop the other psychical systems. It will be seen that there is nothing daringly new in these assumptions; we

> have merely adopted the views on localization held by cerebral anatomy, which locates the "seat" of consciousness in the cerebral cortex—the outermost, enveloping layer of the central organ. (18:24)

This "borderline" is also the site of a chiasmatic crossing of Fechner and Pater, although Freud has widened the terrain and deepened the focus. Freud is no longer much interested in consciousness. He is, like Fechner and Pater before him, interested in the formation of the "threshold" between mind as such, especially in its unconscious functioning, and the world of sense to which it is constitutively opposed. Nor is this model topographical; it is structural and dynamic. It is the full-blown elaboration of the "series" model of *The Interpretation of Dreams*, dramatized in living terms.

Like Fechner and Pater, too, Freud uses the traditions of idealism and positivism dialectically—mind and sense are "reciprocal" or supplemental, like quality and quantity, or like ideas and sensations. But Freud also wishes to go further. He wishes to widen his view to account for the very origin of animate life as we know it:

> Let us picture a living organism in its most simplified possible form as an undifferentiated vesicle of a substance that is susceptible to stimulation. Then the surface turned towards the external world will from its very situation be differentiated and will serve as an organ for receiving stimuli. Indeed embryology, in its capacity as a recapitulation of developmental history, actually shows us that the central nervous system originates from the ectoderm.

Then one of Freud's greatest perorations, the one prefigured by Bergson, all the more moving because, as in aestheticism, its materials are of a grossly material kind:

> A crust would thus be formed which would at last have been so thoroughly "baked through" by stimulation that it would present the most favorable possible conditions for the reception of stimuli and become incapable of any further modification. (18:26)

The similarity with Pater's description of consciousness is not only dramatic; it also reminds us, in startlingly physical terms, that the principle of constancy and the structure of chiasmus are, in Freud, Pater, and Fechner alike, one and the same. Constancy is the psychical counterpart to chiasmus, or, to put it another way, each one is the condition of and for the other. Experience has the form of a specific trope, and a specific trope is, in turn, the very shape of experience in the world. The psyche is, by definition, an achieved balance between inside and outside as such; indeed, it invents this very difference in order to become itself. It no longer has to seek "discharge," as it did in the *Project* or *Studies on Hysteria*. Now the very form of self-realization is one that absorbs and expunges stimulation in a reciprocal rhythm. *Beyond the Pleasure Principle* also allows Freud to restructure his relation to intellectual history. Without his skill as a Paterian surfer, the waves of overdetermination might overwhelm his navigation of endless cross-disciplinary sites. Freud's originality outlasts the opposition by keeping it talking deep into the night. The new model of the psychical apparatus in *Beyond the Pleasure Principle* is, as one might expect, itself an instance of this new combination of sensitivity and absorptiveness. The very distinction between inside and outside to which organic matter's response to stimulation gives rise is a model, in other words, for the retention of influences without the danger of debilitation by any among them.

But Freud and Pater are not, it is also clear, of a single mind. Freud seems to champion the very "habit" toward which Pater casts a wary, drifter's eye. Pater is caught up, at least in the "Conclusion," with the pleasure principle alone, while Freud has, presumably, moved "beyond the pleasure principle." Are Pater and Freud at a crossroads? Certainly not. By moving "beyond pleasure," Freud is not seeking to impose "habit" on "flux"; he is, like Pater, curious to see what "flux" there may be in "habit" itself. Stability is, strictly speaking, a borderline condition. If the psychoanalytic component of aestheticism gives it a heightened precision of thought, the aesthetic component of psychoanalysis gives it a heightened poeticity. Each lends the other a supplement to sharpen the terms of its appeal. Each also kindles a difference that it cancels—the difference between science and literature.

Other questions, however, are near. Fechner's place in Freud's thinking is clear, particularly the roles that psychical locality and the principle of constancy play in it. Fechner is inescapable. Freud shares with him the common shop of "German science," and he is the last of its influences to be expunged. But the question of Pater's influence on Freud must also be raised. If Freud's relation to Fechner is motivated by the anxiety of influence, his relation to aestheticism, by contrast, is one, not quite of parallelism or of congruence, but of overlap. Freud's relation to Pater, unlike his relation to Fechner, about whom he retains more "consciousness," resembles the self's relation to the world in *Beyond the Pleasure Principle*: one in which the absorption of stimulation or "influence" becomes automatic or "unconscious." It triggers no conflicts; it produces no symptoms. Pater is one of a series of impressions that Freud has absorbed. In contrast to the case of Fechner, there is no "scientific protocol," however strategically it may be deployed, that requires him to use his name. Freud uses Pater's name for the simple pleasure of doing so.

4

A supplement to the history of psychoanalysis and modernism

Modernism and psychoanalysis

Beyond aestheticism looms aestheticism's great child, modernism. Inevitable is the question of the relation Freud has to the writing of his own day. What histories structure Freud's wider relation to modernism? And what structures modernism in relation to Freud? Like the "decisive" features of Freud's texts, the "decisive" features of Freud's historical relationships are less certain than they used to be. We know too much about them. The relationships are now more varied and porous—my choice of Bergson in Chapter 2 or Fechner in Chapter 3 is no more privileged than Amacher's choice of Meynert—because they are overdetermined and grow more resonant with time. This gain and loss is also a reflection of the activity of the psychical apparatus, which, like any historiography, has as its chief modality deferred action, and as its first aim the object of survival. Constancy is both its precondition and its goal. Freud's texts, in other words, resemble the objects of their presumable scrutiny, even historiographically. Regarded psychoanalytically, the texts of modernism fall into three distinct groups that are familiar to us, not because they are not overdetermined, but because the overdetermination has an internal historical logic: These three groups correspond to the three phases of Freud's career. It is as though modern literature as a whole is an unpacking of the three stances available to Freud over the years. Each trend or tendency in Freud finds a home in one of modern literature's three versions or modes. Freud's early phase finds its literary locus in the "instinctual" modernism of D. H. Lawrence and its gross materialism. Freud's middle phase, from *The Interpretation of Dreams* to *Totem and Taboo*, before the onset of the metapsychology, finds an unlikely counterpart in the "mythic" modernism of T. S. Eliot and its crude idealism, including its affiliation with Freud's own use of new anthropological models. This is the Freud of what I have called the doctrinal decade, before the metapsychology brings down its assumptions. Freud's later phase corresponds to the "material" modernism of Katherine Mansfield, Willa Cather, and Virginia Woolf, with its notion of the unconscious as that which links "instinct" and "representation"—"sensations" and "ideas"—the way that the later Freud does: through language and society, particularly through the medium of identification. The work of Joyce forms an instructive double pathway between mythic and material modernism. The tripartite mind that Freud describes in *The Ego and the Id* in 1923 is actually a history and compartmentalization of these three views of the unconscious, and presents as summary a picture of modern literature as it does of psychoanalysis. "Id" is Lawrentian "instinct." "Super-ego" is Eliotic "myth." "Ego" is the Woolfian attempt to manage the difference between them—between "sensations" and "ideas."

Despite a tradition of criticism that insists on its newness, modern literature's project is not, we should remember, an entirely fresh one historically in any of its three manifestations, any more than is the project of psychoanalysis. Indeed, Freud's reflexivity should assure us that what is new about modernism and psychoanalysis alike has, like any unconscious structure, deep, and shared, roots in the past. Psychoanalysis also shares with modernism—here is a principle of historiographical constancy—one overriding preoccupation that Trilling has already identified: a preoccupation with "a research into the self." It proceeds, as Trilling has said, from Freud's Romanticism, and from Romanticism's own ironic dependence on models from the Age of Reason that both enabled its rebellious spirit and muffled the very energy it produced.

James and James

As Foucault has shown (1961), among the first great shifts to accompany the demise of religion and the emergence against it of Enlightenment rationality was the division of reason, not from religion, but from madness. A nosological shift—the creation of a new descriptive field available to medical diagnosis—was also an epistemological one: The mind was no longer partitioned into good and evil, but into the rational and irrational. The religious antinomies that precede it historically shadow this new pairing, but its consequences are different. Reason's domain was necessarily psychological. Reason was now the guardian of a soul that was by definition divided, turning the self into its first, and chief, object of scrutiny. So began, to use Christopher Lasch's phrase, the culture of narcissism. The conventional critical emphasis on madness in modern literature is a durable way of showing how clearly modernism descends from the Enlightenment split that Foucault describes (Gilbert and Gubar 1979; Valentine 2003). But modern literature's transgressive energies and liminal orientations—Virginia Woolf is its *locus classicus*—merely heighten what is already at work in the comparatively stable if neurasthenic world of the later novels of Henry James: an emphasis on the self, and the difference between self-knowledge and self-regard.

This shift in the history of modern literature is nowhere more evident than in the shift from James's own early fiction to his later phase. It is a shift that has served generations of critics as an organizing assumption about the history of the novel as a whole, and about modern fiction in particular. In fiction before James, the world predominates; in fiction after James, the mind predominates. Compare the opening sentence of *The American* (1877) with that of *The Ambassadors* (1903). The shift from outside to inside is manifest. *The American* begins with James's fashionable hero in a pose of aestheticist lassitude that borders not only on exhibitionism but also on pretension:

> On a brilliant day in May, in the year 1868, a gentleman was reclining at his ease on the great circular divan which at that period occupied the center of the Salon Carré, in the Museum of the Louvre. (1877, 1)

It is the pose that is ambiguous, not the man. Whether or not a doubleness invades the soul of Christopher Newman we have as yet no idea. We do not know if he is as ambivalent about his mannerisms as the morally impatient reader of James may be about him. How different is the beginning of *The Ambassadors*. Once again the focus is on James's hero, but the terms have changed, perhaps only slightly, but with enormous differences in implication:

> Strether's first question, when he reached the hotel, was about his friend; yet on his learning that Waymarsh was apparently not to arrive till evening he was not wholly disconcerted. (1903, 17)

By the end of the sentence we are firmly established within Strether's mind, even to the point of feeling his ambivalence about his friend's absence ("not wholly disconcerted"). Strether is, it appears, relieved to have some time to himself despite missing his friend's expected company. Nor are we asked merely to identify with Strether. This is free indirect discourse, with the narrator shaping the construction of Strether's thoughts for our consideration as well as simply presenting them to us for the purpose of sympathy. What differences contribute to Strether's ambivalence? If we are asked to know Christopher Newman where he does not know himself, we are asked to know Strether where he presumes to know more about himself than he really does.

It is often to Henry's brother, William, that historians turn to find a way to describe Henry's prose. Here is an influential passage from the *Principles of Psychology*:

> Consciousness, then, does not appear to itself chopped up in bits. ... It is nothing jointed; it flows. A "river" or "stream" are the metaphors by which it is most naturally described. In talking of it hereafter, let us call it the stream of thought, of consciousness, or of subjective life. (1890, 1:239)

We all know this passage. Its terms, however, require a second look. Despite the combination of "comparison" and "suppression" (1:288) required to constitute an object's "fringe" (1:258), as James puts it, or, in a splendid phrase, its "theatre of simultaneous possibilities" (1:288), this process must be one of "consciousness," or, in the decisive assumption, "voluntary thinking" (1:259). Although the mind organizes "tendencies" (1:254) of thought rather than real perceptions, its agreements with other minds are considered agreements about "the same object." "Thought," concludes James—we have been here before—is "cognitive of an outer reality" (1:272).

William James's descriptions of consciousness hardly do justice to the psychical processes that his brother's novels both describe and provoke. Despite James's personal warmth to Freud at Worcester in 1909, James regarded Freud, as he did Fechner, as a rival. No wonder. William's "consciousness" is too limited notionally to account for what his brother's exemplary texts actually do. It is not surprising that historians invoke Bergson to account for the techniques of modern fiction in more detail, especially the relation of the self's fluctuating impressions to language and social myth. Unlike brother Henry, however, even Bergson cannot describe the state of perilous epistemological twilight in which Strether exists. We have seen why in Chapter 2. It is because Bergson cannot give up the idea of "consciousness" any more than brother William can. Nor can either give up the notion that the world is simply given.

Neither Bergson nor brother William will do to describe brother Henry's fiction. *The Ambassadors*—and *The American*, too, for that matter—deals with states and data quite precisely *not* given to consciousness. Whether or not they eventually enter consciousness is the ethical drama that James's novels customarily play out. Like Bergson, what brother William cannot describe in brother Henry's prose is the unconscious: that which exceeds the grasp of any sense of awareness based on the presumption that one can see objectively, without the biases that make us, unconsciously, who and what we are. Formulating the unconscious is the province of European psychology in the nineteenth century, the product of myriad influences reaching back to the Enlightenment. It is just this history that American clinical psychology, following brother William, represses; it is its enabling negation. This repressed history leads, not to academic psychology, but to Freud and psychoanalysis. The tradition of the unconscious is also what joins modern literature, not with academic psychology, but with psychoanalysis, and in a systematic way.

"The life of the blood"

One element in the crowded cultural history that Freud inherits seems far from the discourse of physiology. This is the discourse of race and ethnicity of which nineteenth-century science is a product and against which it is a reaction. Freud's work, too, both emerges from this discourse and criticizes it also. This discourse has two registers, in Freud and modern literature alike, the registers of "instinct" and "myth." They are different, as we have seen, but they are also related by similar epistemological assumptions. They reflect Freud's early romance with libido and his disciples' romance with myth. They also reflect two of the three tendencies that I have suggested are at work in modern literature itself.

Let us take up the discourse of "instinct" first. Simultaneously among the direct progenitors of psychoanalysis and among its targets, theories of ethnic and racial difference and valuation, often tied to the emergence after 1870 of an organic rather than a liberal notion of nationalism, abounded in imperial Europe. Changes in philology toward a view of language expressive of a national spirit or folk accompany this ethnocentric shift in politics, eventually coming to justify it, first in the ethnology of colonialism, and then in the discourse of Nazi eugenics. Even in the United States, Weir Mitchell's rest-cures for East Coast neurasthenics were the consumer counterparts of the belief that the closer you were to nature, the healthier you were. Decisive scholarly texts on the subject included that of Freud's heretical disciple Otto Weininger, *Sex and Character* (1931), but the earliest and most influential of them was Max Nordau's *Degeneration* (1892), a comprehensive description of a causal relation between skull types and personalities, posture and sexual predisposition, facial features and morals. Although phrenology like this was actually the end product of a century's worth of real brain research, it presented daunting conclusions. Nordau showed the "degenerate" personality to be closer to the instincts than the more rational, whose skull is more developed, containing a larger and less constricted brain. He lives further from his feet, and closer to his head. Like it or not, this exorbitant physicalism informed the assumptions of Freud's circle, to varying degrees of spin and reimagination. Nordau was also Viennese, and Jewish, and he and Freud knew each other socially (Jones 1:100). No wonder Freud believed that "primitive" cultures exhibited "instinctual" trends more plainly than did civilized ones. The difference between psychoanalysis and eugenics, however, is that psychoanalysis finds these differences to be those of degree on a common scale of humanity, while eugenics finds them to be differences of kind.

This glorification of the instincts in everything from political theory to philology, brain science to Western rest-cures, has its counterpart not only in Freud's earliest theory of the instincts, but also in one strand of literary modernism. Nordau's physicalism, as we saw in Chapter 1, finds no better literary exponent

than D.H. Lawrence. Lawrence is at his conventional best as prophet of libera-
tion through the "instincts." They are good for you. No matter the complications
of Lawrence's prose, the categorical consistency of his physicalism is undeniable,
even if it is only part of a wider aesthetic strategy. Its familiar vocabulary is
still at work in the posthumous "Study of Thomas Hardy" (1936). There, as in
Psychoanalysis and the Unconscious, Lawrence extols the virtues of "Love" over
"Law" (1936, 476), "instinct" and the "life of the blood" (503) over "pupilage"
(417) and "the social code" (420). This is the truth of "the primal soil" (417), "the
unfathomable womb," "the powerful, eternal origin" (418). Although he uses
the term "consciousness" (446), Lawrence, unlike William James, has in mind a
state of being that far exceeds awareness. It is almost a kind of Bergsonian transcendence. Birkin's labor in *Women in Love* (1921a) rests on making conscious
this deep instinctual state as a path toward human salvation. Like *Psychoanalysis
and the Unconscious*, of course, *Women in Love* is dialogical as well as polemical (see Lodge 1985). This textual doubleness, as I noted in Chapter 1, is what
Lawrence's fiction and nonfiction share.

Lawrence's great trilogy—*Sons and Lovers* (1913), *The Rainbow* (1915), and *Women
in Love* (1921a)—exhibits technically, like Lawrence's criticism, what Lawrence
describes as a "criticism" of its own "system of morality" (1936, 476): a debate about
Lawrentian doctrine among Lawrence's characters. The trilogy is not doctrinal but
reader-directed, measuring response, as do many of Freud's own texts, rather than
imposing it. Lawrence's poems are similarly self-correcting by virtue of their endless
revision of their own earlier tropes (Chaudhuri 2003). Less articulated novels such
as *Aaron's Rod* (1922) or *Lady Chatterley's Lover* (1928) garner no such dispensation.
But a doctrine of the instincts leaves a heaviness behind, even in the great trilogy.
Lawrence's notion of the "equilibrium" of the love-relation, as Birkin calls it (1921a,
139), is his version of the Mitchell rest cure from stress, the redemption from moral
degeneration unavailable in Nordau. Birkin's "equilibrium" is idealist to the extent
that the "being" it discovers is material and, in Lawrence's self-frustrating epistemology, therefore distinct from it. Even awareness must die in Lawrence to vouchsafe the truth of the material to which it must, redemptively, submit. Sensations
are valuable when they become ideas. But once they become ideas, they lose the
Bergsonian purity that made them valuable. The "pure balance" (139) that Birkin
wishes to achieve with those he loves is therefore the only qualified one within the
novel's story. Such a balance is achieved only by the novel itself, which suspends in
"equilibrium" Birkin's impassioned voice and the more conventional novelistic diction to which it is polemically—and constitutively—opposed. As a writer, Lawrence benefits from the very alienation that assails his characters. The gap between
their lives and their self-understanding is, as it is in James, his very subject.

Lawrentian modernism and its presumable primitivism has as its American cor-
relate the reception of another kind of literary modernism, that of the Harlem

Renaissance. This history shows how reductive a single reading of Freud can be. While African American novelists like Zora Neale Hurston or Jean Toomer, or poets like James Weldon Johnson, put in place an "instinctual" basis for black expressiveness—as W.E.B. DuBois had done in *The Souls of Black Folk* (1903)— they do so in order to foreground and criticize it as a mode of racist misreading of both literature and persons. Not so the well-meaning reception of black culture by whites, for whom, as with Lawrence, blackness signifies a savage substrate useful to white culture as a source of energy with which to combat its own lassitude. Indeed, the title of Carl Van Vechten's most well-known novel, popular and important in its time, is *Nigger Heaven* (1926). In a mockery of High Lawrentian Modernism (Lawrence himself gave the book a poor review [1927]), Van Vechten, whose black enthusiasms also included jazz, is at the head of a tradition of honoring black expressiveness for "instinctual" reasons that reaches its apex with the Beats. Jack Kerouac's spontaneous bop prosody (1958) sees in jazz a primal, unself-conscious energy that is most fully expressed by Norman Mailer in *The White Negro* (1957):

> The Negro, not being privileged to gratify his self-esteem with the heady satisfactions of categorical condemnation, chose to move instead in that other direction where all situations are equally valid. ... The Negro discovered and elaborated a morality of the bottom. (1957, 321–22)

Here Mailer's late American modernism reduces Freud's "instinct" to the bottom, too, exercising wit only to the extent that, like Lawrence, Mailer finds in "degeneration" a savior rather than a foe.

Particularly ironic is that the primitivism of Lawrence and Mailer recalls the roots of DuBois's own thinking in the German idealist tradition. While a graduate student at Harvard, DuBois matriculated at the University of Berlin from 1892–93, attending Max Weber's lectures and reading deeply in German philosophical texts. DuBois developed his notion of "soul" among rural blacks in America from the German idealist belief in the connectedness between native land and human essence signified by the notion of *das Volk* or "the Folk." Indeed, DuBois's German thesis was to be a comparison of black and German peasant life, although the German part never materialized, and the thesis itself disappeared (Lewis 1993, 139–40, 142). This manifestly racist estimation of human beings, destined to serve as propaganda for the Third Reich, also served to underwrite a doctrine of black American freedom, as DuBois's biographer, David Levering Lewis, observes (148–49). It is interesting to note that DuBois's term "soul" is really a redaction of *Seele*, the German word that Strachey translates, much to Bruno Bettelheim's consternation (1983), as "mind" rather than as "soul." As in Hurston, Toomer, and Johnson, the formal strategies of *The Souls of Black Folk*, particularly the double epigraphs that counterpoint African American spirituals with European Romanticism at the start of each chapter, render the assertion of "soul" or "folk" more dubious than it may seem. DuBois's term "double-consciousness" (1903, 5) is cognate with Charcot's *conscience sec-onde*. As a trope, it is already to be found in Hegel's *Phenomenology* (1807, 251). It is a doctrine of the unconscious. Like Freud, DuBois saw the effect not only of sensations on ideas, but of ideas on sensations. And like both of the brothers James, DuBois needed a term to describe the varying degrees of self-attentive-ness that it was possible to exercise regarding one's assumptions about things, particularly oneself. In it rests a theory of identification to undo its thrall.

This work, of course, it is left to Frantz Fanon to do. Colonial subjectivity is an especially aggravated form of subjectivity, the Oedipal subject *in extremis*. Here the Oedipus complex is "an inferiority complex" (1952, 18). "There is a complete"—and devastating— "identification with the white man" (145). The "identification" that is salutary in Mann is burdensome in Fanon. Here the gen-uine historicism of Mann's own position becomes especially clear, although, in an imperial context, that is just the problem. The only identifications worth making are those available from the trophy case of colonial tradition. This is to find what Homi Bhabha finds in Fanon (1990), an implacable relation between narcissism and identification in which the colonial subject can win only his servitude. Colonial subjectivity, to use Trilling's words about Freud, shows "how entirely implicated in culture we all are" (1955, 91). Without being valued, or devalued, as inferior by imperial culture, the colonial subject has no value at all. These are the new terms of the global sphere into which the colonial subject has been traumatically thrust. That this identity rests on its social estimation ironi-cally challenges the imperialist claim that inferior identity is instead inherent. Blood and instinct give way, as they do in Freud, to word and image.

"The mythical method"

Next among Freud's customary tropes for the unconscious is an unlikely one compared to the physicalist ones of Brücke's Institute, or even the racialist ones of Nordau. Thomas Mann, Stanley Edgar Hyman, and John Crowe Ransom have already alerted us to it. In the sequence of Freud's career, it comes in the second decade of the new century—the doctrinal decade—between *The Inter-pretation of Dreams* (1900) and *Totem and Taboo* (1912), and before the self-ques-tioning metapsychological phase. It is the trope of myth. A survey of Freud's use of tropes drawn from myth, classical and primitive alike, shows a particular concentration of them in the texts between 1900 and 1913 (see 24:325–26); it includes the term "Oedipus complex," which Freud first uses in 1910, and uses with more and more abandon as his career proceeds. Myth as evidence for the universal truth of psychoanalysis leads to a metaphor for the unconscious different from the instinctual ones of the early phase, and taken from a different field. Drawing on the Cambridge anthropologists James Frazer, Joan Harrison, and E. B. Tylor, Freud found myth, whether African or Greek, Egyptian or Etruscan, or even in the form of fairy tales, to be the universal reflection of unconscious process, which he still identified with primary process. Now the focus is on the image of instinct rather than on instinct itself, on the "representative," to use Bergson's terms, rather than on the "affect."

Here *Totem and Taboo* is the key text, with its view of the father as a rival to his sons. No wonder myth is the version of the unconscious that most appealed to Freud's disciple Jung, who rejected the libidinal theory of the instincts in precisely the year that *Totem and Taboo* was published. Like Otto Rank's, the Jungian tradition is itself a beastly illustration of *Totem and Taboo*, although perhaps it is also the other way around. Ransom has already called our attention to the ambiguities in the "mythical" position; Hyman has shown us the dangers of enthusiasm about it. Mann, above all, has shown the paradoxes at work in mythical thinking. They involve remembering that myth is really a matter of historical identity. This, however, is a novelist and literary critic talking. In Freud's own accounts of the relation between myth and instinct, no mechanism is proffered to explain the relationship between them. Myth is simply instinct's representational vehicle. As we have seen, however, the connection between sensations and ideas is more elaborate than that, even—especially, as Mann insists—in a communal or historical context. It is associational and takes place in time. Representation is defensive for Freud, not expressive.

Freud's handling of myth in *Totem and Taboo* is the best case in point. As Richard Armstrong observes, Freud recurs for his new materials to "Darwinian prehistory" (2005, 233), while Jung as a rule prefers the symbolic histories of Biblical, Hellenic, and anthropological contexts. Freud's materials allow him to take liberties for which Jung will have to pay the price. Because they are prehistorical—organic or cellular rather than cultural or representational in the common sense—they require no evidence of origination. The successful functioning of the nervous system in Freud's readers is proof enough. Freud's materials are their own evidence, an endless representation of their own condition because the texts and mode of reception are one and the same thing. The mythic materials are really an instance of the book's own action as a text. It is a Socratic dialogue, but one written by a Rabelais. It is a carnivalesque—a carnivoresque—that eats up explanations with the same ferocity with which fathers and sons gobble each other down. It is the Freudian parliament of fools. Like *The Interpretation of Dreams* or "On Narcissism," *Totem and Taboo* is not a mimetic account of signification or an example of one. It is not a representation of the truth of "myth," any more than psychoanalysis as a whole is. In Freud's hands, even the truth of myth becomes an instance of how texts work.

Not so classical "myth" criticism. A passage from Maud Bodkin's influential study *Archetypal Patterns in Poetry*, published in 1934, well summarizes the mimetic assumptions about myth present in a Jungian psychoanalytic approach. Describing Jung's "archetypes"—those "primordial images" of "unconscious forces"—Bodkin is very clear about what kind of representation myth is:

> These archetypes he describes as "psychic residua of numberless experiences of the same type," experiences which have happened not to the individual but to his ancestors, and of which the results are inherited in the structures of the brain, a *priori* determinants of individual experience. (1934, 1)

This is familiar. What has happened is presumably real, a kind of grand primal scene that is historical and not fantasized—"experiences which have happened." The only moment of hesitation is the word "residua." It sounds like Fechner's "residuum" and includes the specific worlds of representation that individuals share with both their cultural and species histories. Despite its epistemological realism, however, "archetypal" criticism disavows the specific nature of these "residua"—their formal status as images, or narratives—in favor of a blithe universalism. The tenor of all representation is simply a vehicle, as Bodkin puts it, for "the structures of the brain."

Jung's text of the same fateful year that saw his break with Freud, *Transformations and Symbols of the Libido* (1912), begins the succession of texts that lie behind Bodkin's. *Transformations and Symbolisms of the Libido* is the first book of Jung's independent phase, the foundation of his system and the unmooring of his literary star from Freud's own. Jung's early word-association research in 1904–5 had turned up narratives specific to individual patients and their histories; now he was promoting mythic universals. Rank predates Jung in publishing a less systematic kind of myth criticism—*The Myth of the Birth of the Hero* appears in 1909—but Rank is less effective than Jung in developing a strategy for undoing Freud.

It is not until 1919, in "Instinct and the Unconscious," that the term "archetype" itself is coined. Before that, Jung uses the word *Urbild*, which R.F.C. Hull, Jung's chief translator, translates as "primordial image" (1919, 136). *Bild*—picture—also counts among Freud's terms for psychical representation, although for Jung this *Bild* is not something that we ourselves can see, not even unconsciously, as we can—whatever it means to say that—in Freud himself. In Jung, something else does the seeing: the "instinct," and only the instinct. Jung's definition of the archetype is actually a reversal of Freud's definition of instinct in 1915. For Freud, instinct is the psychical representative of a somatic process. For Jung, the archetype is "the instinct's perception of itself" (1919, 136). It is the problem of representation that Jung wishes to avoid, particularly the mechanisms of its delivery system.

This is already true in 1912. The terms of Jung's original title tell us as much. "Transformation" and "symbol" suggest that there is a psychical tenor ready and waiting to be "transformed" or "symbolized" in a vehicle—a system of expression—distinct from it. "Libido" is a field apart from its "transformations"; it is the origin of their effects and cause of their flow. In Freud, their flow *is* their cause; their "transformations" are the fluidity that defines them. The "libido" is its "transformations." In 1915, Freud will say that "instincts" and their "vicissitudes" are one and the same thing. But this route is not the one that Jung has in mind. It is not surprising that he will reverse Freud so exactly. It is the notion of innate ideas that Freud has most genuinely overcome; it is the notion of innate ideas that Jung most wishes to reinvent. Here they are again, front and center:

> The conscious phantasies tell us of mythical or other material of undeveloped or no longer recognized wish tendencies in the soul. As is easily to be understood, an innate tendency, an acknowledgment of which one refuses to make, and which one treats as non-existent, can hardly contain a thing that may be in accord with our conscious character. (1912, 34–35)

In 1919, Jung is even more forthright:

> The archetypes of perception and apprehension ... are the necessary *a priori* determinants of all psychic process. (1919, 133)

To call the *Urbild* the "mechanism" of "phantasies in general" (1912, 34) is wishful thinking. This is precisely Mann's complaint about mythic thinking in its idealist form: It has no way to account for myth's symbolic labor. Its lack of one is proof of its efficacy. Mann, of course, has shown us how mythic signification really works. It is not unmediated, as Jung describes it; it is not, to use Bodkin's language, "inherited in the structures of the brain." As the Freud of *Beyond the Pleasure Principle* will eventually conclude, it *is* the structures of the brain, conceived in a semiotic way. The mediator of myth—what puts it in place and keeps it going—is representation, whether the shields that cellular life builds against a world from which it grows distinct, or personality's hierarchy of defense mechanisms stored in the "residua" of the unconscious. Myth's mechanism is also familiar. The hero produces the myth by copying whatever myth is available. This is called identification. When Freud applies himself to historical instead of prehistorical myth, this difference is very clear. Moses as an Egyptian is an obvious psychical defense, a wish-fulfillment or turning away from what is at least a social and psychical truth—Jews are Jews. Freud's handling of his mythic materials does not reveal a real event; Moses was not an Egyptian. This is the seduction theory all over again. Myth is a defense, not a memory. In Jung, however, myth remembers for us, and expounds.

Mythic psychoanalysis has its literary counterpart in Eliot and his school. This school shares the psychoanalytic notion of myth, or at least the Jungian permutation of myth, because it shares with psychoanalysis some of its sources in Cambridge anthropology. Eliot confesses how "deeply" he is "indebted" to Jessie L. Weston's *From Ritual to Romance* (1920) in the notes to *The Waste Land* (1922). Eliot's influential review of Joyce's *Ulysses*, published in *The Dial* in 1923, discovers in Joyce's novel what Eliot actually called the "mythical method" (1923). Based on Homer's *Odyssey*, *Ulysses*, by Joyce's own testimony, is serious about what Eliot describes as its mythical correspondences, from the manifest parallelism between the novel's organization and that of Homer's epic to the less obvious mythic alignments produced by Joyce's naming techniques and his use of puns. "In using the myth," says Eliot, "in manipulating the continuous parallel between contemporaneity and antiquity, Mr. Joyce is pursuing a method which others must pursue after him" (1923, 177). For Eliot, the "mythical method" is the *sine qua non* of modern literature because it allows the embattled present to find roots in the deeper strata of the Indo-European past—not in its instincts, but in the "mythic" unconscious that they produce. Unlike Freud's, Eliot's is a somewhat restricted view of universality from a global perspective; not all civilizations, even ancient ones, are created equal.

Eliot's polemical animus as poet and critic alike—what Christopher Ricks views as a strategy of provocation designed to engage the reader to wrestle with him (1988)—has as its justification his belief in a beneficent mythical undertow to human experience that it is the poet's job to express. Despite the dialogical potential of such writing, the poet's function remains hieratic—and polemical—even, especially, in a modern age. Eliot's, like Jung's, is a religious version of the unconscious; Eliot and Jung elevate the mythic side of the Freudian unconscious in order to free themselves principally from the doctrine of unconscious libido. Perhaps more to the point, they elevate the mythic side of the unconscious in order to stem the tide of history. This is the mimetic assessment of myth that they share with Ransom and Hyman, although it is not one that they share with Mann. Myth synchronizes the temporality of the representational achievements it praises. Achievements carved out of time are honored for their specificity by terms that know neither history nor culture. The very historicity of the events is what marks them out as timeless, but this timelessness is what also erases their historicity. How these paradoxes produce rather than somehow express their realities is of little interest to either Jung or Eliot, although they often make up the very material of Mann's novels, such as the difficulties of life in a traditional family, whether in modern Germany or in ancient Israel. Mythic time is not "constant" time—a tolerable life, gained within historical process—but the time of "arrest," to use Joyce's word in the *Portrait* (1916, 205).

"Arrest" is frozen time. The rhythm, or lack of it, is the same as Eliot's. What affirms history also cancels it.

This is also the program of Eliot's poetry. Like Lawrence, he is doctrinal, although in a different way. Both are idealists, also in a different way, but one takes that for granted. And like Lawrence, Eliot, too, is dialogical, thereby provoking not only agreement with his program but also giving his program its own immanent critique. *The Waste Land's* extraordinary suppleness as a poem is challenged by its rude impositions of mythic *doxa* on its shifting materials. "A poem that is to contain all myths," wrote F.R. Leavis, memorably, in 1932, "cannot construct itself upon one" (1932, 81). The poem tries to recontain its polysemy by means of the "mythical method," but the flooding of its mythic correspondences and their unmooring are the poem's chief activities. Eliot separates dialects in value even as he mingles them in the poem's narrative flow. The equivalences do not hold when the candidates are bourgeois. The poem becomes a site of contention rather than a movement toward the harmonization of its plural voices. Nor is the contention only political; it invades all the poem's topoi. Eliot's ambivalence about Madame Sosostoris, for example, Tarot reader extraordinaire, both affirms the horoscope while at the same time damning the nouveau riche context in which it operates (1922, 43–59). Similarly, the nightingale in "A Game of Chess" is a universal symbol for "inviolable voice" (101), as in Keats, although it is precisely Keats's use of the nightingale for rather more specifically ambivalent effects that makes Eliot nervous about the bird's very universalism. The Thames in "The Fire Sermon" is both a mythic repetition of its sweetness in Spenser while also a sign of Eliot's distance from Spenser because of the river's contemporary pollutedness. So, too, Tiresias, or Elizabeth and Leceister. Representatives of the past and therefore valuable, but also measures of our inability to conform to that past, they are measures of a gap rather than figures in a correspondence. The "reverberation" (326) of memory, as Eliot calls it in "What the Thunder Said," is at one and the same time what allows the correspondences to be invoked, and what washes away or unseats the parallels they wish to stabilize. Indeed, the poem's own constant movement corresponds rather exactly to the structure of the shift from sensations to ideas in Freud: the shift from difference to metalanguage, from dialogue to dialectic.

Real history, alas, interferes, as in Joyce, with the neatness of a "continuous" mythic history. *Ulysses*, despite Eliot's review, regularly interrogates just this use of myth. Eliot, whose ultimately medieval and agrarian program grows clearer and clearer in his later criticism, can follow his hero Joyce only so far. While Joyce shares with Eliot's classicist modernism a use of myth, he departs from Eliot in focusing on myth's displacement in real time by ideology, much as our third mode of modernism will do. No wonder Eliot is sad at the end of *The Waste Land*; his myths are piecemeal attempts to defend against the complexities of the real history he abjures: "These fragments," he writes, "I have shored against my ruins" (431).

Comparative examples are instructive. Modernist projects like Chekhov's may also appear to be instances of a mythic, agrarian idealism like Eliot's, but are not. *The Cherry Orchard* (1903) is a case in point. A seeming tragic melodrama about the destruction of nature and the feudal order by industry and the bourgeoisie, the play is, by virtue of its insolent and transgressive dialogue, especially by servants and intellectuals, really a criticism of its own apparent aims. Unlike *The Waste Land*, *The Cherry Orchard* aggressively undoes the agrarian myth it appears to put in place. A similarly revised reading might be given to another canonical early modernist text like *Moby-Dick* (1851), which, like *The Cherry Orchard*, seems to lament the troubles that befall the heroic mode in industrial modernity. Considered dialogically, however, the novel, like Chekhov's play, is a different affair. Ahab's quest-romance is an *idéologème* imbricated within the discursive vortex of the crew's carnivalesque, which unseats the quest's centrality from a linguistic point of view even as it supports it from the point of view of plot. Ishmael is the ambivalent mediator between the two modes. Is there such a dialogical modernism in the twentieth century that rivals its more familiar counterparts in blood and myth?

"This double life"

Like blood or mythic modernism, dialogical modernism has a historical scrim against which it emerges. It also corresponds to Freud's third and most elaborated notion of the unconscious, the material and social unconscious—the unconscious of *Beyond the Pleasure Principle*, *Group Psychology*, and *The Ego and the Id*. This notion of the unconscious has, as we have seen, emerged, by necessity, out of the internal logic of Freud's thought. It also emerges as a function of Freud's relation to yet another tier of influence in the sedimentations of his literary and scientific unconscious. Freud's materialism, like that of materialist modernism as a whole, has a long history. Unlike English and French Romanticism, German Romanticism, which precedes them both, included Novalis, a doctor; British Romanticism counted a professional apothecary surgeon, Keats, among its chief poets, and among its intellectual sources the associationist psychology of David Hartley, medical doctor as well as philosopher. The hard division between science and poetry that emerged in the early twentieth century with the rise of technical research (Whitehead 1925) was not yet in place when Fechner began his second career in the 1860s as Doctor Mises, journalist, spiritualist, and literary entrepreneur.

Psychology's earliest modern terrain is not science but philosophy, especially the sensationalism of John Locke, which prefigures Hartley's associationism by more than a century, and which provides Fechner's thought its widest condition. Psychology's presumably intimate relation to idealism is already a problem for Locke, who rejects it. Sensory experience builds the mind as well as the body. Imagine Freud's astonishment when he read in 1912 that his chief disciple Jung believed in ideas innately conceived. Even Bishop Berkeley's first investigations, like Fechner's more than a century later, place epistemology on a footing that actually combines Lockean psychology with physiology, a study of the mechanism of vision (1709).

It is easy to let Berkeley's presumable idealism obscure what he shares with his Enlightenment cohort. Vision, unconscious and the effect as much of judgments that come from memory as from direct experience, is mental as well as sensory. The two intermix, says Berkeley, especially during reflection. "When the mind perceives any *idea*, not immediately and of itself, it must be by the means of some other *idea*" (1709, 15). An "idea," says Berkeley, is simply "the immediate object of sense, or understanding, in which large signification it is commonly used" (33). There are "tangible" ideas and "visible" ideas (33), although the associations that provide transit between them make this difference more descriptive than categorical. The model is already familiar to us from Freud: the hierarchical stacking or storage of one "idea" on a prior, presumably more "tangible" one. "Sensations" are "ideas" in a "tangible" sense. Although Hume will reverse this kind of proposition, its structure will remain the same. In Berkeley's *Theory of Vision* at least, there is always a continuity between sensations and ideas. Even though Berkeley wishes to conclude that "objects of vision constitute a universal language of the Author of nature" (81), he cannot. One can speak of a "universal language" only because we all "regulate our actions in order to attain those things which are necessary to the preservation and well-being of our bodies … to avoid whatever may be hurtful and destructive of them" (81). This is the reason that the nervous system grows to some small degree conscious: because it is "useful," as Solms puts it, for it to do so (Solms 2002, 91). No wonder Berkeley drops the distinction between "universal" and "habitual" languages later in the same passage. Note especially his emphasis on the mechanism of signification in vision and language alike:

> It is by their information that we are principally guided in all the transactions and concerns of life. And the manner wherein they signify, and mark unto us the objects which are at a distance, is the same with that of languages and signs of human appointment, which do not suggest the things signified, by any likeness or identity of nature, but only by an habitual connexion that experience has made us to observe between them. (1709, 81)

With Hume, Locke's epistemology and Berkeley's mechanics find a synthetic site. Hume's distinction between "impressions" and "thoughts or ideas" (1748, 96–97) readily looks forward to the Victorian distinction between "sensations" and "ideas." For Hume, "impressions" are "sensations" (99). British impressionist thinking such as Pater's in the next century has a clearer—and more systematic—filiation than we customarily afford it. "Resemblance" and "contiguity" are the chief mechanisms for the association of ideas (101). Resemblance and contiguity are, of course, also metaphor and metonymy, condensation and displacement. Although Hume wishes "causation" to be a third category (101), "resemblance" and "contiguity" are between them the agents of their own "causation." "Effect," in Nietzsche's sense, is its own "cause" (101), the motion of its own mechanisms. Experience alone is both the motive and the medium of their activity. "Necessary connexion" (145) is Hume's correction of Berkeley's "universal." "Necessary connexion" is, as it will be for Pater, "habit":

> The mind is carried by habit, upon the appearance of one event, to expect its usual attendant, and to believe, that it will exist. This connexion, therefore, which we feel in the mind, this customary transition of the imagination from one object to its usual attendant, is the sentiment or impression, from which we form the idea of power or necessary connexion. (145)

In order to explain "fresh" impressions, "necessary connexion" becomes a part of what Hume calls "a customary connexion" (147) in a hierarchy of association. "Customary connexion" is really a recognition of sameness in a field of otherwise slightly different "impressions" (147)—the second-order construction of ideas that have many contributing originals, but no single or unique one. As in Derrida's description of the Freudian psychical apparatus, "fresh" impressions may occur simultaneously with the retention of past ones. This is hardly a philosophy of consciousness. Consciousness is superogatory. Hume has already invented a doctrine of the unconscious.

If Berkeley's psychophysics prefigures Fechner's, David Hartley's *Observations on Man* (1749) provides the best link between sensory philosophy and the beginnings of the science of the brain. Like Freud, Hartley starts as a physician, unlike Locke, who is belatedly certified to practice medicine in 1674, and for whom medicine is, as it will be for Hartley, the inevitable counterpart to a speculative philosophy of mind. It is not Hartley's associationism that is new. The bond between sensations and ideas is already familiar from Hume. What is new is the connection between associations and "vibrations," the latter understood in a medical sense: as an "active" power in the "medullary substance" (1749, 1:4). Although Hartley chooses the medulla rather than the cortex for the location of this activity (1:7), he nonetheless predicts neuroscience in another way. "Vibrations" are neurotransmitters. Not only as in Hume do sensations and ideas form a bond. Now sensations and vibrations also form a bond at the originary or physical end of the cluster of what are otherwise only psychological associations. This is where and how one first experiences impressions. In Hartley, associations are, as they will be in Freud, actually connected to the tissues of the brain by the simple facts of human development. For Hartley, the brain is "the seat of the sensitive soul, or the sensorium" (1:31), the initial receptacle of sensations from which the rest of the mental structure derives. The continuous structure of brain as it turns into mind and back again is now fully programmatic. Ideas which "resemble" sensations are "ideas of sensations," or "simple ideas"; "the intellectual ones which are formed from them" are "complex ideas" (1:56). "Simple ideas," in other words, "run into complex ones by association" (1:77). Language, and signification in general, is a matter of complex association in which words "annex" "ideas" of the "circumstances" "associated" with them (1:275). The stacking of structures in a hierarchy of complexity, from the sensory to the ideational to the linguistic, is familiar from Berkeley and Hume, although its combination of specificity and sweep in Hartley looks forward more exactly to Fechner and to Freud.

These are conversionary structures of a non-neurotic kind, the transformation, to restore Jung's term to a medical context, of the somatic into the ideational. Othello's epilepsy and his open nature provide a good example. They betoken the same insufficient structure of neural defense. Psyche and soma predispose each other. The modern psychiatric category coprolalia is also a good example. Here, a neural overload produces a stream of obscenities reflecting a preoccupation with fecal matter. Even the patient's language shifts to the pathways of association required to replicate the underlying neural condition that prompts it. The verbal tic is not a discharge of the condition so much as it is an instance of it, at an only quantitatively or structurally higher level of complexity. It is a symptom of the condition, not a catharsis or abreaction of it. By necessity (Hartley called his doctrine necessitarianism), the role of memory is expanded: "Memory is that faculty, by which traces of sensations and ideas recur or are recalled" (1:iii). As in coprolalia, the "traces" leave "a perceptible effect" or "vestige" once we see them as a system. Their permanence or feebleness is to be measured in proportion to their strength or "repetition" in a continuous series, from the histological to the psychological (1:57). If Hume provides a doctrine of the unconscious before the fact, Hartley provides a blueprint for neuropsychoanalysis.

As Fechner's psychophysics has shown, the simple division between idealist and materialist never structures the history of modern psychology in the first place. Contemporary with Hartley is the widespread development of interest in the brain and nervous system (Richardson, 2001). Brain science is the overt and institutionalized link between the sensory philosophy of Locke and Hartley and the materialism of a literary tradition from Keats to Pater that takes body and brain to be continuous rather than at odds. By 1820, phrenology, despite its notorious future as a cult practice and locus of popular assumption about intelligence, has emerged as the first attempt to map the brain. Writers like Nordau are witness to its durable popularity. Its background is the discovery in 1781 of "animal electricity" by Galvani and the notion that mental activity could be broken down into component parts and actually studied. The anatomy of the soul had replaced its salvation. In the hands of a physiological philosopher like Hartley, the notion of "association" therefore included the physiology that underlay the mind's psychology. Like Hartley's "vibrations," Galvani's electricity strove to connect physical stimulation with events in the mind using the "association" as the mediator among sensation, ideation, and feeling. Erasmus Darwin, in *Zoonomia* (1794–96), also uses the term "sensorium" to describe a connectedness of brain and perception that is no longer simply ideal. Franz Joseph Gall in turn gives us the notion of the brain itself as a systematic organ. The emergence of the brain as the biological source of thought, feeling, and sensation therefore complicates the otherwise idealist air of Romanticism, British Romanticism in particular, and likens the neural atmosphere that surrounded Romanticism with the neurological atmosphere, including railway spine, that, later in the century, surrounded both aestheticism and the birth of psychoanalysis. Brain science had already made both Romanticism and psychology materialist affairs, not by becoming mechanistic, but by situating ideas in a relation to the "sensorium." Keats's hands-on involvement with the sciences of the body has produced generations of scholarship preoccupied by the connection between his emphasis on sensation and his experiences as a surgeon actually holding the material of his own metaphors.

The step from this tradition to that of Freud working in Ernst Brücke's Physiological Institute as a young neurologist from March 1881 to July 1882 is a very short one. Thinking under these assumptions in Brücke's laboratory as he dissected everything from crayfish to the nervous systems, including the brains, of human cadavers, the young Freud was taught to regard neurological processes as reflexive discharge, the body's way of relieving buildups of tension. For Fechner, however, as we have seen, this was an improper way to understand the "conservation" of Brücke's comrade Helmholtz. "Conservation" was not a process of reflex or discharge but of "constancy." The organism seeks equilibrium through absorption rather than through discharge, which, for Fechner, is a pathogenic state. The body expunges stimulation rather than absorbs it only when stimulation is toxic or unassimilable. This key structure of influence has, as we have also seen, required Freud to postulate a "residuum," to use Bergson's term, or, to use Freud's own later one, a "dynamic" unconscious. In the laboratory, in other words, even before the *Project*, lay all the terms and solutions of Freud's final phase.

Our third, material modernism is the Freud of this summary phase. Its art is not an art of consciousness at all, as is Eliot's hieratic art, or Lawrence's hortatory and pedagogical art. It is an art of the sleeping self that awakens just in time to survive. It is a more influential modernism—it has produced more actual idiolects in history, both literary and cultural, than the other two—and it is more Freudian because of such an ability to influence, in deep and pervasive ways. Nor should its social or political side be overlooked. In Freud, the third phase emphasizes social interaction because it is concerned with symbolization, particularly identification. Its concerns with symbolization also lead to concerns with gender. This third modernism, in other words, is also a feminist modernism. Its tradition can be traced from Katherine Mansfield, émigrée from New Zealand, through both Willa Cather in New York and Mansfield's close friend Virginia Woolf in London. Cather's essay on Mansfield (1936) shows how Mansfield's particular focus is on what Cather calls the "double life" that everyone leads:

> Even in harmonious families there is this double life: the group life, which is the one we can observe in our neighbour's household, and, underneath, another—secret and passionate and intense—which is the real life that stamps the faces and gives character to the voices of our friends. (1936, 109)

It is as though Mansfield—and Cather—had actually made James a novelist of the Freudian unconscious. Here is a theory of images and the way they connect sensations and ideas through the identifications that the social life of the family provides. We are back to very central Freud indeed. The "double life" is the Freudian unconscious in its most mature form: "the material and social investiture," as Cather puts it in "The Novel Démeublé" (1922, 40), out of which the self emerges by resisting. What is the mechanism of "material investiture"? Nothing less than the dialogue or dyad of narcissism and identification. Like colonial subjects, subjects at large are, to use Althusser's word, interpellated into the world by means of the cultures with which they are identified. Cather and Woolf show us this process among adults; Mansfield, as Klein will, shows it also among children. Knowledge for Mansfield and her school, as it is for Freud, is not objective knowledge of an external world. It is knowledge, to use Pater's words, of the truth of one's impressions. How the ego, or the soul, manages to regard these impressions, particularly the idealizations to which the losses of life give rise, is the drama that psychoanalysis and the novel most exactly share as forms.

An emphasis on Mansfield's influence on Cather and Woolf not only suggests a new way of mapping the history of modern fiction, particularly a sound relationship between British and American modernism. It also suggests that neither psychoanalysis nor the techniques of literary modernism are an extension of idealism either as a philosophy of mind or as an aesthetic practice. An aestheticist regard for inwardness is not at odds with the social sphere to which its concerns are presumably opposed. Mansfield, Woolf, and Cather draw common inspiration from Walter Pater. But neither, as we have seen, is Pater an idealist; his sense of perception is resolutely material, especially in the "Conclusion" to *The Renaissance*, where the vocabulary is very often a scientific one. Indeed, the materialism of Mansfield, Cather, and Woolf evidences a continuity with the materialist Romanticism of Hartley, Keats, and Pater all alike, a Romanticism from which the quite distinct careers of Lawrence and Eliot have led us away.

Mansfield's influence is key to showing us what Cather and Woolf share. The material and social "investiture" of the self is represented in Mansfield's own stories as early as "The Tiredness of Rosabel" (1908) and as late as "Bliss" (1918) and "Prelude" (1918). Mansfield's world is the shifting boundary between sensations and ideas, often among children, and the social identifications that allow children and adults alike to protect themselves against the very social order from which they are in symptomatic flight. For Cather and Woolf, this "investiture" is played out in different national settings and under different suns. For Cather, the key relation is between country and city; for Woolf, it is between the neural and the noumenal. But the focus of representation is a common one that highlights the relation between sensations and ideas, as it does in Mansfield herself. For Cather, this relation is best studied in the young person's inscription into the protocols of local community that may or may not be adequate to her. Some of Cather's heroes simply change their surroundings, like Thea Kronborg or Lucy Gayheart; others reinvent local community by recasting its terms, like Jim Burden or Tom Outland. Only in an active relation to landscape, as in the focus on farming in *O Pioneers!* (1913), or to ideology, as in the focus on business law in *A Lost Lady* (1923), can the self's materiality and sociality come into being. *A Lost Lady* even provides the psychosexual grounds on which these later modes of social inscription are propped. For Woolf, "investiture" is best studied in Clarissa Dalloway's ambivalence, or Mrs. Ramsay's fluctuation between Victorian hostess and Paterian aesthete. The striking of London's clocks in an inexact relation to the strokes of Big Ben in *Mrs. Dalloway* (1925) is a fine emblem for the way in which the self's particularity is a function of the separate peace it makes with the social order. As in the writings of Freud, this proceeds in Woolf's novels through identification, with *Jacob's Room* (1922) inaugurating this tendency in Woolf's classic phase by regarding idealization as the source of depression, much as Freud himself does in "Mourning and Melancholia." This is the exact focus of *To the Lighthouse* (1927).

Mrs. Dalloway and the first volume of Freud's *Collected Papers* in English were published by the Hogarth Press on the same day—May 14, 1925. Lytton Strachey's younger brother, James, had begun his career as Freud's chief translator and editor of what would become the *Standard Edition* of Freud's works. Strachey's career proceeded at the very center of the Bloomsbury Group's daily life. Woolf's brother Adrian Stephen was also a psychoanalyst, as were other Bloomsbury habitués like Joan Rivière, who served as first translator of both "Mourning and Melancholia" and *The Ego and the Id*. That the material production of English Freud was a physical labor of Woolf's immediate circle of friends is the last and best historical instance of the very real relation between modern literature and psychoanalysis. Let us turn to it now.

5

Strachey the Apostle

Discipleship

The Bloomsbury production of the *Standard Edition* is a splendid instance of historical overdetermination, and of the overdetermined ways in which cultural production both occurs and is received. It proceeds under particular conditions and over periods of time, mediated and, in the case of psychoanalysis, constituted, like religions and poetic histories, by the histories of institutions. As Walter Kendrick and I argued in 1985, the *Standard Edition* needs no apology. Its organizing power proves its influence. All other editions, even the German collected works published by Fischer, use it as the most thorough and compendious of the texts of Freud. English Freud is treated, for all intents and purposes, as original Freud. A passage from Strachey's "General Preface" is worth quoting at the start of any discussion of the translation:

> When the *Standard Edition* was first planned, it was considered that it would be an advantage if a single hand were responsible for shaping the whole text; and in fact a single hand has carried out the greater part of the work of translation, and even where a former version has been used as a basis it will be found that a large amount of remodeling has been imposed. This unfortunately has involved the discarding, in the interests of this preferred uniformity, of many earlier translations that were excellent in themselves. The imaginary model which I have always kept before me is of the writings of some English man of science of wide education born in the middle of the nineteenth century. And I should like, in an explanatory and no patriotic spirit, to emphasize the word "English." (1:xviii–xix)

Even the apology for burying earlier translations under the "preferred" "single" one shows how reflexive the translation is: Its structure, too, doubles that of the psychical apparatus. As with the unconscious, what is "discarded" in the "remodeling" process nonetheless remains behind as a series of memorial traces, much as Strachey's phantom "man of science" presides in ironic solemnity, a totem without a taboo. This is, of course, the protective spirit of Darwin, Freud's only scientific "English" influence.

Psychoanalytic history as a whole is a series of literary discipleships structured by anxieties of influence. It would be foolish not to place Bloomsbury Freud within this wider context first. To regard psychoanalytic history in this way, including Bloomsbury's role within it, is to discover another of its endless redoublings as a discursive practice, not only in the analytic session and on Freud's page, but also in the way that Freud's shadow falls on the pages of his disciples'. Wilhelm Reich's *Mass Psychology of Fascism* (1933) is the best instance in all of analytic history of the projection of such difficulties. Freud's *Totem and Taboo*, of course, is Freud's own. Reich's book is a manifestation of the disciples' collective fear of Freud's own authority or status as *Führer*. It includes the fetishization within the analytic movement of Freud's very body in the 1930s (hence, too, the fascination with his decaying health), and one not, alas, unlike the procedures that characterized the simultaneous advent of fascism proper in the culture that had already produced psychoanalysis. To argue that psychoanalysis and Nazism are the twin and opposed products of Max Nordau and Otto Weininger is hardly new (Mosse 1964, 1978; Gilman 1993).

The familiar schismatic tendencies that elaborate rather than inhibit the history of analysis are likewise a sign of Freud's own transferential intent rather than of a grossly Napoleonic ambition. Considered strategically, the maintenance of orthodoxy was not for Freud as straightforward as analytic history may make it seem, nor, of course, as naïvely fascist as an aggressive history could. Jones's biography represents the first position; Paul Roazen's defense of Victor Tausk's apostasy represents the second (1971). Freud wished heresy among his disciples, much as he wished his reader to argue with him. As the history of analysis goes on to attest—and as we have already seen from a formal point of view—no single reading of Freud has ever—can ever—succeed in maintaining itself as wholly just or authoritative. Since Freud knew this, the implication is plain that Freud's apparent willfulness during his lifetime to preserve a theoretical orthodoxy, no matter the personal cost or the apparent expense in the repression of influences both local and international, disguises his arguably real desire to produce rival discipleships. Transferentially, the resistance that Freud prompted was directed at the customary interdependence of narcissism and identification symptomatically hypostasized among his disciples. Because the professional situation involved psychoanalysis, their work aggravated rather than relieved, by means of sublimation, the structure of family-romance conflicts. This is the classical usefulness of professionalism, and one that has a specific structure for writers, as I will show in Chapter 8. Freud's disciples have the very real disadvantage of being psychoanalysts.

Hence the extraordinary literary history of psychoanalysis. Alfred Adler, like Jung, is a familiar Freudian renegade; their stories are equally reflexive. Adler's "organ inferiority" and "masculine protest" misread Freud as a rival rather than as a father, while Jung makes the mistake of treating Freud just the other way around. Jung's achievement, in contrast to Adler's, is very considerable: even its transcendentalism is a direct rather than displaced response to Freud's own secularism. Rank, who weakly precedes Jung with an interest in myth, presents a similar story, but its terms, like its power, are different, less rugged than Jung's and more provocative than Adler's. If Adler protests, Rank projects. His mythic hero already has a thousand faces, too many to choose from if one of them is to be taken seriously. The dramaturgy of the mythic stance goes unacknowledged compared to Jung's; the performance is positively shy. The title of *The Trauma of Birth* (1924) expresses a desire to return to the womb, free from the trouble that the book seems to invite. By contrast, even Jung's early bibliography reads like a literary yellow sheet. His first book, on the psychology of occult phenomena (1902), betrayed the interest in spiritualism hidden beneath the rigor that impressed Freud in Jung's word-association experiments. In 1909 follows a paper on the significance of the father; in 1910 a paper on the psychology of rumor. Psychoanalytically, these are projections of the break to come; literarily, the break to come is the Wildean effect of these texts and their history. Jung's love for myth only reconstitutes, in an idealist's vein, the kind of family-romance sagas he had presumably dismissed in his rejection of Freud's theory of infantile sexuality. Jung's apostasy we have already seen in its technical or procedural differences from Freud's. Here, as with the other disciples, its allegorical nature from the point of view of literary priority comes to the fore more readily, and with a more businesslike affirmation. Jung's metaphysical profile is a handy mask for his desire to incorporate the father under cosmic slogans and a refreshed and more attractive psychoanalytic vocabulary. In addition to "complex," in *Studies in Word-Association* (1906), Jung had contributed "imago" (1913, 134), six years before "archetype."

If Jung is Freud's radical theologization, then Lacan, beginning in the 1930s, is his radical historicization. Between them they are a fine example of the poles in Mann's description of the two contradictory currents whose dialogue or dialectic makes up the Freudian picture of mind. For Jung, what the mind gains in power it loses in understanding; for Lacan, what it gains in understanding it loses in power. If Jung reads Freud through theology, Lacan reads Freud through phenomenology, the effect of Koyré's seminars on Hegel at which he was joined by the young Sartre (Roudinesco 1993, 88). Refracting Freud's trio of psychical agencies through dialectic, ego, id, and super-ego become, in a wholly nonparallel relation, Imaginary, Symbolic, and Real. This reimagination alone, especially the exact positioning it gives to personality's relationship to social and historical process, is singularly vivid. Its empirical reliability is betokened by its endless usefulness. Its inaccuracy as a reading of either Hegel or Freud is betokened by Lacan's originality. Lacan's subject, in order to survive and succeed, must misunderstand its sources.

Freud's loyal inner circle is even more literary in structure. The intensity of its discipleships recalls the intensity of those of minor poets such as the Pre-Raphaelite Brotherhood in their complex relations to Ruskin. Sandor Ferenczi hugs his patients in Budapest, including the young Melanie Klein, who goes on to Berlin to work with Karl Abraham, who focuses on the sexual stages of childhood. In different but equally regressive positions in relation to Freud himself, Ferenczi and Abraham are both infantilized. They predispose Klein to regard the analyst as a mothering figure rather than as a father surrogate because they project their own wish for help and protection from Freud onto her and her promise. Freud, of course, is the absent father, and they are good enough psychoanalysts to know that in Klein alone will Freud find, however much he will resist it, the only one of his disciples worth having. No wonder Klein goes on to elaborate the notion of projective identification. It is a memory of what happened in her analytic sessions with these men. The terms of Klein's own more bracing relation to Freud himself are much clearer than those of Ferenczi's or Abraham's. She is, of course, the daughter but, doubly disabled as she is—as a daughter, not a son, and as a disciple of disciples—she cannot expect a direct relation to Freud. Nor does she want one. She is not Anna Freud. Unlike the other disciples, she does not respond to Freud personally. In the close quarters of London, her relation to Anna Freud remains sublimated. She responds to Freud—both of them—as a writer. She takes the only role left to her as the kind of daughter she is, and the only one given to her by her own analysts—that of the mother, and the mother's world. The refusal to theorize in her essays is the primary example in her prose of her *ascesis*—her self-curtailment in relation to Freud's own far more grandiloquent writing. Belated as Klein's position in psychoanalysis is, it has one advantage that none of the others do: Her approach precedes, or seems to, well enough, Freud's own presumable focus on the sexual stages, this by pushing the earliest symbolic dramas back to the breast. Mothering as a theme is not an expression of Klein's goodness. It is the subject matter that emerges when she takes her opportunity to come earlier than Freud as a writer. This is on Freud's own part a shrewder means of securing immortality than that of requiring mere assent, since it allowed for—indeed, fostered—the expression of schisms inherent in his theory, and, in the process, disseminated his teachings at increasingly diffuse levels of debate. Foucault is right. Freud is the initiator of a discursive practice, with all the anxieties that attend it. Foucault himself, as we shall see in the next chapter, is one of its beneficiaries as well as one of its causalities.

Nor does French feminism escape its discipleship to psychoanalysis. Julia Kristeva's case is exemplary. The distinction between the semiotic and the symbolic—between the pre-Oedipal joy of mother and child and the Oedipal nightmare of the law of the father—leads to an epistemological cul-de-sac of the kind we have seen in our reading of "On Narcissism." It requires valorizing the notion of natural rhythms as opposed to social ones, and linking the rhythms of the female body with nature itself. This the terms of psychoanalysis forbid. This is the unreflective side of French feminism and the point at which it cannot sustain the ironies that bring it into being. Kristeva's work is a displacement of her literary anxieties. The opposition of the semiotic and the symbolic is really the opposition of Klein and Lacan in her literary unconscious. Indeed, the very struggle between Klein and Lacan reproduces the structure of the family romance in—as—analytic history. Klein is the mother, emphasizing the mother's role in her teachings; Lacan is the father, emphasizing the Name of the Father. Anna Freud's study of the ego's mechanisms of defense (1936) shows what is at stake in the face of these difficulties by naming what they require. Luce Irigaray hypostasizes the difference between the semiotic and the symbolic far more egregiously than Kristeva does, although that is because she has already chosen Klein, or at least a misreading of Klein. Kristeva's own study of Klein (2000) rights the balance to the extent that it shows how Klein and Lacan are continuous rather than opposed. If one accents the preoccupation with symbolization that they share, Freud's own influence, in Kristeva's case, remains screened by these later influences, which both protect her and prevent her from taking on Freud himself, as no good disciple would.

Freud's influence on Bloomsbury, however, is no greater than Bloomsbury's influence on Freud. This is another way in which Bloomsbury exercises its historic rights, second only to Woolf's prose style. Bloomsbury has remained controversial in the half century that has seen the demise of its last members, although in a way different from that surrounding its initial modern fame. While this study of Freud is not a social history, it is important to frame any discussion of the *Standard Edition* with a brief indication of the changing status of Bloomsbury in Britain, and its contrast with the durably popular Bloomsbury that continues to thrive in the United States. Today, in Britain particularly, Bloomsbury represents the durability of aristocratic patronage. By the standards of Terry Eagleton's Marxism and the work of Raymond Williams behind it, it falls short of its own progressivism, a failing underscored, perhaps caused by, its aestheticism. For Williams, aestheticism is no more than "the sovereignty of the civilized individual" (1978, 165). This social criticism sounds surprisingly like the Leavises' resentment toward Bloomsbury in the 1930s, and suggests a similarity between Left and Right that many hesitate to acknowledge. Both Marxists and Leavisites are moralists not only because they believe in perfectibility, but because of a view of literary language that regards it as transparent, and therefore capable of unproblematic referentiality in its quest for truth. The new Penguin translations of Freud are a combined function of antipathy toward Bloomsbury and a belief in a mimetic notion of both language and translation that, as we shall soon see, Strachey himself, like Freud, does not hold.

The Strachey translation will provide a very close look at Bloomsbury's own view of literary language and will show how wholly misconstrued its presumable problems are. Strachey's "liberties" are actually examples of why the translation is a good one. Strachey, like Freud, sees that, like the psychical apparatus, language does not refer to stable objects outside itself. It produces those objects from the start in a vast web or network of consensual—or almost so—social significations. Language is not mimetic but constitutive. Woolf's landscapes, both of mind and of England itself, are this web's Wordsworthian manifestation. For Strachey the translator, the semantic fields of different languages produce different objects and different subjects; translation can never be a "better" or "worse" approximation of an original text because, as I will show, different languages construct different worlds. Bloomsbury's social and aesthetic virtues are actually related, as we have seen in Mansfield and Woolf. A material reading of aestheticism should also serve as a good platform from which to mount, cautiously, to be sure, such an argument about Strachey and his translation. And because aestheticism has so much in common with psychoanalysis, it is natural enough to turn, not to Bloomsbury's official literary production—chiefly novels and essays—but to Strachey's translation to show Bloomsbury's aesthetic materialism in its Freudian form.

English Freud

If Woolf's chief literary anxiety is Pater (Meisel 1980), then Strachey's, of course, is Freud. Indeed, Strachey's anxiety defines our collective discipleship to Freud in the Anglophone world because of the translation. How is Strachey's transference resolved by the translation? What is his theory of translation? What is his theory of transference? And what is their relationship? Translation, as it turns out, is another instance of the structure with which both deferred action and the dream-work have made us familiar. Let us backtrack. The modality of psychoanalytic knowledge at large is that of retrospection or *Nachträglichkeit*. While it may appear that deferred action is the structure of the patient's memory alone, it should be evident that it is also the structure of the analyst's knowledge of the patient. Freud's narration doubles rather than simply reports that of his patient. In fact, the two narrations are in the final instance inseparable. What comes later—Freud's *récit*—effectively puts into place what comes before it—the apparent quiddity of, say, the Wolf Man's *histoire*. As the text of the case history graphically attests—especially if we are attentive to the almost comic revisions to which the primal scene is subject as the narrative unwinds—Freud's vaunted primacies are actually later constructions. The primal scene is a representation after the fact of something that happened only because it was required to happen.

We have already seen these narratological configurations in literature. *Paradise Lost* is probably the frankest instance in English of a text that freely admits how and why the putative immediacies that give its narration the aura of presence are the function of contrast or negation. The garden, innocent man and woman, all the poem's prelinguistic primacies are, like Freud's unconscious, really the result of fallen—that is to say, belated—modes of narration. Milton broadcasts his "erring" but necessary reversal of temporal priorities ("a new train of intermediate images," as Dr. Johnson describes it [1779–81, 365]) in the construction of the poem's *histoire* by explicitly announcing, even exploiting, its retroactive production by means of its anthological *récit*. The structure of literary reference, in other words, is equivalent to that of psychoanalytic thought and practice. Much as the play between *récit* and *histoire* produces the illusion of a Miltonic world, so the play between patient and analyst produces the ground of the subject's interiority in tandem with its production of the analytic discourse that tautologically signifies it. Like a literary text, the transference in analysis becomes in retrospect not just an instrument that works on objects or states of mind it may come upon, but is also the self-engendering ground of the discursive scenario in which they emerge. As we already know, Freud's various speculative origins or primacies—the unconscious, the primary process, even the originary father—are similarly produced as retroactive functions of their symptoms or effects—consciousness, the secondary process, the son.

The structure of the transference is no different. Strachey's classic essay on the transference, "The Nature of the Therapeutic Action of Psychoanalysis" (1934), takes these parallels up in no uncertain terms. The dynamic of the transference lies in the double action produced by the bond or, as Strachey calls it, the "mutative" play (1934, 369), between the patient's immediate relation to the analyst as a person in his or her own right and the patient's relation to the symbolizations the analyst acquires during the analytic procedure. Such a play or relation, Strachey argues, is the very pivot of the action of the transference. The psychoanalytic narrative is, in other words, both about itself—the patient and analyst in their actual state—and about something else like it—the patient and analyst in transferential or mediate, not immediate, relation. The premise of the transference is its ability to motivate and mobilize symbolization for the patient. The analyst is who he or she is because he or she is someone else. This is a familiar enough proposition in narrative poetics: Thanks to *différance*, a sign is, by definition, what it is by virtue of its ability to stand for what it is not. Authority—the analyst's, for example—is what it is by virtue of what it can be by contrast, in the symbolizations to which the analyst lends his or her plasticity. To the extent that such symbolization comes to a halt—a function as it is of the relation between the two planes on which the analysis has proceeded, the immediate and the transferential, very like the two planes of *récit* and *histoire* in narratology—the tension that drives the narrative of the analysis also comes to a halt. Once the difference that allows symbolization to occur collapses, relations between patient and analyst grow normal. The analyst is now no more than "a real figure, and not an archaic and distorted projection" (376n18). Then, ideally, the analysis, or at least one in a series of movements in it, is terminable.

Once, in other words, *récit* flags, the symbolizations that produce an analytic *histoire* assigned to the patient's primary process also flag. Its difference from the *histoire* it supposedly only recounts withers away, rendering the analytic scenario all that it had ever been anyway: the byplay of a series of *récits* and interruptions, all designed to evoke the always absent causality of the unconscious factors to which they appear to refer. The transference, in other words, produces primary-process material as a function of the analyst's interference with the patient's discourse, whether by speech or silence. Transferential authority serves as a kind of marker or algebraic variant by means of which, scene to scene, *imago* to *imago*, the patient is conduced into an associative and inferential realm of elaboration, both in his or her reactive speech and in the silence beyond the session that the analyst never hears. This is what situates, by definition and after the fact, the primariness the transference's mutative play has succeeded in rearing. To arrive at the "immediate"—for Strachey, the straightforward relation between consenting adults rather than the mediate symbolizations between them—is to arrive at the terminus of an analysis. The trajectory of the transference dissolves its authority as the sign of its success.

More than a theory of the transference is at work here. Strachey's mind is an extraordinarily unified one. The translation follows these very principles. Psychoanalysis in English—Strachey's English—is itself an example of psychoanalytic process. The reasons are both procedural and epistemological. Here is the deep, and very psychoanalytic, logic of the *Standard Edition*. It is governed by deferred action. Strachey's translation is informed by a theory of transference and a theory of reference each as systematically Freudian as the other. Freud's German, the ghostly original, is like the unconscious, never present but always constitutive, producing its translation as a shadow effect, as secondary process to the primariness of the German that is lost. The pure, traumatized original emerges only later, as a function of the abusive translator. Translation itself may be described as the production of a lost primacy or purity by deferred action. The Homeric original, for example—Arnold's great cause, and Joyce's great jest—

gains its authority precisely because we receive it belatedly in at least two ways, one inescapable even if the other is not. Without Greek, we receive it simply in translation; but even without translation, we receive it as the direct effect of a fall from the fullness of oral speech into the secondariness of writing. The secondariness of Homer's founding epics in relation to themselves is in fact the constitutive irony on which their authority durably rests. And on such a decidedly secondary original—the kind of phenomenon that even in 1800 Wordsworth, in the first preface to *Lyrical Ballads*, can only describe paradoxically as "originally derived" (1800, 245)—we customarily bestow a phantom legitimacy, granting it a fullness, as we do the unconscious, to which its translator bears witness only rhetorically. The translation is the "idea," to use Bergson's vocabulary, of which the original is the inexpressible "sensation." This fugitivity of the original and its exoticization are effects that come only after translations have been made, making time, our benefactor, our enemy instead. One risks turning epistemological necessity into moral melodrama. Such institutional opera takes on a power of its own, as the reception of the *Standard Edition* has.

Translation, then, like the transferential embarrassments of analytic history, redoubles the analytic project itself. Much as analysis produces its originals—the unconscious and its brother variations—as the belated effects of its narration of them, so translation produces the original behind it as the price of its own success. Of course, weak translations—literal ones that believe in punctilious correspondence rather than imaginative equivalence—are victim, like vulgar analysis, to the notion that there really is an original—a fathering text, like a genuine primal scene—to which the belated translator or disciple must remain strictly faithful. This is the tradition of Bettelheim (1983) and Ornston (1982, 1992). By contrast, strong translation, like Strachey's, is the kind that reimagines and reinvents, in the awesome shift from the signifying fields of one language and its history into another's.

We should remember, too, that all texts—Freud's originals included—are profoundly unstable to begin with—semiotically porous, deconstructible. Even an empirical attempt to maintain the fixed, fathering status of Freud's German is therefore doomed to failure. Bettelheim's outbursts are a combination of nostalgia and resistance. That strong translation is agonistic is already clear to that ironist, Wordsworth, in his revised preface to *Lyrical Ballads* in 1802. "A translator," says the poet, "endeavors … to surpass his original, in order to make some amends for the general inferiority to which he feels he must submit" (1802, 257). That translation is transferential is also clear. The translator, says a Joycean Wordsworth in the same passage, actually "deems himself justified when he substitutes excellences of another kind for those which are unattainable by him" (257). A genuinely effective poetics of translation presupposes that language, even that of an original or primary text, functions, like the unconscious, as a set of mutable relations, not as a lode of presence. The origin is a function of its own derivation.

Three examples will do. Strachey grants Freud's *Seele* (making it "mind" instead of "soul") and *Trieb* ("instinct" rather than "drive") more leeway in our English fields of reference than one would think justified. But this is because German already allows for such latitude in these constructions. An exact English translation, occupying a different system, cannot find Freud's spectral meanings in the same term, as Freud and German usage can. *Seele* is an even more complex affair than Bettelheim insists. Strachey chooses to translate *Seele* as "mind" in order to de-idealize it. Even the growing use of the term as a medical one in German, particularly as an adjective, had the same effect. Similarly, Strachey must split the term *Trieb* into a semantic doubleness in English that retains, as *Trieb* does in German, the flavor of a natural event while also coloring it, from above, as it were, with a less anthropomorphic notionality. Such a middle ground might find a suitable period analogue in Hardy's *The Dynasts* (1904–8), in which "The Immortals"—Hardy's version of the powers that be—are suspended in their portraiture between personification and mocking caricature. "Soul," an implicitly Christian notion in German and in English, implies a split between body and soul, while "mind," as we have seen, leads to the possibility of a continuity with the body rather than an eternal contest with it.

In our *Bloomsbury/Freud* (1985), Walter Kendrick made a particularly fine defense of Strachey's notorious "cathexis" for Freud's *Besetzung*. It is worth recalling here as a good third instance of the translation's process. This is, says Kendrick, "a decision whose strategic brilliance continues to elude the comprehension of Strachey's more vociferous critics" (1985, 319). Strachey's appendix to Freud's "The Neuro-Psychoses of Defence" (1894) was Kendrick's evidence:

> The German word is one in ordinary use, and, among many other senses, might have some such meaning as "occupation" or "filling". Freud, who disliked unnecessary technical terms, was unhappy when in 1922 the present editor, in the supposed interests of clarity, introduced the invented word "cathexis" (from the Greek κατέχειν, catechein, to occupy) as a translation. He may perhaps have become reconciled to it in the end, since it is to be found in his original manuscript of his *Encyclopedia Britannica* article. (3:63n)
> *Besetzung* is, after all, a polyvalent term to which no English word exactly corresponds. James's options included a range of partially adequate translations—"occupation," "investment," or "filling"—none of which would precisely represent the nuances of psychoanalytic usage. He might also have translated *Besetzung* differently according to each of the many contexts in which Freud uses this crucial formulation. Such hairsplitting, however, would have amounted to an act of interpretation (reductive at that), not translation.

Confronted with a case where no English word would suit Freud's German exactly, Strachey chose to invent one stripped of all reverberations except its equivalence to Besetzung. He went to a classical language here, as English traditionally does, as well as in his translation of Fehlleistung as "parapraxis," Schaulust as "scopophilia," and Anlehnung as "anaclisis." In such instances, Freud had followed the proper German practice of yoking together two common words to produce a new one. Freud, in short, wrote proper German, and Strachey wrote proper English. Critics of the Greek derivation of Strachey's terms fail to observe that many now-familiar English neologisms have been formed exactly the same way. (Meisel and Kendrick 1985, 319–20)

My concerns in the present volume also require us to have a look at the panoply of terms in German that Strachey largely reduces to a single one in English: "representation," and sometimes the parliamentary "representative." In German, "representation" has two principal thrusts: *Darstellung*, as in "depiction," and *Vorstellung*, as in "imagination" or "idea." The first inclines more toward the visual than does the second, but falls short of *Bild*, which means "picture." Freud favors *Darstellung* until the metapsychology phase, when he begins to prefer *Vorstellung*, which Strachey renders "idea" when it is not part of a compound word (14:201n). Strachey has actually sharpened the focus of Freud's own idea of representation here. Freud himself obviously wishes to render "conditions of representability" more problematic than they are. "Representability"—*Darstellbarkeit* in the German—now becomes less reliant on visual factors but, with the play of "idea" in the English, more rather than less so there. We are in deep and not particularly healthy waters here. Do these different German inflections of what in English are fewer things tell us anything about representation itself? It tells us first that there is no ideal notion of representation variously copied by all languages in their different ways. Freud's two words constitute what representation is in two very different ways, and what in English is unrepresentable. Does representation, then, have a mechanism? This is the question that the "mythical" Freud left us in the dark about. Do the German distinctions help us to see such a mechanism, or is it as obscure in German as it seems to be in English? "Depicting" (*Darstellen*) and "imagining" (*Vorstellen*) are divided in German as single words, while in English no "translation" can go any further than either "idea" or "representation," or sometimes "image." Strachey's English actually gives us a better sense of the mechanism of representation than the German does. "Idea" in particular returns us to the origin of the mechanism in the link between "idea" and "sensation" worked out in Bergsonian fashion in the *Project*.

Bloomsbury's sometime fellow traveler from Cambridge, Wittgenstein, reflects on these very distinctions in the *Philosophical Investigations* (1953), which are a familiar topic of discussion in his native German-language context. Wittgenstein has the same anxieties as Freud, but takes them out in a different way. "The image of pain"—the "*Vorstellung*," in Wittgenstein's German—"is not," he says, "a picture" (1953, ¶300, 101). "A *Vorstellung* can represent," writes A. Donagan of Wittgenstein's reading of the term, but only "indirectly"; a *Vorstellung* is a kind of "imaginative representation," but not a visual one (1966, 331). *Darstellung*, of course, is much closer to the sense of "depiction," but, even here, the decidedly visualizing tendencies of the English word "representation" (I will discuss these in Chapter 10) still do not predominate in the semantic inventory of this German alternative.

A moveable feast

Given Strachey's Paterian "scholarship" as a reader of Freud, can we also find in Strachey an analogue or even a model for the mechanism of reading as a whole? Behind Strachey's essay on the transference lies another, earlier essay, like a more primal theoretical scene behind a screen. "Some Unconscious Factors in Reading" was published in 1930. If Strachey's translation consumes the letter or wafer of Freud's text, the metaphor of ingestion also turns out to be the way Strachey tropes the act of reading itself. Strachey is particularly concerned here with what he calls "obstacles to reading" (1930, 323), and with finding the "unconscious factors" at work in them (324). What are they? Reading, says Strachey, is actually an act of resistance. The reader wishes to ingest the text, but has problems in doing so.

Why? Why does the reader resist? Because, as a mode of "ingestion," says Strachey, reading "is actually a method of taking someone else's thoughts inside oneself. It is a way of eating another person's words" (326). The neurotic case instances to which Strachey alludes function, as they do in Freud himself, as hyperbolic instances of normative processes or "trends" (324). When reading as a smooth, sublimated activity experiences an interruption, says Strachey, it is because "each word is then felt as an enemy that is being bitten up, and, further, for that very reason is an enemy that may in its turn become threatening and dangerous to the reader" (327). Reading is "coprophagic" (329)—a form of ingesting excrement. Reading, says Strachey, has an "oral-sadistic basis" (330). He locates its origin, not in the first oral stage, which is fringed with joy and "pre-ambivalent" (326), but in the second— the "oral-sadistic" phase—when ambivalence rears its head. The child, as it were, bites back, to protest any withdrawal of the breast, and any incursions against infantile narcissism, which now begins to encounter frustration of its pleasure thanks to authorities other than itself. We have seen this byplay and its implications in Chapter 2.

The link to transference and to the question of authority is an associative step away. In the child's mind, the father not only interrupts the narcissistic bond with the mother in the first oral stage. By doing so, the father initiates the anxieties that will lead to the Oedipus complex later on. Oedipus's shadow is already here, as we have also seen in Chapter 2, at the beginning. The father's influence already makes the child anxious because it is he, presumably, who takes the mother away, at the outset, in the interruption of the otherwise blissful dyad of madonna and child.

Reading as resistance is therefore a form of ambivalence that recapitulates in its structure not only the structure of the Oedipus complex, both also the structure of both translation and discipleship in Strachey's later essay. It prefigures Strachey's theory of translation because it shares with it the same theory of reference. Both are based, as we have seen, on anxieties about the elusiveness of presence and immediacy. The emphasis on the "second oral phase" (327) and its ambivalence shows us that Strachey's emphasis on reading as a form of orality is not, to use Derrida's term, logocentric. Unlike Kristeva or Irigaray, Strachey does not assume the mother to be simply there, given, unattended, unmediated in her presence. The mother is never bound to directness or immediacy. Far from it. That is the precise disappointment that defines not only the second oral phase, but also the first. There, to be sure, is a mythology to preserve. The first oral stage is pure pleasure—direct, presumably, and unmediated. Only in the second does ambivalence appear and, with it, the disruption of the ideality of that now-fugitive garden state, the "pre-ambivalent" joy of oneness with the mother. But symbolization was also there, from the start. Is this structure familiar? Of course it is. It is not only the sad destiny of narcissism in its own presumably primary state, seeking identifications as its transient cure. It is also deferred action. These primacies are actually effects of their later violation by the father in his numerous symbolizations.

But it is not only primary narcissism and the purity of the first oral stage that are rendered secondary by the interruption of the child's nourishment and the feeling that the child is being made to ingest something unpleasant rather than something good. Here resistance also prefigures the structure of discipleship to authority at large. Authority, as we have seen in *The Ego and the Id*, is not based on a "first" or unitary father, but on the father as a function of what are actually a series of moments which belatedly and retroactively constitute him, chiefly by his effects. This may be a key mechanism of the family romance, but it is hardly unique to the family. It is true, as *Group Psychology* tells us, of all group bonds, the family included. Hence the father's authority is all the more frightening, since it is, like that of Foucault's Panopticon, everywhere and nowhere at once. Worse yet, it is not based on the father's personality, or even his person, but on his mere role. The child's rage is even hotter than it might be, because it may have an aim, but it does not have, at least where the father is concerned, a calculable object.

Translation, reference, transference, discipleship—all share a common structure in Strachey. As translator, Strachey's discipleship to Freud occupies a sphere apart from the two seemingly most influential ones historically, Jung's on the Right, Lacan's on the Left. Strachey does not, like the child—or like Jung or Lacan—take on the father directly. He does so indirectly. The real power of the translation turns on an irony so strategic that it loses in glamor or fame what it gains in influence: anonymity. While the terms Jungian or Lacanian are commonly used, the designation Stracheyesque never is, even though English Freud *is* Strachey, and the *Standard Edition* the most encyclopedic of our editions of Freud, including that of the "original" German. Strachey's anonymity is, ironically, the very sign of his influence. It is more pervasive than that of any of the other disciples, because no choice is required of the reader except that of simply—simply—reading Freud in English. One is even inclined to submit that Strachey, alone of all the disciples, resolved his relation to the psychoanalytic origin, to the Freud to whom we can never return, in a successful way. Whether or not a real act of parricide is behind the subsequent totem by which Freud assures us of the crime's prior reality in *Totem and Taboo*—as though to prefigure his own ambiguity as to the question of the reality of such primal scenes in the Wolf Man—Oedipus is, of course, always a question of how murderously the father is to be handled by the disciple. In Strachey's case, the answer to the question, "Does the father, Freud, retain priority?" is a surprising one. It need not be asked. As with the father in *The Ego and the Id*—or in the first oral stage—the father is not really "first" at all. In the case of the translation, the father, Freud, is now one in a series that Strachey, too, can recast or split—German and English, original and translation. The *Standard Edition*, in other words, is a totem. It is also a totem—a signifier—that is, as it turns out, actually more rather than less capacious than the father whose death it signifies. That is because the *Standard Edition* is his tomb, and must contain him even as it exalts him. In a decidedly Protestant Christianization of totemism, Strachey as translator consumes Freud's spirit—his text—rather than his body—the biographical body of Masson, for example, or, in the same tradition, that of Freud's physician, Max Schur (1972). For Strachey, Freud is not rude clay but a play of signs, or molecules, the real structure, as Pater and Freud have alike shown, of mortality itself, and of a heightened, quickened sense of it. Strachey's discipleship consumes Freud's original text entirely. It replaces the original to which it refers. Its English referents are not those of the text translated, which has been brought instead into the thickets of the history of English usage and a history of the English past that Freud himself does not occupy, despite his identification with Shakespeare and his love for Milton.

The ambivalence toward Bloomsbury to which I alluded at the start of this chapter is, of course, a rather more vulgar or pedestrian instance of Strachey's own ambivalence toward Freud himself. In addition to Strachey's own class anxieties (they ran the other way), there are interpretative ones. The *Standard Edition* presents difficulties not only of a pedantic kind, but of an epistemological kind. To engage the question of translating Freud is a question of psychoanalytic process. As a question of psychoanalytic process, translating Freud, to use Freud's own metaphorical language of defense, appears in the light that it should: as a project that is overstimulating, and fraught with the dangers of disorder and decay, an enterprise perhaps too close to the death instinct to cause the psychoanalytic community anything but the anxiety it has shown on the subject. Strachey's own affiliation with Melanie Klein, to whom "Some Unconscious Factors in Reading" alludes in its last pages, is another instance of these anxieties. The Strachey alliance with Klein was itself an attempt to achieve a kind of constancy in the history of psychoanalysis. Klein's sponsorship by the Stracheys in England did not come without blood. Strachey's second analyst (the first had been Freud himself, from 1920 to 1922) was a fellow member of the British Society, James Glover, with whom he began sessions in 1925, and which continued until Glover's untimely death the following year. Strachey's wife Alix had also survived the death of her second analyst, Karl Abraham, the year before. Klein, whose analyst had also been Abraham, arrived in England less than two years later. The Stracheys, and Klein, who had encountered considerable resistance to her ideas at the Berlin Psychoanalytic Society, were, inevitably, a primal horde. Is Klein's discipleship a heretical one, or an elaboration of Freud? To say that Klein's discipleship resolves this kind of problem satisfies no one, as it should not—we are all in the depressive position. Indeed, the object-relations school to which Klein gives rise in Britain is a reflexive locus for these problems. Bion and Fairbairn map the mind's sense of its objects, not—as no proper analyst would—the objects themselves. In the same way, the history of British analysis—or French, or American—is likewise a play of the impressions Freud makes rather than of an actual Freud, corpus intact, whether textual, or biographical, or both. There is, alas, no Freud.

6
Freud and Foucault

Typhoon

If we fail to regard the history of psychoanalysis as a history of writing, we are often guilty of the same sin in regard to the history of criticism. We may read Derrida from the point of view of the history of philosophy, but we do not read Barthes, for example, from the point of view of the history of French aestheticism. With Foucault—he has haunted these pages—we do not even read from the point of view of the history of history. That we should read Foucault in relation to Freud is, presumably, inconceivable, as Stephen Greenblatt's embarrassed response to just such a query from Suzanne Gearhart attests (1997; see also Gearhart 1995). It is surprising that so fine a reader as Greenblatt can find a writer as elegant as Foucault lacking in the customary dynamics of influence. It is even more surprising when the writer in question is a virtual magician in the balancing of the influences that determine him.

Foucault is a typhoon of influences. What is surprising, however, is not his lack of generosity in acknowledging them—no good writer does that—but the extraordinary petulance involved in their repression. Neutralizing his principal influences, Marx and Freud, is central to this petulant success. Marx and Freud are the usual influences. Lacan's efficient genius, as Althusser tells us, manages to find the one in the other. For Foucault, Marx, however—quite surprisingly—is less of a problem than is Freud. The reason is a simple one: the *Annales* school. Rather than confront Marx directly, Foucault can take on his French surrogates, and easily overwhelm them. Invented by Lucien Fèbvre and Marc Bloch in 1929, *Annales* historiography accords a place to the downtrodden, particularly the rural poor, rather than concentrating on the bogus hegemony of diplomatic or intellectual elites. But Foucault does not even take *Annales* historiography on. He takes it further. This is how he leaves its downtrodden in the dust. He does his own version of peasant history by focusing on those marginalized by society in other ways—the sick, the insane, and the transgressive. Despite it all, Foucault is also, like his mentor, Georges Canguilhem, an intellectual historian, a historian of power. He is nonetheless also a champion of the oppressed. He gets to have it both ways at once.

Foucault's republic

With Freud, however, the situation is different. There is for Foucault no buffer to contain him, no school to punish. The opposition is too organized, even in its disagreements. Foucault has told us as much in "What is an Author?" With Freud, the blow must be taken head on. Foucault's anxiety about Freud grows more intense as his career proceeds. So do his defenses against him. In *The Order of Things* (1966), where Freud is beside the point, he is praised; in *Discipline and Punish* (1975), where Freud is important, he is ignored; and in *The History of Sexuality*, especially the first volume (1976), where Freud is decisive, he is brutally attacked. Freud is "pivotal" in *The Order of Things* (1966, 361) for introducing the problematic of subjectivity in terms that will later on become Foucault's own in *Discipline and Punish*. In *The History of Sexuality*, however, "the good genius of Freud" (1976, 159), as Foucault puts it there, is relegated to that of a minor function within a longer history of the constitution of the subject. This is surprising. Freud's "pivotal" position in *The Order of Things*—like his decisive role in "What is an Author?"—is suddenly reduced. What was once invented by psychoanalysis is now begun in late antiquity. In this longer history, psychoanalysis comes to perform a belated and conservative rather than an original and revolutionary role. Freud simply codifies what the ancients had to say. In *The History of Sexuality*, psychoanalysis is taken, not as the rupture it marks in *The Order of Things*, but as a simple necessity—"Freud, or someone else," as Foucault puts it (56). Freud is part of a curve whose shape is determined long before him.

One would also expect Freud to be the primary exponent of what Foucault calls the "repressive hypothesis" (10 passim), which he condemns: the notion that "repression" is the way that culture keeps nature down, particularly libido, and particularly libido in its sexual mode. But Foucault will not blame Freud for the "repressive hypothesis." Everyone else does. Lawrence does. Even Derrida does, at least when it comes to early Freud. But for Foucault, Freud was never that naïve; he never believed in a struggle between "Law," to use Lawrence's terms, and "Love." Freud is not, according to Foucault, a purveyor of the "repressive hypothesis." He has something else to sell. It is a newer technology of the self. Here "Law" and "desire" (81), to use Foucault's own terms, are not at odds, as they are in the "repressive hypothesis." They are interdependent and reciprocal.

The "repressive hypothesis" is a fiction. "Law" and "desire" are chiasmatic, as they are for Pater and Fechner. They produce each other. No wonder Freud is not attacked. He codifies the link between law and desire. Rather than opposing law and desire, says Foucault, Freud articulates their interdependence:

> The idea of a rebellious energy that must be throttled has appeared to [psychoanalysis as] inadequate for deciphering the manner in which power and desire are joined to one another; [it] consider[s] them to be linked in a more complex and primary way than through the interplay of a primitive, natural, and living energy welling up from below, and a higher order seeking to stand in its way; thus one should not think that desire is repressed, for the simple reason that the law is what constitutes both desire and the lack on which it is predicated. (81)

Foucault's Freud is already the Freud of the late phase, after the difference between ego and libido has been deconstructed, and the reciprocity between repression and drive well established.

Freud's insistence on the dependence of desire on the law rather than despite it should make him a welcome antecedent, consistent with the generous portrait that Foucault affords him in *The Order of Things*. And yet in *The History of Sexuality* he is not. Why? Because Foucault has a borrowing to conceal. Freud can be neither antecedent nor foe. He must, like the Marxists, be neutralized. The origin of Foucault's own leap forward, beyond the logocentric "repressive hypothesis," is Freud himself. He uses late-model Freud to overturn early model Freud, and claims the work to be his own. No labor is necessary. This work has already been done by Freud himself. The metapsychological phase has already deracinated "instinct" in psychoanalysis, and expanded the notion of "defense," blowing Freud's own "repressive hypothesis" to smithereens. Eros and civilization are no longer at war, as Freud and Foucault agree. What Derrida shows to be the self-critical arc of Freud's own career Foucault claims to be his own critical arc in relation to Freud.

No wonder the great matrix of Foucault's technology of self bears a striking resemblance to the one he describes as Freud's own. It is Freud's own. The description of the Foucauldian subject in *Discipline and Punish* is actually more Freudian than any of Foucault's descriptions of the subject in *The History of Sexuality*, even without a discussion of sexuality. The return of the Freudian repressed has not yet arrived in this earlier text, either in the selection of subject matter or in the preoccupation with the practice of psychoanalysis. Its real subject, of course, is subject-formation itself, and its strains are very familiar. Instead of a medieval site of physical torture, modern punishment "is not the actual sensation of pain," says Foucault, "but the idea of pain. Punishment has to make use not of the body, but of representation" (1975, 94). Foucault's subsequent description of "the mind" as "a play of representations and signs" (101) is irrevocably Freudian, and in a very literary way. Even Foucault's terms—"sensation" and "idea"—intercept those of Freud's early, Bergsonian years. The coincidence of vocabulary well demonstrates Foucault's skill as a historian of the nineteenth century. It shows how faithful he is to the terms of his subject, including those of Freud and his circle. Even more, to plot the subject in this way is to have followed Freud deep into the later phase of his career. What else would a Foucauldian "politics of the body" (103) be but a psychoanalysis keyed on representation (see also Mitchell 1974)?

Why does Freud rate such generosity? The strategy on Foucault's part is considerable. It is not confined to masking early Freud with late. It involves a wholesale use of Freud to go on, in *The History of Sexuality*, to depose him. Now, Foucault is obliged to deny psychoanalysis precisely what Freud means by "defense," the term that Foucault prefers to its more revealing synonym, "repression":

> But let us assume in turn that a somewhat careful scrutiny will show that power in modern societies has not in fact governed sexuality through law and sovereignty; let us suppose that historical analysis has revealed the presence of a veritable "technology" of sex, one that is much more complex and above all much more positive than the mere effect of a "defense" could be; this being the case, does this example—which can only be considered a privileged one, since power seemed in this instance, more than anywhere else, to function as prohibition—not compel one to discover principles for analyzing power which do not derive from the system of right and the form of law? Hence it is a question of forming a different grid of historical decipherment by starting from a different theory of power. (1976, 90–91)

Indeed, by Foucault's own testimony in *The Order of Things*, it is just this strategic and productive rhetoric—call it Freudian "defense" or "primal repression," or call it Foucault's "positivity" (1966, 372)—that marks the psychoanalytic rupture, and that makes Freud the decisive figure that he is. In *The History of Sexuality*, this insight is denied to Freud. Here, once again, is the voice of that earlier Foucault, in *The Order of Things*:

> The subject and the object are bound together in a reciprocal questioning of one another; but whereas, before, this questioning took place within positive knowledge itself, and by the progressive unveiling of the unconscious by consciousness, here it takes place on the outer limits of object and subject; it designates the erosion to which both are subjected, the dispersion that creates a hiatus between them, wrenching them loose from a calm, rooted, and definitive positivity. (1966, 372)
>   There before us [is] an existence at once real and impossible, thought that we cannot think, an object for out knowledge that always eludes it. (375)
>   Bearing in mind that Freud more than anyone else brought the knowledge of man closer to its philological and linguistic model, and that he was also the first to undertake the radical erasure of the division between

positive and negative (between the normal and the pathological, the comprehensible and the incommunicable, the significant and the nonsignificant), it is easy to see how he prefigures the transition from an analysis in terms of functions, conflicts, and significations to an analysis in terms of norms, rules, and systems: thus all this knowledge within which Western culture had given itself in one century a certain image of man, pivots on the work of Freud, though without

—and here we see the caveat out of which *The History of Sexuality* will emerge—

leaving its fundamental arrangement. (361)

The chiasmatic structure of Freud's "defense" or "repression"—long ago recognized by Burke and Trilling as a productive rhetorical structure—is, alas, precisely the structure of Foucault's own "positivity," the mechanism or technology by which the Freudian subject—and the Freudian narrator—produces a world by defending against it. Foucault could not be clearer. Nor is it possible to be more sophisticatedly Freudian. Even the way in which "subject" and "object" question each other "on the outer limits" and constitute themselves by virtue of their mutual elusiveness is an elaboration of *Beyond the Pleasure Principle*. Freud's later name for this technology of reciprocity is, of course, "negation," a name that Foucault exactly, symptomatically, reverses by renaming it, with considerable stress, "positivity," and keeping the notion. It is most familiar to us as Freud's "primal repression."

Whether "positivity" is simply a redaction of "negation," however, is not, finally, the point. Not, at any rate, for Foucault. This is how he swerves once again from the problem at hand. The question instead for Foucault is whether or not this Freudian invention is metaphorically appropriate in its ability to represent what it claims to represent. In *The History of Sexuality*, Freud's representation of the link between law and desire—his great achievement in *The Order of Things* — is, says Foucault, trapped in an outmoded system of representation. It is useless. It cannot represent what it presumes to represent. In Freud, says Foucault, "power" is imagined as centralized, "juridical" (1976, 89), paternal, the function of a "king" (91), or of "sovereignty" (193). This representation, says Foucault, is inadequate. Whether or not "power"—*pouvoir*, that endlessly problematic word in Foucault—is itself an appropriate metaphor for the Freudian representation of the relation between law and desire has sparked considerable debate (see, especially, Butler 1997, 83–96). The debate is easily solved, and Foucault's own question easily answered, by translating *pouvoir* as "enablement"—that which puts subjects in place through a constitutive relation to objects. Foucault, however, insists on accenting the political connotations of *pouvoir* despite the new perils it creates for him. The reason is once again plain enough: not to be in the position of repeating Freud. Hence the broadside that begins in Foucault's preface to Deleuze and Guattari's *Anti-Oedipus* (1972), and that culminates in

The History of Sexuality. The "juridical" representation—Freud's Holy Family in particular—"is increasingly incapable of encoding power, of serving as its system of representation" (1976, 89). "To surround desire with all the trappings of the old order of power"—that is, to represent it monarchically, to give it a center or "head-quarters" (95) signified by the royal figure of "the Prince" (97)—is no longer possible given the movement of history. Foucault's *Annales* spirit is still alive and well. One is surprised to find that Foucault remains such a republican.

What does Foucault's rejection of the metaphor of central, paternal authority repress? What does the dissolution of the category of the father in favor of a plural notion of power mean, from both an empirical perspective and a poetical one? What in Freud does Foucault's rejection of Freud repeat? And what is it about the Freudian characterization of power as paternal that so irks Foucault? What do the paternal and the "sovereign" share? The attribute of authority as such. Is authority—*pouvoir*—identical with the paternal and the sovereign, or are they just among its manifestations as *pouvoir*?

Foucault's primal scene

The notion of the univocal sovereign father is indeed a problem in Freud. We noted it when reading *The Ego and the Id*. Even there, the father is undead. It is not that the father is not to some extent a regulatory figure. He is. It is because he is not the only one, and certainly not, as Freud says he is, the first such regulatory figure. Here Foucault's objections return in a more reasonable light. They are not, however, the objections of either Kleinian feminism—the mother comes first—or of a classical emphasis on narcissism—one's self-figuration comes first. No, Foucault's objections are bathed in the light of a different kind of irony, the irony that surrounds the disciple's ire. It is amusing that this reaction takes the form of a rejection of the Oedipus complex as a notion. Foucault's difficulties with Freud's notion of the father, like his objections to the "repressive hypothesis," are both already difficulties in Freud himself. Foucault's misrepresentations of Freud are ineffective because his palinodes of Freud are Freud's own. As in the other redactions we have noted, Foucault is, as a rule, preempted by his great precursor. For is it not Freud, prior to Foucault, who insists not only on productive defense but also on the necessity of overdetermination? What is Foucault's plural notion of determination? It is Freud's overdetermination.

"Sovereignty," as we saw in *The Ego and the Id*, is never in place anyway. Never in place, that is, for more than a moment, or moments, in time. It is never more "first" or fixed than, say, Freud's own father, Jakob Freud, and his shifting status in constellations of later influence in which, because Breuer, or Fliess, or Brücke is decisive, he, Jakob, must be their prototype. This kind of interpretative deferred action may well be designed to protect, in a manner that Foucault quite properly objects to, the causal status of the real or biographical father. The father, however, is never more stable than any other Freudian subject is, in all its peril. But deferred action has no place in Foucault's scheme of things. Foucault is blind to the fact that the father, the sovereign, the "first," is also produced by deferred action. The sovereign is constituted belatedly from among a series of later evidences, particularly, in the case of the artist, professional ones. These concerns will be central to my chapter on biography and literary history.

Cogent as Foucault's objections to the father may be, of course, they have already been announced by Freud himself in a stentorian voice. Once again. It is not a shift that we have to be punctilious about finding in a reading of *The Ego and the Id*. It is obvious in *Group Psychology*, Freud's revisionary dialogue with his own first assessment of "sovereignty" in *Totem and Taboo*, at the flood tide of psychoanalysis. *Group Psychology* revises *Totem and Taboo* by shifting authority from the figure of the father to that of a super-ego held in common. This notion of authority is that of a political unconscious that is based, as Freud suggests, on collective social identifications that exceed those available in the family unit, but which the family may represent. This is Freud's rather Foucauldian notion of "the libidinal constitution of groups," as he calls it in *Group Psychology* (18:116). Here "a number of individuals ... have put one and the same object in the place of their ego ideal and have consequently identified themselves with one another in their ego" (18:116). If the super-ego is the "precipitate" or "residue" of the Oedipus complex, as Freud puts it in *The Ego and the Id*, it is because the father himself passes on, not his personal authority, but the collective authority with which he is, deservedly or not, invested by culture *as* a father. Like the mother, but in another way, he is real because he is symbolic.

What is the real role of "sovereignty" in Freud's thought if its endless destabilization is so self-evident? For Foucault, what is "sovereign" represents all the vices mixed into one: canonicity, the paradigmatic, the totalizing, the "juridical." As opposed to these are overdetermination, the dialogical, the subversive carnivalesque. The Oedipus complex, as even Deleuze and Guattari know, has a very specific role. The Oedipus complex recontains libidinal economy when it exceeds the bounds of regulative subjectivity. Not for moral reasons, of course, but for reasons of survival. There is no subjectivity where there is no law of the father. However metaphysically absurd, it is the only organizing discourse that culture knows. To think otherwise is to reconstitute the fantasy that Trilling identifies in "Art and Neurosis." This fantasy is reasonable enough as a popular estimation of Freud and as a radical critique of him. They are after all one and the same thing. But it is not reasonable in the sober world of Foucault's historiography. It is too poetical.

Foucault's critique of "sovereignty"—and here is the final irony—is in the service of a far less complex historiography than Freud's own. Foucault's myth—it is surprising—is that of univocal determination in history. It is his presumable target, but it is also his goal. No wonder New Historicism, despite Foucault's deconstructive propensities, can find in him the basis for a new positivism. Although we think of Foucault as the great historian of overdetermination, the truth, alas, is different. While from *Madness and Civilization* forward, Foucault gives expression to more rather than to fewer discursive systems, he regularly totalizes them. He does so by reducing their mechanisms to duplicable homologies—madness and reason, disease and health, desire and the law. These constructions are not, protests Foucault, uniform sets of oppositions, but endless differences. In the case of sexuality, "there is no single, all-encompassing strategy, valid for all of society and uniformly bearing on all the manifestations of sex" (1976, 103). Sexuality "appears rather," he writes, "as an especially dense transfer point for relations of power: between men and women, young people and old people, parents and offspring, teachers and students" (103). This is how the subject is created in all its acknowledged differences. But the mechanisms are always oppositions—"men and women," "young" and "old"—while the results are always differences. Sexuality's mechanisms are homologous even if their effects are not. Homology of mechanism yields heterogeneity of population. This is familiar, too. It is Freud's reading of desire and the law as chiasmatic.

But Foucault cannot account for the subject's experience, even if he can give it a grammar. The temporal dynamic is missing in Foucault's technology. The passage from opposition to difference is the passage from structure to time. Foucault may plot this difference, but he does not narrate it. He remains a structuralist, despite the appearance of doing deconstructive historiography. It is Foucault's final repression of Freud. Freud is actually more plural than Foucault is, and, of course, actively focused on time itself as a condition. Foucault's refusal to think chiasmatically—to temporalize his oppositions—is an old habit: "The original error of psychoanalysis," writes Foucault in 1954, is the same evolutionary one made by Darwin and Spencer: that "the truth of man" is "in his development as a living being" (1954, 30). So easy, and so hard: The axis of *langue* and *parole* in structuralism already solves this problem. Apprehended in time, the play between what is given or implicit ("truth," the body, *langue*) and what occurs ("development," biological process, *parole*) produces the subject. It is a chiasmatic play, which alone historicizes. Neither side of the opposition can come into being without the other. No wonder Sartre criticized Foucault for failing to supply a role for what Sartre called "temporality" (1966, 94). The method is "non-dialectical" (90). The self-produced is "passive" (92). Like the regulative histories of which they are products, Foucault's subjects, unlike Freud's, are automatons. They are not Freudian subjects because they are not even Darwinian subjects, who, in their difference from Lamarck's, respond to the environment. Foucault's subjects are influenced; they are determined. They are made. They do not fight back.

Let us remember that Foucault's texts, splendidly written as they are, are literary in their own right. They are part of a long tradition of French bohemian writing that, as I noted at the start of this chapter, also threads its way through the work of Barthes. Foucault's notion of "sovereignty" is a very broken kind of sovereignty, one constantly under siege, as it should be. Foucault insists on a "sovereign" or univocal structure of historical determination no matter the context and no matter the period. This is his own hidden transcendental ahistoricism, his own secret life. Foucault's texts are thereby instances of the histories they claim only to write. They are broken against themselves as witness to the ruination that they represent. They recall the Romantic hero in ruins—Goethe's Werther, Keats's Hyperion, Byron's Cain. To personify Foucault any more than this would lead us well beyond even the phenomenologist's assumption of a "world of Michel Foucault," and dangerously close to psychobiography. With Foucault, let us simply remember that his republic bans the very thing that it is means to celebrate. This is paradoxical, of course, but whether it is constitutive, as are Freud's paradoxes, it is hard to tell. Perhaps it is only symptomatic.

Foucault's ambivalence, including his ambivalence about Freud, reaches back to his boyhood, when, as he told me in Paris in 1978, he heard the boots of the Nazi patrols outside his bedroom window in occupied Poitiers. This nocturnal legacy is Foucault's primal scene. It is the space between the family and the public sphere that is the very focus of his writing. So he eventually said (see Miller 1993, 38–39, 369). No wonder the Foucauldian subject cannot respond. It is split between two worlds of authority, neither of which can protect it against the other. Without the domicile of time, it remains homeless.

7

Representation and resistance in Mansfield, James, and Hardy

Psychoanalysis and literature

As I noted in Chapter 2, Freud likes his reader to argue with him. It is his way of drawing the reader into the world of psychoanalytic process in a flash, and of producing not only a quickly working belief in psychoanalysis as a discourse, but doing so by requiring the reader to resist it. The reader is the site that dramatizes Freud's truth, brings it into being. Does this strategy sharpen our sense of Freud as a writer? One test is to see whether this strategy is at work in other writers. This test, as I noted in my preface, brings us, finally, to the return of this book's repressed: the question of Freud *and* literature.

Does fashioning resistance, as Freud does in his writing, appear as a strategy in literary texts at large? Freud makes narrative propositions to which we dubiously respond. This turns out to be a constructive rather than inhibitory dimension of his prose. "Narrative" may seem an unlikely word to append to the dry "proposition," but the incommensurability between the two terms nicely sets out an aspect of both Freudian narrative and narrative as a whole that as a rule—and, as we shall see, by definition—it is designed to repress: the reader's constitutive resistance to narrative propositions. A text, in other words, narrates the reader's resistance to it. In Mansfield, James, and Hardy—our test cases, as it were—the precise mechanism of readerly resistance is what I will call "counterrepresentation." Good fiction narrates its own counterrepresentations in order to be absorbing. Good fiction is absorbing because it narrates its own resistance. By representing the reader's own defenses, the narrative clears its path by virtue of clearing the reader's.

The status of the reader

Let us also clear our critical path before we begin. It would be a mistake to over-look what affinities this notion of reading may have with other ones. Although Judith Fetterley's reader is a "resisting reader" (1978), her model for reading is not psychoanalytic. René Girard's influential model of reading is (1961). It is, however, triangular rather than dyadic in structure. It is based on desire rather than survival. Our own trio of psychoanalytic categories for reading—defense, overdetermination, and constancy—is based, not on desire, but on survival. Constitutive resistance—the kind the reader exerts in relation to Freud's texts, or to reading fiction—is also the trope in *Beyond the Pleasure Principle* for primal repression, and for the emergence of life itself—a turning away that produces even as it deflects. Will these terms survive an assessment of Girard? And will they survive a subsequent assessment of Barthes' notion of the reader before we turn at last to fiction?

What is Girard's third term that mediates between text and reader? It is evident in the case of Don Quixote; here "the disciple pursues objects which are deter-mined for him, or at least seem to be determined for him." This is "the *mediator* of desire" (1961, 2), provided by custom, or by psychology, as though they were different. What Girard calls "external" and "internal" mediation may be suf-ficiently distinct to describe the world of realist fiction, but not to represent as exactly as Freud himself does the spots at which desire blushes the most, in any kind of literature. For Freud, it is the play between ideal ego and ego-ideal that is the source of desire, not simply secondary "mediations" of it. It is not the tri-umph of what Girard calls the victorious "Other" (33) that makes "mediation" real in either psychoanalysis or in fiction. It is because the difference between self and other is so hard to find. "Mediation" as a notion is problematic for the same reason. It presumes a transaction between two existents—a subject and a world, whether in novels or in psychoanalysis—that are never in place except for other subjects. In our model, such a third term cannot precede the encounter between text and reader, since this encounter actually produces the third term, the "mediator," in its very activity—as a buffer or "skin" between self and world, whether for a character in a novel, or for a text and a reader.

Nor is the genteel critical tradition any more useful in providing a good model for our purposes. Christopher Ricks is too generous in giving T.S. Eliot sole propri-etorship of "provocation" as a way of stirring a reader into life (1988). All writers do this, some better than others, although not all do it as Eliot does—by appeal-ing to the worst in us, so as, presumably, to call out the best. Freud does just the reverse. Borges, to describe this phenomenon at its most procedurally exact, uses the term "counter-book" (1941, 29): Every writing requires its opposite or reverse so as to be what it is. Unlike Eliot's, it is not a moral but a formal activity, in the widest sense. A "counter-book" emerges from the reader's resistance to the story. Narrative not only uses the reader's resistance; it can also—as in Philip Roth's *The Counterlife* (1986) or Martin Amis's *Time's Arrow* (1991)—actually narrate it. Indeed, in postmodern fiction, this mechanism is often thematized. The anti-novel of Robbe-Grillet is, of course, its prototype.

Donald Barthelme's "Paraguay" (1970) is a superb American example. It relies almost wholly on yanking the reader out of normative defense at the very moment it is employed. As a place to map, the tale's referent appears to be no undiscovered country at all, but—naturally, or so it seems—Paraguay, the Paraguay designated by the story's title. We all know Paraguay; or do we? Barthelme has a surprise for us in the second entry, "Where Paraguay Is":

> Thus I found myself in a strange country. This Paraguay is not the Paraguay that exists on our maps. It is not to be found on the continent, South America; it is not a political subdivision of that continent, with a population of 2,161,000 and a capital city named Asunción. This Paraguay exists elsewhere. (1970, 130)

Like Borges's Uqbar and Tlön, or like Barthelme's own "Robert Kennedy Saved from Drowning" in *Unspeakable Practices, Unnatural Acts* (1968), Paraguay, in Barthelme's signification at least, has no referent as such—no preexisting set of codes to which it points as a signifier, and certainly no discoverable, self-sufficient, extrasemiotic reality to which its name merely appeals the way the ordinary map or diary appeals to places and events we all know, at least from our reading. As static representation or ethnographic project, the story has no proper objects to work on, even though we think it does. Barthelme delights in disrupting our neat little assumptions. This breakdown and resistance on the part of the reader is the story's real landscape.

Of course, to say "on the part of the reader" is to presume too much. We come at last to this question—even at the outset. Such a figuration presupposes a reader—a phenomenological reader—already in place apart from a text to which he or she comes as though it were an object. Let us assume no such reader and no such text, but something else. Let us assume the dynamic relationship between what we call text and reader to be one between representation and resistance. Roland Barthes' well-known words in "The Death of the Author" (1968) make it clear that texts produce readers anyway, not the other way around:

> The reader is the space on which all the quotations that make up a writing are inscribed without any of them being lost; a text's unity lies not in its origin but in its destination. Yet this destination cannot any longer be personal: the reader is without history, biography, psychology; he is simply that *someone* who holds together in a single field all the traces by which the written text is constituted. (1968, 148)

Barthes' proposition should alert us not so much to the interpretative demands a text may make, but to the demands that it actually makes at the more basic level of technique.

The fluid nature of Barthes' idea of readership, however, raises a difficulty. Prose fiction, as a form, tends to require the direct exercise of a reader's judgment in relation to the thematic problems that novels and stories as a rule present. What kind of woman is Emma? Is Stephen Dedalus fatuous or cunning? Where is the line in Dickens between melodrama and real Romanticism? How do we reconcile this normative demand of novel reading—the exercise of judgment—with its fluid, polysemous condition—its dialogical carnivalesque as a form? Here, in fact, is where the reader's defenses are ignited. The reader's responses take the form of moral responses that organize for defensive purposes these polysemous fields of otherwise overstimulating reference. They turn quantity into quality. Even in the presumably stable world of the Victorian novel, polysemy—overdetermination, or overstimulation—can, in the blink of an allusion or association, take us anywhere if we are not careful, and, alas, everywhere if we are. Nor, as I have suggested, is this for reasons of a phenomenological kind. Reading as defense or resistance is defensive in a key familiar to us: ordering stimulation as a means of simple protection. This is how the text hatches its reading subject, in a birth like the one in *Beyond the Pleasure Principle*. This is also where questions of interpretation in fiction and questions of technique in the writing of fiction finally become one and the same. The writer produces a world by requiring the reader to exercise judgments about it. The reader does not resist because of disagreement, but because of having to process and balance too much. The reader is overdetermined, overstimulated. The reader seeks constancy, and gets it in defense.

Mansfield and resistance

But we are getting ahead of ourselves. Let us see how resistance works in three fiction writers, beginning with Katherine Mansfield. After Mansfield I will turn to her great precursor, Henry James, and then to Thomas Hardy. Is a mechanism like goading the reader into argument at work in these writers' prose? The rather rough terms I have used to describe Freud's own boxing with his reader may not be the kind of metaphors we should use. We might be surprised to find a kind of psychical defense at work in fiction that is, in its own ironic action, as searching as Freud's own, but which acts less aggressively, that is to say, more naturally, or seemingly so.

If we have seen the theoretical side of Mansfield in Cather's essay on Mansfield's materialism, let us turn now to another, more familiar dimension of Mansfield's work, her technique. Though we customarily honor Mansfield for her craft, we too often let its mechanisms elude or escape us. How do her texts provoke, assuage, upset, pacify? How are they made as narrative structures? Two stories will do better than one, especially if they are very different.

First published in 1919, Mansfield's ironic and unforgiving tale, "Je ne parle pas français," may strike us as galling and even cruel, certainly in comparison with the almost superhuman pathos of a tale like "Bliss," first published in 1918. If we read the stories in relation to each other, however—they were begun less than two weeks apart, in late January and early February, 1918, respectively—we may be surprised by the kind of implicit dialogue they entertain. Made explicit, this dialogue shows us something precise about the way Mansfield's stories function, particularly their use of the moral or the judgmental, not to produce allegory, but, rather, to stabilize the reader. This Mansfield does by appealing to the most familiar kind of constancy there is, that of faithfulness, not simply in love, whether children's or lovers', but epistemologically—using the reader's moral reaction to set the reader in place, and thereby regulating the reader's economy by virtue of the narrative's technique.

While "Bliss" is, of course, well known, "Je ne parle pas français" presents special and unexpected complexities. The story itself is simple enough: Raoul Duquette, a twenty-six-year-old French writer of astonishing pretension and surprising success, befriends a foreigner visiting Paris, an English writer named Dick Harmon. Raoul secures rooms in Paris for Dick on his next visit, which he makes in the company of a beautiful and delicate woman—his fiancée, as it turns out—who, at least by her own testimony, does not speak French; as she puts it, in the only line delivered in French in the story, "Je ne parle pas français" (1919, 162). The *frisson* of the tale comes when Dick deserts her, leaving behind a letter that she shares with Raoul, and with us, giving as the reason for Dick's desertion his mother's unwillingness to accept the match. The beautiful and delicate woman—she is given no proper name, only the generic nickname Mouse—is left desolate and alone in Paris, with only the dubious friendship of Raoul. But though Raoul promises to return on the morning after Dick's flight, he fails to do so. He announces his decision to us with a perverse pride in collapsing all decency of feeling—the kind of pride that marks his attitude toward everything in his derisive monologue, which is at one and the same time out of keeping with our customary sense of Mansfield, and yet somehow peculiarly representative of certain impulses in her fiction.

The story's real tradition is not so much that of the reflexive or self-conscious *récit*—a story about writing a story, though it has sure elements of that—as it is of the bad or unpublished tale. The story is a sort of burlesque on both bad fiction and the pop mythology of the rakish aesthete which is among the very real raw materials of the Parisian demimonde that the story represents. It particularly mocks the unsavory Raoul, against whose ugly nature we rather automatically react.

And so Mansfield locates her reader. Look at the overstimulation involved in the silent work the reader is called on to perform at the level of judgment again and again. Hope dies hard where decency is concerned in Mansfield's world. In what direction does the story's viciousness cut? Where is its irony to be located? Or, to put it another way, where does its irony locate its reader? One way of answering such a question is to say that what the reader knows in "Je ne parle pas français" are all the things that the story itself derides: an innate sense of compassion, a sense of human worth, a sense of human sharing. The reader, in other words, counterrepresents rather than records the text. All the things that the pretentious narrator maintains *are* the case are *not* the case, cannot possibly be the case; all our decency says no. This is the pivot of Mansfield's technique. Invoke what is absent to stabilize what is present, both for the tale and for the reader. Judgment here functions in an executive rather than properly moral way. Perhaps there is not much difference between the two anyway.

Central to the web of reactions the story breeds is Raoul's notion that people are, as he puts it, like portmanteaux:

> I don't believe in the human soul. I never have. I believe that people are like portmanteaux—packed with certain things, started going, thrown about, tossed away, dumped down, lost and found, half emptied suddenly, or squeezed fatter than ever, until finally the Ultimate Porter swings them on to the Ultimate Train and away they rattle. (159)

Echoing E.M. Forster's indictment of modern life as the "civilization of luggage" in *Howards End* (1910), Raoul's metaphor has a presumable authority to it, although it collapses, like his other stances, once the reader knows that this haphazard registry of human souls produces no sorrow at all in Raoul himself.

Only such a cynical belief would allow for the callousness of Raoul's behavior, and yet it is a belief that is sustained throughout by a consistent if distasteful vision of how experience is structured. Raoul elaborates, through the logic of his figures of speech, an entire theory of character that is extraordinarily cogent from an abstract point of view. "People are like portmanteaux," like pieces of luggage, devoid of innate or indwelling essence, because life, or at least our perception of it, is structured in or by a temporal chain whose functioning requires the contrast and comparison of moments of time one with another. "You never do recover the same thing that you lose," says Raoul. "It is always a new thing. The moment it leaves you it's changed" (163). While this may sound, on the one hand, like a lively theory of the constant freshness of experience—and to some degree it is—it is, on the other hand, an unnecessarily desperate theory of the evanescent flux of all things beneath our feet. Only by the play of relations, between one moment and another, can what we call an essence or a quality be established as such. The theory of signification implicit here is one familiar to us under the names of *différance* and deferred action. Mansfield's own vocabulary, of course, derives from the Romantic tradition of Pater and his privileged moments (the suspicion with which "habit" is viewed is, as one may remember, very Paterian indeed), and, before Pater, of Wordsworth and his "spots of time" in Book 12 of *The Prelude*. We have seen that this Romantic tradition and Freud's own often overlap historically to the point of identity. Raoul, however, wishes to complain about time's flight, and to place the blame elsewhere: He explains, disparagingly though logically enough, that his bitterness against life is, as he puts it, the "direct result of the American cinema acting upon a weak mind" (161). Life is a function of the ideologies into which we are inscribed rather than of any indwelling sanctity it may be said to muster from beyond the bounds of culture. "Everything," says Raoul, "is arranged for you—waiting for you" (161). Hence one's character is, from the ground up, a "pose," as Raoul puts it, which becomes a "habit." Even poor Dick does not just "look ... the part," whatever part that may be; "he was the part" (173).

How far we are from the delectable universe of Bertha in "Bliss," where the human soul, as Mansfield puts it there, has a "shower of little sparks coming from it" (1918, 145). Once again there is an allusion to Wordsworth, this time to the language of the lazy Intimations ode, an allusion, quite unlike that to a late book of *The Prelude*, to the time of childhood. In Bertha's "bosom," says Mansfield, there was "a bright piece of ... sun" (145). The difference between "Bliss" and "Je ne parle pas français" could not be more exact. Bertha's tropes—"shower of sparks," "bosom"—insist on a human essence, recalling Wordsworth's wishful image of the human spirit before the realities of time and experience overtake it. All the same, however, "Bliss," too, is structured by irony. If "Je ne parle pas français" makes the reader feel, by the reactive thinking irony induces as a rhetorical device, that just the reverse of what is asserted is true—that there is a human soul, not just people as portmanteaux—then "Bliss" also requires an equal and opposite reaction. Despite its manifest claims, there is no Wordworthian or Platonic "shower of sparks" in "Bliss" any more than there is in Raoul's tale. Indeed, poor Bertha is disabused of precisely the comforting notion that there is when her recognition of Harry's secret arrangement with Miss Fulton—an almost High Victorian moment of knowledge, perhaps the reason Virginia Woolf felt obligated to criticize the story—punctures Bertha's bliss at tale's end.

If in "Je ne parle pas français" the reader is all love and goodness, in "Bliss" the reader is all worldly guile and suspicion. The very first line of the story makes us prophets of caution and doom. Bertha's pace is so breathless—like her running in the scenes she imagines—that we want to slow it down for fear she will fall and hurt herself, as she indeed does at the story's close. Here at the start, however, the story finds the suspicion first and foremost in *us*, by the force of its negation:

> Although Bertha Young was thirty she still had moments like this when she wanted to run instead of walk, to take dancing steps on and off the pavement, to bowl a hoop, to throw something up in the air and catch it again, or to stand still and laugh at—nothing—at nothing, simply. (145)

By contrast, the opening lines of "Je ne parle pas français" fill us with the kind of gray rain we later associate with Jean-Luc Godard's early *hommages* to film noir. The story finds the sunshine in us by the force of its negation: "I do not know why I have such a fancy for this little café. It's dirty and sad, sad. It's not as if it had anything to distinguish it from a hundred others—it hasn't" (1919, 159).

In "Bliss," what the reader knows is that people are indeed like portmanteaux. Despite Bertha's radiant optimism, they do not wear their essences on their sleeves; their sleeves are packed away in portmanteaux like those that Raoul describes. Portmanteaux are the rhetorical tokens by means of which narrative allows us to know people and by which it allows Bertha to know people through a painful education. Both in the reader and in Bertha's mind, Mansfield provokes a constitutive resistance to the story's idealizations so as to generate the dramatic tension that makes the story absorbing. Indeed, "absorbing" is the appropriate word: Mansfield's narrative economy solidifies her drama by widening the reader's sympathies to include, like the Freudian psyche, more and more, including the perspective of a Raoul to stabilize one's sense of a character like Bertha. Bertha's fatal blindness or innocence of vision is in reading her surroundings, her husband included, too straightforwardly, reading them as though there were no necessity for reading. Not, that is, until the secret is made so palpable as to shock Bertha into such a realization, which makes her, belatedly, a reader, too. In this sense the story is an allegory of reading, disabusing the reader as well as Bertha of the notion that human personality—whether in life or in a story—is stable and secure. Mansfield's technique shows us how such stability or constancy is put in place by resistance in an overdetermined and overstimulating world. What the reader knows in "Je ne parle pas français" is that people are not at all like portmanteaux. What the reader knows in "Bliss" is that they are. These are the tugs of the heart against which the stories work. It is as though Bertha's wishes are fulfilled by the negation of Raoul's view of the world, and Raoul's wishes fulfilled by the negation of Bertha's. This kind of dialogical play between the two stories is potentially endless.

How can both of these tales' clais be simultaneously true? How can the reaction prompted by one tale be the opposite of that prompted by the other?

How can one writer exhibit so discordant, so internally divergent a sense of what we ordinarily call character? How can Bertha's naïve Platonism give way to a darker sense of the instability of essences, while Raoul's nasty sense of the instability of essences gives way to a brighter, perhaps even genuinely Platonic, sense—in the reader, at least—of the real stability of essences? Well, if each reaction produces its opposite in the play of the reader's mind, it is likely the case that each category needs the other to be what it is. Both can be true at the same time because the claim of each—so Mansfield's epistemology goes— needs the other for what coherence each may be said to have. One is reminded of Harold Bloom's paradox that if God created the world out of nothing, then he must have created the void at the same time that he created the world. In a curious but implacable logic, Raoul's irony requires the truth of the heart he rejects, much as Bertha's belief in essence requires its violation by a duplicitous world. Each notion of the world depends for its sense on the other.

But this structure is true of more than the epistemological. Or, to put it another way, it shows how and where the epistemological and the psychological mix: in the structure of readership that texts like Mansfield's produce. In both cases, what is dramatized is not so much discordance as the calculated orchestration of irony in a very precise way: the enactment of the reverse of what is narrated in what the reader knows rather than in what character shows or tells. Each story represents a falling away from the state that it names, this by means of the reader's supervening moral judgment. For Mansfield, the importance of the reader's activity cannot be overestimated. It is the reader that is the active instrument or channel supplementing what is lacking in the two tales we have read. Bertha, Raoul, Harry, Mouse, even the Norman Knights, who humorously enough invade Bertha's home in "Bliss"—these are all figures in the reader's mind, the result of the work the reader does to produce verisimilitude, which exists nowhere else but in the reader's apprehension. By this unconscious work on the reader's part, the story takes on what mimetic attributes it may have, the result, not of an unmediated mimesis, but of Mansfield's technique, which orchestrates the play of her reader's moral assumptions. The reader produces the fiction's world by resisting or counter-representing it, achieving stability—and its own coherence as a "reading," educable subject—through judgment. This judgment, however, does not operate as a moral act but as a protection against the field of stimuli—in Raoul's case, the noxious stimuli—that Mansfield's texts disseminate. In the case of "Bliss," the reader's dark side is summoned, not to countermand the story, but, yes, to protect it, too, by taking the worst that can happen to its world on its own shoulders.

Semiosis and judgment in Henry James

Mansfield's relation to James is a complex and uncharted one, although a comparison of their technique yields not only some interesting similarities between them, but also a shared similarity with Freud himself. The modern novel enjoys a particularly faithful display of heightened indeterminacy and provides a clear and delimited role for the exercise of moral judgment in trying to control or stabilize it. In the case of Proust, say, or James himself, the textual environment is actively, sometimes aggressively overstimulating. This kind of behavior has earned for modern literature Eliot's designation of *"difficult"* (1921, 289). "Difficulty" is an ambivalent term, and well measures the split response or resistance that overstimulation requires of the subject that it puts in place. The traditional judgmental point of view we bring to the reading of novels as a form therefore produces a curious tension in the reading of modern novels, as with modern poems, between an admiration for irony and a predisposition to moralize. What is really at work, especially in James, is that the judgments provoked are defenses against textual polysemy. This is, as it is in Mansfield, an epistemological and psychological rather than a moral project.

James's *The Golden Bowl* (1904) is an exemplary instance of a "modern" novel that actually thematizes its own structure as a text. By calling attention to the play of semiosis and judgment, it also calls attention to this double operation on the part of James's reader. In *The Golden Bowl*, readers and characters alike are immersed in a semiotic play that provides whatever ground there is for both. James's parlously conscious characters live altogether in a world of signs made figurally identical with the structure of a text by virtue of James's metaphors: "They might have been figures rehearsing some play," thinks Maggie of the book's other protagonists, "of which she herself was the author; they might even, for the happy appearance they continued to present, have been such figures as would, by the strong note of character in each, fill any author with the certitude of success" (1904, 454). As in Freud, narration and story, *récit* and *histoire*, are adequated by virtue of the identity of activity in the narrative and the language of narration. James is reflexive by virtue of his realism; he represents a world in the process of representing itself.

James elucidates the semiotics of the four lovers by making the world of the novel a world of "differences," as he habitually calls the structure of human relations and feeling, and by habitually likening it to the play of tropes in a text: "Our marriage," says Mr. Verver to Charlotte of Amerigo, "puts him for you, you see— or puts you for him—into a new relation, whereas it leaves his relation to me unchanged" (168). "Unchanged" or not, this world is endlessly shifting because, no matter the stability of given moments, it functions by means of relationships alone. In fact, the worlds of narrative and narration, story and reader, are not just similar in *The Golden Bowl*—they are concordantly the same. Both inhere in James's language, the precondition and the medium for the semiosis within which reader and characters mix. Famous for the quality of its absorption—the word is once again exact—Jamesian narration identifies reader and character by requiring each to share a common field of usage, inflection, and association. In what precise accents do the Ververs, do Charlotte and the Prince, speak or think? How do we as readers of James understand these accents, these inflections of sound and sense in a discourse alien to both its characters and its readers? Here James's incitement to counterrepresentation emerges very clearly. Located not in similar but in the same semiotic field of a certain period English made up of a peculiar Anglo-American literary idiolect, the reader and James's characters are all outsiders to the laws of this language, although with an achieved fluency that renders it negotiable, in different measure, to each of them in turn. Three Americans and an Italian in England, none native to the landscape in which the action occurs, all speak an English not natural to them, just as James's English is not native to the histories of prior British usage. Even Fawns, the rented English nature of the Ververs' country house, is less pastoral refreshment than another site of dialogical contention, the novel's sociality drowning the visionary connotations its landscape also exudes. But how is this fluency acquired? As a function of resisting this semiotic field. Such negations mark out the novel's tropes of character; they also fashion the novel's reader. As in Mansfield, in James, characters and readers alike situate and steady themselves by means of counterrepresentation.

That this is a defensive process from the start is made perfectly clear at the beginning of the tale. The novel's opening describes the play of semiosis and judgment very exactly:

> The Prince had always liked his London, when it had come to him; he was one of the modern Romans who find by the Thames a more convincing image of the truth of the ancient state than any they have left by the Tiber. Brought up on the legend of the City to which the world paid tribute, he recognised in the present London much more than in contemporary Rome the real dimensions of such a case. (1)

"These," concludes James, were the "grounds of his predilection, after all sufficiently vague" (1). Like Amerigo, the reader is in possession of the "truth" of an "ancient state"—the "grounds" of James's world—only by virtue of a double displacement constituted by a double difference. Prior Rome helps Amerigo grasp present London because, for Amerigo, it is present London that helps him grasp prior Rome. Presence, either way, is the function of a ghostly comparison—here, very specifically, a counterrepresentation—that makes the present sensible and significant only to the extent that it is calculated by the past. Of course, the past has the same structure, too. The past is the past to the extent that it is calculated by the future. It is hard not to see that deferred action is the novel's ruling trope. Here it is in the service of two counterrepresentations rather than, as it is in Mansfield, only one. Like Amerigo, James's reader is inscribed into the field of Jamesian narration by counterrepresenting it with the mythologies he or she brings to it from elsewhere—if not by means of the absent rule of Rome, then, like the American Adam, the absent rule of American City. The novel, that is, gives us interior models for the kinds of relation that any institutionalized or coherent reading—English or American, male or female—may bring to the text so as to provoke it into the illusion of life. Indeed, the novel as a whole is structured as a counterrepresentation of itself. It flips over in the middle; the second half tells us exactly what the first half makes us want to know: What is Maggie thinking while all this is going on behind her back?

As a trope, Amerigo's "sufficiently vague" world is structured like a defense. It puts in play a world that is at once "vague" enough to require further elaboration, and yet "sufficient" enough to allow such elaboration to proceed. This is true for James's reader as well as for James's characters. As we saw with Mansfield, counterrepresentation in fiction often takes the form of judgment. Hence the destabilizing paradox that attends the judgment required to stabilize semiosis by means of counterrepresentation. Because it is the text's incompleteness that requires the supplement of judgment, the basis on which the work of judgment is propped or supplemented is itself unstable, thereby throwing the ground of judgment into jeopardy by virtue of its exercise. Incomplete by virtue of the need for judgment, the text is also complete by virtue of what ground for judgment it affords. In the play between them emerges the "sufficiently vague" world of Jamesian representation, for character and reader alike. Semiosis and judgment are recast in relation to each other. The destabilization of judgment by polysemy is necessary for the stabilization of polysemy by judgment. There is neither text nor reader—nor story nor character—only the one by means of its relation to the other. This is also the classic structure of Freudian defense, which, as a shield against overdetermination, produces an internal world to defend itself against what it has managed to render external.

Amerigo is not alone, of course, in representing the reader's resistance allegorically. In describing the double bind in which Maggie finds—or fails to find—herself, Colonel Assingham also describes the paradox that structures any presumable call to judgment in the novel: "I don't quite see," he says of Maggie's relation to Amerigo, "why that very care for him which has carried her to such other lengths … hasn't also, by the same stroke, made her notice a little more what has been going on" (275). And yet it is just this recognition that eventually dawns on Maggie, and causes her to suspend the very judgment it otherwise enables. Judgment cannot be made as such until, in Maggie's case, enough time will have passed for her to see the structure of events that requires it. When she does at last judge, she chooses not to judge because judgment risks the very field of her judgment. This, rather than privilege, emotional or otherwise, is what she does not wish to lose. She is a genuine aesthete. Once Amerigo and Charlotte's activities become clear to her late in the novel, her assessment of her relation to things doubles the Prince's own at the novel's start. The "freshness" of her new emotion of "disgust" means that she must "give them up"—give up what friends and family she has. And that is, says James, "not to be thought of" (455–56).

If Maggie's moral dilemma is bound up with a wish that is, of course, ambivalent—maintaining her field of life may mean losing love, or at least attention—her dilemma is not unlike that of the reader. The reader, too, is perpetually ambivalent. The reader also risks dismissing the novel's action on moral grounds as a function of his or her ability to see the situation it produces. To realize what Amerigo and Charlotte are up to requires a traditionally immoral counterrepresentation. But to summon such a counterrepresentation is to threaten the delicate situation that it allows us to represent. When Maggie can judge, then, she chooses not to do so, in a sublime—and sublimely sublimated—aesthetic—and ascetic—detachment. Maggie sums up James's heroines by taking the final condition of her life—one that she even assesses as a kind of psychical progress—as a perpetual play of tensions. She acknowledges the paradoxes of judgment that constitute, and frustrate, all things, and responds to them without appeal to a stabilizing term outside the paradoxes to alleviate or resolve their play. And while Maggie, like Mrs. Assingham, may earn a privileged purview in the novel, each of James's other principal characters—Adam and the Prince certainly, and Charlotte perhaps—still articulates the paradox of judgment in his or her own way: Adam, by measuring the newness of American City by means of the antiquity of the museum pieces he brings there; Charlotte, by measuring the immediacy of love by means of institutions; and, of course, Amerigo, by measuring London by historical Rome.

Judgment, so the lesson goes, is always insufficient because its ground is all too "vaguely" sufficient, thanks to the porousness or abundance of the semiosis that prompts it. The reader's relation to the novel is the pedagogical counterpart to Maggie's relation to the world she comes to understand. James describes what he declares by leaving semiosis suspended in a productive undecidability. The reader's uneasy luxury in James's prose is like that of the characters in their restless repose. We all come to know too much. Thinks are okay in *The Golden Bowl* only because everyone agrees that things are not okay; peace depends on an acknowledged acceptance of a state of warfare. So, too, is the text of the novel in place only to the extent that the reader perpetually, dynamically absorbs its endless discriminations and judges them. In this exact way the text is pedagogical, and in a surprisingly American fashion. James educates his reader with the end in view of having his reader educate him. Both technically and thematically, James is afraid of the very stimulation that his impressionism seems to cultivate. In this sense, he is an overwhelmingly Freudian novelist, and one leaning toward the bourgeois, not bohemian, side of Freud's influence. James is nonetheless an aesthete, as Freud himself certainly is, although both, as we have already seen in Freud's case, are different from Pater. If Pater shuns "habit," then James, like Freud, wishes to discover what play there is in habit itself. For Pater, we fail when we form habits. For James, our failure—it happens to everybody—is to lose faith in them.

The conversation

What are the material components of the structure of reading as a mechanism of defense? The materiality of the signifier, and of reading as an institution. Much as texts find their coherences in restructuring the literary past, so readers find themselves in deciphering them by recourse to the codes of one or another interpretative community. If writing comes into being as a defense against its overdeterminations as a medium, reading comes into being as a defense against this defense. If the poet is a member of a presumable school or a reaction to one, so the reader is a member of—let us not draw a distinction where there is none—one interpretative market or another.

Hardy's *Jude the Obscure* (1895) is a fine site in which to explore some of these questions. Not only does *Jude* engage questions of the materiality of signification and the history of institutions by means of its language. Hardy's shifting, and shifty, language, in all the novels as in the poems, excavates and puts into various relationships histories of usage—philologies (Taylor 1993)—to create a sense of time from the sounds of the dead. *Jude* does this thematically, too. Indeed, *Jude*, more than any of Hardy's novels, directly engages questions of its own intellectual origins by ridiculing the central site of British intellectual authority. This is accomplished by Hardy's materialism in two ways. First, Hardy apprehends Oxford as superstructure rather than as the cause of anything. It dehegemonizes Oxonian discourse by making it simply one discourse among many. The novel irritates Hardy's reader, almost neurologically, into resisting anything and everything because of the absurdity any presumption to authority has. Arabella's earthiness, Phillotson's loving-kindness, Christminster's aura—all are not so much deceptive as they are, well, self-regardingly "sovereign." The novel's contentiousness, manifest in the ebullient relationship between Sue and Jude, finds its counterpart in the reader's own Barthelmean confusion of response that may begin in the moral sphere but that eventually becomes epistemological. What one is arguing about, especially in the novel's second half, becomes, to use Hardy's phrase, the "second silent conversation" (1895, 161) that one is actually having with oneself as one reads. The novel becomes an assault on assumption itself.

At first sight, *Jude* seems to be a perfect instance of a novel that takes its power from what I have called counterrepresentation. The reader, especially a British reader, simply reacts with sympathy to the young Jude's scholarly ambitions, knowing, as he or she does, the realities of the class system and of nineteenth-century admission to Oxbridge. No one in Jude's position can aspire to what Jude aspires to; the foreboding that hangs over the schoolmaster Phillotson's dreams in the novel's early pages prefigures how such aspirations will be vexed even for those in a position more fortunate than our hero's. The negative judgment of Phillotson is as peremptory as the one that the master of Biblioll College later renders on Jude himself (94).

This is also the story of Hardy's own life. The young Hardy, like Jude, was socially barred from entrance to Oxbridge because of his compromised class position. As a member of the vanishing yeoman class in Dorchester (his father was a builder), Hardy stood no chance of admission had he tried to gain it. Apprenticed to an architect in Dorchester, Hardy's aesthetic aims nonetheless found easy expression. But Hardy did not enter, as he later would the tradition of letters, the tradition of architecture as a committed professional. Architecture provided, apparently, no opportunity to move beyond the family romance; literature did.

How are we to regard the rather simple cause-and-effect mechanism for reader-response that our assumption of Jude's social ignorance and its authentication by Hardy's biography provide? As the cause of our initial sympathy for Jude, it is clear, but suspiciously so. This sense of why we sympathize with Jude is not sufficient because it is not, to use James's phrase, "sufficiently vague." Though one may assume that Hardy was no more than a melodramatist, even as late as *Tess*, something else is afoot in *Jude*, something different than in his earlier works. Jude's serious—that is, fanciful—adventure with the administration of Christminster is complete by the end of Part Second, and is no longer the primary vehicle for the story's emotional dredging of its reader at any point beyond it. Secondarily revised, the entire narrative does seem to have been the effect of Jude's initial failure. Then again, secondary revision is a defense (it is also a useful way to describe the dangers of paraphrase), designed in this case to keep the novel itself simple—typically Hardyesque, we might say—rather than real and complex.

If the early Christminster sequence makes melodrama and pathos suspect, it also makes suspect a familiar epistemological assumption. This comes in a minor incident at the end of the novel's first half. Jude, having grown enamored of a new hymn written by a local composer, decides to track him down and visit him, assuming, by strict cause-and-effect logic, that such a man as the author of this deeply moving music must be a worthy from whom one can gain wisdom. The composer, of course, turns out to be not only cavalier, but entirely commercial in his views about his work. Defeated again, Jude feels that something has at last snapped, this as the book itself takes its turn into its second half, beginning with Part Fourth. What has happened is a break in the chain of cause and effect—here, an exemplary break in the cause-and-effect relation between author and text. The reader feels it in his or her exasperation with Jude's durable idealism—it is our last moment of self-righteousness before the Flood. Like *The Golden Bowl*, *Jude* flips over in the middle and revises itself.

What happens in the novel's second half? The oppositions that organize the first half are no longer fixed, even though it takes Jude and the reader some time to see it. How does the novel change? Like the reader, Jude's all-too-familiar world has suddenly become overstimulating. It is nostalgic, full of echoes. Its languages, like those layered in Hardy's prose, reflect a somber overdetermination. Here, the simpler world of the novel's first half has grown more complex. "Light" and "contrast" (102), for example, is not quite an opposition, although we might have thought it was, back in Part Second, as though it formed the pair "light/dark." Even a Hardyism such as "Nature's law" (244) is an oxymoron from the point of view of the dichotomy between mind and matter, ideal and material, that the trope is designed, presumably, to overcome. If nature stands against society viewed as the rule of law, how can nature itself be a law? But while this kind of semantic toxicity is often unnoticeable, it has its noxious effects. It leads not only to the irritable exchanges the reader now has with him- or herself. It also leads to the irritable exchanges, most representatively, between Sue and Jude in the novel's second phase. Here an endless semiosis replaces the rule of fixed codes, which appeared to reign in the novel's first half. As in Mansfield and James, judgment is required to stabilize things. This "silent second conversation" induces the movement to judgment between Sue and Jude, and between reader and text, simply to stabilize the semiotic field. It is a different kind of readerly relation to the text than that at work in the novel's first half, which makes us think that codes of fixed correspondence are stable. Back then, the reader sat in the easy chair of class and privilege, doting on poor Jude. Now, like Sue and Jude themselves, the reader must judge because the world is no longer stable. It never was. Even in the novel's early pages, we are in a destabilized world without realizing it. Every moment requires counterrepresentations, large and small, referential and formal. Much as Jude and Sue counterrepresent each other both intellectually and emotionally, so the reader counterrepresents them as the price of the slowly exhausting relation to be established with them over the course of the novel. Overstimulation, defense, constancy—the movement of psychical defense in its rudest form. Hardy's texts, like Freud's, exact a reflexive investment from the reader. The heightened degree of responsiveness that we experience is the novel's real surprise, its endless invention of the worst upon the worst.

Reading as a mechanism of defense

At the end of my chapter on Strachey, I suggested that transference was a reasonable model for the process of reading, since the two share so much, including a constitutive place for resistance. After our discussion of Mansfield, James, and Hardy, is such an assertion still reasonable? A transferential model for reading is well enough suited to a narratological point of view that simply wishes to identify *récit* and *histoire* as reciprocal and chiasmatic. We have been largely satisfied with this point of view so far, even in our reading of Freud. But with the presence of resistance or defense at the heart of the reading process, the need to supplement this perspective is obvious.

Representation *as* resistance is an inevitable formulation from both a psychoanalytic point of view and a literary one. Any screen, *imago*, transference, ideal (choose among Freud's terms for this kind of activity) is, by definition, a defensive reaction to the stimulation it encounters. Representation is the function of resistance, its fruit or yield, as it were. An object's reception is always an object-relation. A text is the mode of its reception. The reader's activity is that of the perpetual infant, struggling for simple constancy under the banner of judgment. Primary narcissism, the kind that has survival as its goal, is no more sinful than the rush to judgment with which we traditionally read prose fiction. With narcissism in mind, can we say that resistance has an even more specific literary form? What would it be? Let us turn to biography, an old topic, and to pornography, a less familiar one, to see if they can help us conclude our discussion, and, in the process, return us to Freud himself.

8
Biography and literary history

What is an author?

Foucault's primal scene presents all the elements we need to construct a model for biography and its relation to literary history. It may begin in psychobiography, but it will not end there. Any summary of the psychobiographical approach immediately encounters two related obstacles, whether the example is Erik Erikson on Luther (1958) or Leon Edel on Henry James (1953–72): that the work is an expression of the author's unconscious, and that the author's unconscious is to be viewed in relation only to the private family romance. Georges Poulet and the Geneva School at least managed to separate the "world" of the author from the author's personality. Not surprisingly, however, Foucault, like Barthes, rejects the notion that the text is a mimesis of the psychological subject who writes.

What is a text, and what is its relation to the various forces, including the "author," that produce it? What is an author, and what is its relation not only to the texts it produces, but to the histories that produce it? Recall Eliot's presciently Bloomian description of how poets become canonical in "Tradition and the Individual Talent." Eliot's description of tradition's porousness and overdetermination is surprising. It is, as we saw in Chapter 2, a Freudian moment. Like the Freudian subject, the poet reconstitutes the past by refiguring it later on. And like the Freudian primal scene—as I have noted, the Jacobean poets of "The Metaphysical Poets" are Eliot's version of such a primacy—the fullness of the early is also a function, as prehistory is in Milton, of belatedness from it. And as for the figure of the father, the later poet, says Eliot, situates the earlier, precursor poet. The later poet, says Bloom, echoing Eliot in Eliot's single moment of lucidity, makes the earlier poet strange and different. The later poet changes the very conditions that produced the earlier work by reconceiving them—inevitably. Such events—psychoanalysis is one of them—change the past because they change the future that looks back on it. The aesthetic of "impersonality" that Eliot shares with Pound and Wyndham Lewis is almost Foucauldian, in the best sense. The world is a world of language and historical structures that form both self and poet, each of whom, in different ways, addresses their prior determinations rather than a real object-world. Self and poet alike—and here is their single real likeness—respond to object-relations rather than to objects. The overstimulation that the self experiences, like the overdetermination that burdens the poet, is precisely this phantom array, in the mind, of past authorities, paternal or poetic, at once awesome in their enabling power and hateful because of it.

The structure of Eliot's temporality, of course, is deferred action. But Eliot is a stubborn man. Like Foucault, also a stubborn man, he will not, consciously at least, acknowledge deferred action to be the modality he describes. I have described this contradiction in Eliot at some length before (1987). With Eliot's later and unlikely *confrère* across the Channel, the situation is similar. There is, as we have seen, an internal conflict leading to a blockage or repression. Foucault has been helpful in describing Freud's authority by calling him the initiator of a discursive practice. In his assessment of psychoanalysis in *The History of Sexuality*, however, we have found him to be insufficiently psychoanalytic. As we noted, what is missing from Foucault's historiography is an understanding of deferred action as the modality of his own historiography. In being insufficiently analytic, Foucault is also insufficiently Foucauldian.

The question of temporality leads us back to the question raised by Foucault under the name of "sovereignty"—the presumption of control. It is also a preoccupation of Eliot's. Recall Eliot's projective remark in *The Waste Land*:

> … your heart would have responded
> Gaily, when invited, beating obedient
> To controlling hands (1922, 421–23)

In Eliot's case, sovereignty's difficulties are lamented and lionized; in Foucault's, they are mocked and humiliated. But, in both cases, the anxiety is overdone. Eliot and Foucault know that the "sovereign" is a sham, a figure of delight in the hands of the artist who controls where no one else can, who lies at will. Despite Eliot's altruistic concern for wisdom, and despite Foucault's altruistic concern for pleasure, the sovereign—whether author or subject, precursor or real father—has already met with an unlikely demise. No anxiety about the father is necessary. He has already been transformed into a retroactive construction based on later effects. "Sovereignty," too, is structured by deferred action.

Despite their common anxieties about authority and sovereignty, however, Eliot and Foucault have learned their repressed Freudian material well. So decisive is Freud to them both that they reconstitute his principal trope in their resistance to him. More than that—and despite their shared hesitation to be interested in the biographical subject—Eliot and Foucault have actually helped us to see a difficulty in Freud that, as Trilling has suggested, is puzzling. It is Freud's notion, in his psychoanalysis of art, that the work simply expresses the subject, or produces a mimesis of the subject's mental functioning. Even as sublimation, according to Freud, the work of art—*Hamlet* is always the best example—simply expresses the poet's unconscious wishes. Here the poet and the subject do not intermingle; they are the same thing. Hence, a slip of the tongue and Hamlet's stuttering speeches are little more than another equivalence between art and neurosis.

Freud is an uninteresting psychoanalyst of art because he treats the work as a mimesis, not of the world, but of the subject who produces it. Just as the unconscious must be somehow interpretable to consciousness in order for consciousness to put the unconscious into place, so the work must be a distortion of the subject who produced it in order that the psychoanalytic critic of art has a subject to put in place from its interpretation. This gives Freud his customary rhetorical advantage. A reader of tropes when he is inspecting his patients, Freud becomes a ghastly reader of themes when inspecting figures with whom he identifies—Leonardo, Michelangelo, Shakespeare (for a different view, see Kofman 1970). Does this thematic stance conceal something in Freud's own mirrors of himself?

What, for example, is the relation of *King Lear* to *Hamlet*? *Hamlet* expounds the son, *Lear* the father. Is this because the older Shakespeare of *Lear* is himself a father, not only of a family, but of a new tradition of writing? Shakespeare was already a father when he wrote *Hamlet*, the memorial to his recently deceased son, Hamnet. The autobiographical reading of both plays is therefore incoherent. Its terms do not match up according to the myth of art as an expression, as a mimesis of the psychical processes of its author. The plays do not stand as autobiographical expressions except as single entities. In *Hamlet*, Shakespeare identifies with the son; in *Lear*, with the father. Not even a dialectic between the plays is available; they merely cancel each other out in stance. Not even a phenomenological reduction in terms of Shakespeare's "world" is available here. "Shakespeare" has a different relation to different materials both private and public in the case of each play. The only sense one can make of the career is generic, not biographical.

Surely there is more to be said about the relation between subjectivity and art than this. One wonders if a more formal approach to an author's production yields patterns of a more genuinely psychoanalytic kind. Let us remember

Foucault's primal scene and the way it crosses public and private in a chilly double exclusion of the child from two orders of comfort ordinarily supplementary and therefore secure. Does this give us a model for personality in a dialectical rather than nonexistent relation to the public sphere even in the earliest years? Indeed, the public sphere, as it does in Freud, makes the private sphere. They are interdependent. How does such a relationship work?

"Or someone else"?

"Freud, or someone else," says an insouciant Foucault (1976, 56). But it was not "someone else"; it was Freud. Why not "someone else"? The "specificity" that New Historicism calls for is here, at its source, deemed unnecessary. Specificity, however, is all. Why not "someone else"? We have already seen why, in Freud's case. The influences are both wider than most for a writer, and more skillfully handled in the defensive structure—psychoanalysis—that Freud builds to process this overdetermination. For the first time, a conceptual apparatus has been constructed that is a genuine instance of what it represents. It does not represent Freud, the man; it is an apparatus, and one that Freud "himself" may, in accounts of himself, come to represent. This is because psychoanalysis is not, as we have seen throughout this study, a project that relies on representation in the mimetic sense. I will, as I have promised to do, return to the question of representation in the next chapter, on pornography. For the present, other questions are more pressing. Let us stay focused on the relation, or presumable relation, between personality and literary production. What do we mean by authorship, and, most of all, expressivity? Does the subject express him- or herself in his or her work, or is the structure of writing—a profession—different from the structure of personality as such?

Among the enabling mythologies of psychoanalytic history is that the death of Freud's father, Jakob Freud, in 1896, allowed Freud to write *The Interpretation of Dreams*. Notoriously, perhaps even self-regardingly ashamed of his father's fearful attitude toward Gentiles during his childhood, Freud exchanges the authority of his real father for what turns out to be the more tangible one of professional culture. His father's death, in other words, allows him to enter a tradition outside himself and that of his family, a tradition by means of which he can escape it. And in the beginning was the death of Jakob Freud. We have seen the series of Freud's paternal transferences over the course of these pages—Brücke, Helmholtz, Meynert, Fliess, and Breuer, to name only the principal ones in Freud's early professional circle. And each, as we have also seen, provided Freud not only with a scaffold for psychoanalysis, but also one with a Focauldian contrivance that executed each precursor in turn. Freud regularly slayed the bearer of each paternal gift—physiology, neuropsychoanalysis, and Anna O.'s "chimney sweeping." Freud's pretence that these people abandoned him is a screen memory that hides the fact that he abandoned them. After all, each ran out of things to give him. These admittedly minor influences on the early Freud have never been taken entirely seriously by any Freud scholar. That they simply reenact the happy death of Jakob Freud is hardly surprising.

Who, then, remains alive as real anxieties of influence for Freud? As we have seen, within his own nonimmediate professional tradition, Fechner and Bergson are the chief contributors. I have noted how Freud treats Fechner with eventual generosity after a long period of silence extending back to *The Interpretation of Dreams*; Freud owes Fechner too much to be entirely quiet about it. Bergson, by contrast, who does a great deal of preliminary work in describing problems that Freud himself will solve, merits no more attention in the bibliography to the *Standard Edition* than the single reference to his book on humor. Any number of poets, chief among them Shakespeare, are, as we all know, Freud's more over-arching precursors. But to formulate their role in Freud's imaginative makeup in terms as specific as those at work in Freud's relation to Breuer, say, or to Bergson, is more difficult because the influence is more diffuse in its transmissions. Freud encounters the poets—and the essayists and the novelists—through a screen that the professional poet does not: science. And Freud encounters science, as we know, including the tradition of philosophical psychology, through the screen of literature. What looks like a problem is actually a solution. Literature makes science a play of tropes, while science makes literature a play of atoms. Science and literature produce a richer version of each other by means of what presumably separates them. We have seen how Freud and Pater, for example, supplement and illuminate each other in precisely this way. Freud's various agons with the literary predecessors who join his scientific ones—Goethe, Milton, Shakespeare—produce an overdetermined number of such mutual or reciprocal sites within the corpus of his work.

Is the model for both influence and authorship that we have seen at work in Freud's texts useful for reading other texts? Freud's readerly mechanisms are, as we saw, at work in the novel. Are his mechanisms for structuring influence also at work in other writers? Freud's texts regard influence as both enabling and threatening. Overdetermination, in other words, is the biographical analogue to overstimulation. The text that is the response to such overstimulation—the defense against it—separates itself from the environment, as the protist does, in order to make itself new as a matter of sheer survival. Perhaps this puts less of a commodity premium on the notion of authorship and more a kind of inevitable necessity regarding life and signification. Is such a structure helpful in seeing how other writers emerge? Foucault's primal scene adumbrates the very kind of paradigm we need—the endless play between *Idealich* and *Ichideal*, between the

Imaginary and the Symbolic. It is an unremitting site of influences, felt in time. This ceaseless exchange rather than the bourgeois stasis of life under the super-ego "proper" is the life of writing, and all the arts. It is an exchange that keeps *Ichideal* and *Idealich* in constant motion, each one supplementing the other, and doing so in the dimension of history.

The professional

The temporality of the play between public and private in Foucault's primal scene locates Foucault's writing as a displacement of the double and originary lack that his primal scene dramatizes. It gains him some protection from its twin exclusions. As an author, he—"he"—compensates for rather than expresses the structure of his emergence as a person. We traditionally consider author and subject homologous; they have remained homologous even after a structural revision of our understanding of them, and a renovated sense of their means of emergence. Even political assessments of subjectivity and art presume such a homology, not because of their structuralism, but because of their mimetic assumptions about signification. Can a compensatory view of writing make a difference?

The writer, like any professional, has a double burden—structuring his or her personality, like the rest of us, and structuring texts. Rather than assume a cause-and-effect relation between personality and text, as in classical psychobiography—and, thus, an expressive or mimetic dimension to the work of art—let us ask the question in another way. What is the real relation of life to work, and work to life? What is the defensive dialectic between work and life that makes the work sublimation and compensation rather than expression and mimesis? Indeed, it is really only the first question that we are interested in, since we attend to the lives of artists, by and large, to try to account, alas, for their work. Where, first and foremost, is the career of any artist really made? Not in the life, but in the medium. Auden's description of this problem in "Psychology and Art To-day" is pertinent:

> A medium complicates and distorts the creative impulse behind it. It is, in fact, largely the medium, and thorough familiarity with the medium, with its unexpected results, that enables the artist to develop from elementary uncontrolled phantasy, to deliberate phantasy directed towards understanding. (1935, 337)

But how does the writer pass from the "medium" to the life, and back again? To represent these processes, of course, means to anthropomorphize. This is the young Foucault, alone at night. Is that not what an author's name is, a personification presumed to bestow magical powers? Such a verbal icon is more efficient in its evocative sweep than one of Pater's Wordsworthian churchyards.

Why representation and personification are linked will be at issue in Chapter 9. My argument here requires me to ask, more simply, what are the identifications made by the artist, and how does their choice function as a defense or a compensation for loss in the life? But this is to put the question too conventionally, and from the wrong end.

How does the artist enter tradition, and how does tradition enter the artist? Experience does not disregard tradition, as normative psychobiography presumes; even in nonartistic subjectivity, various traditions engender the subject to form it by reactive response. Lacan's Aimée, the pop fan of his dissertation (1932), remains the best example. How does the structure of the artist do the same, and—so as not to fall into the error of homologizing subject and artist—do more? The shift from the life to the medium gives the writer a kind of second subjectivity, no more, but no less, stable than the first. Every writer knows how the fashioning of a textual apparatus redoubles rather than expresses the psyche that produces it. This second subjectivity is, however, no longer a subjectivity in the normal sense of the word. That is the point.

What is this compensatory shift from life to art that makes a professional a professional rather than simply a personality or a subject? The poet begins with the child's usual fantasy as Freud describes it: to have been born of noble parents. "I shall be among the English poets," says poor Keats as he lingers before death. The shift to literary parentage accomplishes this fantasy. Keats, son of a stableman, became Milton's son instead. What distinguishes the good from the bad poet is that, for the good poet, the fantasy ceases to be a fantasy. It becomes quite real. The subject becomes a poet, a professional. How does this occur?

Poetic or literary subjectivity is not identical with being an author. The author is a second-order mythology propped on the first-order mythology of the text. As a notion, it serves the market, not the workers in the field. As an activity, it is a historical formation specific and overdetermined in each case, some authors being more efficient and therefore more useful in relation to processing the past than others. In Barthes' little model, to which I have already alluded in my discussion of hysteria (1959), the sign of a first-order semiological operation becomes a signifier in the second. What signified, or signifieds, does a text call forth to complete the mythology of authorship? Something that allows the self to divide itself in relation to something else that is different from it, and with which it seeks a relationship, and takes one on. To use Bloom's vocabulary, it curtails itself, ironically, in order to overcome itself. Whatever model we use, however, even Kristeva's "intertextuality," it is obvious that the relation between self and author is dialectical, not expressive, immediate, or mimetic. Despite contemporary pedagogies of writing, the self does not become an author by speaking through the transparent medium of language. Language is not transparent, but, to use Pater's words, full of "recondite laws" (1889, 12). It is a second landscape, beyond the personal, to which the psychological self, as it does in any professional scenario, must submit.

Conrad, whose constant subject is professionalism and its relation to selfhood and flux, is helpful here, and no text is more helpful than the late *Shadow-Line* (1917). Despite its basis in autobiography, what *The Shadow-Line* shows is that professional command and personality are not only distinct. The expansion of self or personality that results from command comes from command, not, as we might think, the other way around. Indeed, this myth of "good character" is Conrad's constant target throughout his work—*Lord Jim* (1900) is the best example of it—with the practical reality of command or "control" standing over against it as something different in principle and in practice from the law of the heart. The young captain in *The Secret Sharer* (1911) hides Legatt even though Legatt has killed his own captain and is technically an outlaw. But Legatt, surpassing any law of the heart, has killed because Archbold, his villainous captain, has violated the law of command by putting his ship—his profession—at unacceptable risk.

Conrad's biography tells us why the need to distinguish between the personal and the professional matters. It is not because Conrad joined the French Merchant Marine at the age of seventeen. It is because his mother, who died when he was seven, and his father, who died four years later, were replaced by his Uncle Thaddeus, who, in addition to love, provided his nephew with profound book-learning and an avenue through books to a mode of compensatory control in relation to loss. It is based on entry into the impersonal medium of literature, the profession that labored within Conrad until his preparatory labor as a seaman and, later on, as a captain, had come to an end. In *The Shadow-Line*, the nameless young captain's surrogate father is Captain Giles. Through a series of puns, Conrad makes Giles the Muse of both the new captain's first quest and of the book itself. Giles, in other words, is Uncle Thaddeus. He is all mediation. Here, in dangerously mimetic fashion, is whatever parallelism there may be between life and work. But in both, the structure contains an element of compensation that keeps the work of art and the life nonetheless staggered and distinct, the one taking up for the other's loss, and drawing only that relation between them. What is key, of course, is that the shift between life and art enables a change in the structure of the subject that, as it were, takes the subject out of its biography. The aesthetic precursor must be a member, not of the disciple's family, but of his profession. He, or she, must be another writer, another worker in the fields. But a shift—a dialectical shift—must be accomplished in order for this exchange to occur. The real father must be exchanged for a literary surrogate, who, Virgil-like, leads the disciple into art, where he can gain some control. In the process, and retroactively, the disciple gains another form of identity.

For Conrad, this surrogate father is, first and foremost, Flaubert. But Conrad chose to repress the French as well as the Polish predeterminations, moving into English as though a free man. If the shadow of Uncle Thaddeus can be glimpsed in Captain Giles, in Stein, and perhaps in Marlow, the shadow of Flaubert is expunged when Conrad inaugurates his actual writing career. In the early *An Outpost of Progress* (1898), the two Belgian clerks, Kayerts and Carlier, are incompetent. Conrad has already concerned himself with professional incompetence in *Almayer's Folly* (1895) and *An Outcast of the Islands* (1896). Kayerts and Carlier, however, are different. Their savage imbecility is a direct and vicious parody of Flaubert's two retired and endearing clerks in *Bouvard et Pécuchet* (1881). In one of his first texts, in other words, Conrad reverses the arrangements of Flaubert in his last. There is nothing funny about these clerks. They are pure loss.

The English novel is rich with such instances. Conrad's example is a very clear one. We would be amiss to leave out Virginia Woolf, whose father Leslie Stephen, editor of the *Cornhill Magazine* and founder of the *Dictionary of National Biography*, was an agnostic. "An Agnostic's Apology" (1876) was the most famous of the pro-Darwin tracts. Stephen was also, as reparation for this sin in regard to his own Evangelical parents, a profound moralist, despite, or, rather, because of, his agnosticism. He therefore attacked Pater in *The Cornhill* in 1875, in an essay I have mentioned. It is no wonder that Stephen closely supervised his daughter's reading until she was sixteen, wishing to keep her free from aesthetic ways of thinking. Woolf's hatred for her father, fueled by his indifference to the assaults on her by her Duckworth half brothers, is well known. What, then, compensated Woolf for the losses in her life, and gave her a profession in exchange? In 1898, Clara Pater became Woolf's classics tutor, balancing both her father's anti-aestheticism and unkindness with art for art's sake and simple warmth. By 1902, Woolf had engaged Janet Case, a feminist activist, to replace Clara, able now to reclaim her father's own political orientation without having to set aside the aesthetic. The real father's primariness has become a function of the daughter's retroactive placement of him as decisive or not. He is left behind by the choice of a rival precursor, Pater, who is also left behind by a return, with a difference, to the real father. In both cases, the disciple leaves the father behind. In the poetic scenario as opposed to that of the life, the ambivalence is manifest rather than repressed. But Woolf can now borrow from both fathers at will. She is political—that is to say, moral—but she is also impressionistic—aesthetic. It is the problematic structure in the life that art repairs by such restructuring of the imagination. As with Conrad and Flaubert, the poet both loves and hates the precursor at the same time. Ambivalence toward the real, or dead, father, by contrast, can only be experienced as pure loss or, as in Woolf's case, pure conflict. With the precursor, it can be transformed into a mode of power.

Scott is Hardy's precursor as a novelist. He allows Hardy to imagine his own father as what he wished him to be: a member of the landowning gentry, an aristocrat, and therefore a fitting object of both his filial love and hate. His own father—slight, benevolent, and a yeoman by class—needed this supplement to become a sufficiently strong Oedipal *imago* with which the ambitious son could do battle. And battle, of course, is what Scott provides, quite literally. It is Scott, his father reimagined, that Hardy revises as a novelist. Indeed, the difference between Scott and Hardy is the one that Bloom describes as the internalization of quest-romance. The medieval quest has become a psychological one, which accomplishes such an internalization by means of the shift from the allegory of love to endless allegories of desire. Wessex is not as antique as it seems. Of course not. Unlike Scott's Highland settings, with the real place names preserved, Hardy's Dorset settings are reconceived under the specific imaginative priority of Hardy's "Wessex" inventiveness and renaming. Although based on an ancient name, the name no longer refers to its proper historical earliness, but to Hardy's reconception of it. Everything British subsequent to it must be viewed by Hardy's reader from the point of view of this heightened belatedness. No longer a restriction, belatedness, as its historical reach shows, is, in the hands of a writer like Hardy, a powerful opportunity. Hardy's poetry is also part of the bargain. As a poet, Hardy's precursor is Wordsworth, Scott's great antagonist in the shifting definitions of Romanticism in the nineteenth century (see Daley 2001). In his double career as a novelist and poet, Hardy can play his novels off against his poems because he is playing Scott off against Wordsworth. Like Freud, Hardy refigures the overdeterminations that assail him by recasting their terms into ones that he can control or manage.

Biographical material, then, does not serve to clarify the work so much as the work serves to clarify the biographical material. The author does not produce the work—we have known this since Wilde. The work produces the author. This is deferred action, too. This is not an antimaterialist formalism. It is, on the contrary, a way of organizing the perished and porous clay of our literary ancestors into shapes that allow us to justify our personification of them when we speak of their texts and their durable legacy. This may be psychoanalytic criticism, but it is not criticism of the author. It is a reassessment of texts as the junction of psychical defense and traditions of various kinds. Only such junctions put the author—the survivor, not the originator, of the tale—into place. All writers are Scheherazade, whose mythology arrives in Europe in the late eighteenth century, coterminous with anxieties about inspiration in early European Romanticism.

Why, then, is Freud himself so poor a psychoanalyst of art? Why is he mimetic and rarely formal in his assessments? It is a strategy, a kind of playing the fool. But toward what end? To repress, as do Eliot and Foucault, but on a far grander and more coherent scale, the means of his literary will, and to prosecute the myth of both his imaginative potency and its location in his physical body. Materialist, and also ideal. This splitting of the Freudian persona is in the service of Freud's narcissism. Bodies need representation, and representation needs bodies. Let us turn to pornography to revisit the problem of representation, and solve it by a return to Freud.

9

The ontology of the pornographic image

Reading pornography

Ordinarily, our attitudes toward pornography are measured on a political scale. We argue about it, as though, even where sexuality is concerned, civil rights and civil safety should remain sovereign in our understanding. Perhaps a psychoanalytic approach is more useful. To apply it, the camera must, as it were, be pulled back, to give us a wide shot of the field and its concerns, and a sense of what is customarily absent from the discussion.

It is, of course, punctilious from the point of view of common sense to quibble about what pornography is, empirically. Pornography is the representation—I use the word advisedly, and will change it later on—of copulation and masturbation, a definition that leaves the object gender-adjustable and, I think, both comprehensive and simple. Here, masturbation also includes the symbolic displacements of the so-called perversions, because of their aim-inhibited economies.

To be sure, Walter Kendrick cautions us, in his groundbreaking history of pornography, *The Secret Museum* (1987), that pornography—or "pornography"—is not a "thing," as he puts it. It is actually a shifting social category; its uses are to produce and control sexuality. The word itself means "writing about prostitutes"—*pornographê*—although its entrance into English in the mid-nineteenth century carries, says Kendrick, a double sense. In 1857, the *OED* used it to signify medical writing about prostitutes. In 1850, however, C. O. Müller, in *Ancient Art and its Remains*, borrowing the term from the second-century compiler Athenaeus, used it to describe the unseemly excavations at Pompeii. The term signifies, in other words, the very ill it means to cure, at one and the same time.

Subsequent readings of pornography remain largely within Kendrick's historical frame, sometimes with great self-congratulation. The early fascination with the pornographic object—Steven Marcus (1966), Susan Sontag (1967), and Morse Peckham (1969) are chief among the critical pioneers—has, ironically, been repressed by the liberationist scholars and historians. They do not pay sufficient attention to the durable center of the conundrum: the pornographic image itself. In the critical literature on pornography, which is now vast, even if I leave aside the legal and the behavioral, we are told that pornography's value lies in its courageous exploration of the "transgressive," particularly in gay pornography, and in bondage and sadomasochistic pornography (Williams 1990, 1992; McClintock 1993). We are told that pornography presents a good opportunity to study high HIV rates in an occupational environment more controllable experimentally than a population of prostitutes; we are even told that pornography is educational (Peckham 1969, 182; Straayer 1993; McNair 1996).

Feminist film criticism has labored a great many hours over pornography, and its conclusions fall into two main groups: a descriptive criticism, bent also on showing how "transgressive" its subject is; and an interpretative criticism, focusing, as Linda Williams does, on pornography as a grammar, or set of codes. Like Kendrick, Williams regards pornography as part of a wider historical movement. It polices, in its historical emergence as a category, the production of normative desire, including the subjugation of women. For Williams, the facial cum shot—the "money shot"—is the fetish, as she calls it, that organizes normative, heterosexual porn, and that shows it to be a manifestation of the identity of sexuality and power in the sexist male. "Transgressive" porn, by contrast, and the emergent lifestyles it represents—gay, bondage, S&M—challenges the rule of the straight male, and democratizes sexuality. Libidinal economy is thereby released from phallocentrism.

Although this stance appears to find its theoretical authority in Foucault, as Williams claims (1992, 261), Foucault's project is actually closer to Freud's own. The culprits here are really Deleuze and Guattari, in the *Anti-Oedipus* of 1972. Even Judith Butler warns against this position: "There is no free-floating attachment which subsequently takes an object," she says; "rather, an attachment is always an attachment to an object" (1997, 208n). The question is whether or not the Oedipus complex is still an empirically relevant notion, given the presumable alternative to it of libidinal economies like homosexuality and sadomasochism. These latter supposedly bypass, in more than a defensive way, the law of the father and the classical family, or what we may call, as we can regarding the shift from Scott to Hardy, the Family Imaginary in the feudal mode that characterizes bourgeois capitalism. The bourgeois family is the living residue of feudalism, a subject I will explore at greater length in my discussion of Freud and Shakespeare in the next chapter. This Imaginary, in Lacan's sense, is what is required to mediate the relations between bourgeois subjectivity and the capitalist Symbolic by providing a mystification of the human relations, or lack of them, that structure capitalism. Market conditions are the real milieu of a liberated libidinal economy, which actually loves the marketplace, erotogenically. This libidinal economy is identical with the very capitalism it rebukes. This is because its presumably "free-floating" desire is identical with consumerism.

Allegorical though it is, this perspective, however, has its virtues, except for one thing. Even "transgressive" porn, like "transgressive" behavior, requires rules from which to deviate. Where is an account of the normative scenarios that the "transgressive" presumably questions and disrupts? Where, one wonders, is the normative pornographic image, that of the copulating dyad? And where is the image that we all grew up with, that of the centerfold, looking at the camera seductively? Here, a more contemporary historical perspective is helpful.

A teleology of pornography

Three developments stand out in the history of pornography in the years since the first commercial showing of *Deep Throat* in 1972, the customary benchmark for the legalization of pornography in the United States: the increasing beauty and glamor of the porn star; the unchanging fourth-wall illusionism of commercial pornography; and the emergence of pro-am pornography—"professional amateur" video and cyberporn—which features solo rather than couple performances, and which presents the pornographic actor in the alternative posture of looking *at* the camera, as do the commercial centerfolds and calendar girls of photographic pornography who are their generic ancestors. The modality, or the problem, that each one of these developments brings to pornography will help us to organize our discussion regarding the pornographic image in general and the normative one in particular.

Glamorization comes to filmic porn in the late 1970s, with Seka, often a costar of John Holmes, the early porn actor who died of AIDS in 1988. While the glamorous model has always been central to pornographic photography, Seka is the first glamorous star of cinematic pornography. Seka's chief contribution to the medium—certainly compared to Linda Lovelace, and even to Marilyn Chambers—is her richly achieved look, especially her tasteful and professional makeup, nails, and hair. Before Seka, the porn star was au naturel, a fact reflected by the industry's first base in the Bay Area, before moving to Los Angeles. Laurie Smith is an excellent example of the pre-glamor porn star who subsists well into the 1980s—handsome, with a modest bosom, and no makeup. The natural look has endured, but it has been categorized and commodified. By the mid-1980s, however, glamorization is in full swing, with Traci Lords, for example, and Ginger Lynn, beautiful, smart, and rather good actresses. Lords and Lynn have both gone on to regular movie careers. The last phase of glamorization, in the late 1990s, sees the rise of tasteful implant-breast beauties like Brittany Andrews before the industry's surprising return to the natural look, particularly the return to natural breasts; Allison Wyte's boyish plainness grows complex next to that of Jackie Ashe. The subsequent diversification of pornography has made it no longer possible to delineate such trends. Especially in cyberporn, trends proceed from the consumer rather than from the producer.

Our second development, or lack of it, lies in one of pornography's most interesting technical symptoms. The spectator's position is, as a rule, limited by the director's unquestioned belief that the camera is, as the saying goes, a fourth, transparent wall—an instrument of simple mimesis, and not a partner. Almost never, in high-production feature-length pornography on film, video, or DVD is the fourth-wall injunction lifted.

In pro-am, however—our third development—this injunction is challenged and removed. Even more than commercial pornography, pro-am carries the signature of its directors, who define the mode by using in different ways the star's expanded potential as a performer, now that the star may engage the camera directly. Stars like Andrews or Shay Sweet cross over between commercial pornography and pro-am; the differences in procedure are, as we shall see, manifest. Indeed, solo porn has, as we shall also see, a psychical aim different from that of couples or ménage porn.

How do these three developments in the history of pornography help us to understand it? What principles of the medium do they suggest? What unconscious structures are at work in pornography's unfolding imagery, and what strategies of response are at work to put them in motion for the spectator?

Faith and faithlessness in *A Lost Lady*

Let us use a literary example with which to begin our little exploration. We have seen Willa Cather at work as a literary critic. Let us turn now to one of her novels. Published in the same year as *The Ego and the Id*, 1923, Cather's *A Lost Lady* is one of the most compelling accounts of sexuality ever written. Cather's novel locates the mechanisms of desire in a series of key fantasies and images, particularly that of the glamorous woman and the responses she evokes in those around her. Niel, the young boy whose consciousness is the technical center of the novel, is the framework through which we experience the novel's action; it is Niel's consciousness that receives these key, and repetitive, fantasies and images, and that registers their effects. Niel's ego, particularly its sexual side, has been, in good measure, developed since his youth by his relation to the handsome and charismatic Mrs. Forrester, the novel's heroine, and wife of Captain Forrester, the retired railroad magnate whose house and hospitality are famed throughout the West. The real question for Niel, and for the reader, is, why is Mrs. Forrester so sexy? The question preoccupies Niel. The fantasies and images that overwhelm him explain his preoccupation.

First, however, we should remember that Niel is without his own parents over the course of the story. His mother dies when he is five, and his father leaves him in Sweet Water to be raised by his maternal uncle, Judge Pommeroy, while he moves to Denver to take an "office position" (1923, 24). This is the last we hear of Niel's proper parents. The Forresters replace or stand in for them, and produce for Niel the Oedipal situation that is missing in his actual biography.

The novel's introduction to Niel's sexual preoccupation is indirect. It comes in its apparently desultory preoccupation with questions of fidelity, or faithfulness, in civic relationships, and in love. Inquiring into this question, however, very quickly unravels the bond on which any presumable fidelity or faithfulness actually, and ironically, depends. Fidelity, in the book's very first discussion of it, turns out to be based on bad faith, or a lie, on the part of one of the partners involved.

Indeed, betrayal is a theme in the novel at large. For the novel's villain, Ivy Peters, the Forresters' tenant farmer who eventually comes to own their property, cheating is, as it is for the West's newer and unprincipled businessmen, the normal way of doing business. Cheating Indians out of their land is the new West's particular vocation. Against Peters and the younger generation stand the men of principle who built the old West, men like Captain Forrester and Judge Pommeroy. Captain Forrester is the epitome of principle, refusing to cheat his old workmen out of the full value of their investment in his bank when his bank fails. A true Romantic, Captain Forrester pays for the loss himself, ruining himself both financially and medically because of it.

But this image of a purer, earlier pioneer West is also largely a myth. While Captain Forrester pays for his principles, in more ways, as we shall see, than one, Judge Pommeroy's loyalty is demystified only by Cather's language. His servant, Black Tom, is his "faithful negro servant" (23), as Cather tells us early in the tale; indeed, Tom is in attendance, faithfully, throughout the novel. But at one point, late in the story, expressing himself fully one night after dinner, Judge Pommeroy, arbiter of the law, also descends into unfaithfulness, on the very site of the presumably "faithful" bond between his servant and himself: "The difference between a business man and a scoundrel," says Judge Pommeroy of the older, better West, "was bigger than the difference between a white man and a nigger" (76). The old, principled West here requires the judge's denigration of his servant in order to be represented, as it were, properly. In this instance, Cather undoes the principles on which the lives of her characters are constructed simply by representing them. These principles turn out to be fissured or double-edged in their constitution.

Nor should we forget that faithfulness is also a chief player in our assessment of the verisimilitude of an artistic representation, in a novel, for example, or in painting, photography, film, or video. Here, Cather joins her modernist contemporary in English, Ford Madox Ford, who, in *The Good Soldier* (1915), not only makes the question of narrative reliability an overt problem in the formal structure of his novel, but also links it to the question of sexual fidelity, or infidelity, in the novel's represented world. Ford's John Dowell does not know that his wife is unfaithful to him throughout a first-person narrative that turns out to be thereby unfaithful to the story it tells. Cather, in a redaction of Ford's reflexive narrative, spares Niel the humiliation that results from Dowell's unknowingness by requiring Niel to witness the kind of unfaithfulness that Dowell sees only after the fact.

Fidelity in the civic and aesthetic spheres, in other words, has its counterpart in the sphere of love: faithfulness to a partner. Niel's preoccupation with Mrs. Forrester is based, as it turns out, on a fascination with her potential for intimacy with other people. Chief but hardly "first" in such a series is her husband. It is a potential that secures her charm and her warmth, but that also presents something more unsettling and exciting. Mrs. Forrester, as we begin to suspect even early in the novel, is unfaithful to her husband, and has been on more than one occasion in the past. Whether or not this is another evidence of her determination by sexism or of her rebellion against it is an undecidable question. It is both and it is neither. It is rather a description of how entirely implicated the very fact of gender is in the law of culture, which is patriarchal (for an elaboration, see Cousineau 1984).

Niel figures that Captain Forrester knows of his wife's infidelity—a projective identification with the father, whom he thereby becomes, but whom in the process he also disempowers. He can imagine things from the father's point of view only by imagining the father as betrayed. The father is not a participant in the primal scene but, like himself, a voyeur or betrayed son. All men are created equal. When Niel hears Mrs. Forrester with her lover, Frank Ellinger, later in the novel—hearing is often the medium, says Freud, of the primal scene—a new possibility occurs to him: The potential for betrayal that allows Mrs. Forrester her intimacy with Frank is also what is behind her intimacy with him. The special relation she grants to Niel, or, indeed, to her husband, is made possible, not by some special choiceness in her lovers, but because, as a principle of life, Mrs. Forrester seeks out special relations with more than one man at a time. Her femininity is, to use Joan Rivière's term, a masquerade (1929).

Niel's realization, then, is twofold. The first is the requisite Oedipal disappointment, as he stands, like a Brontë figure, at the Forresters' window:

> He heard from within a woman's soft laughter; impatient, indulgent, teas-
> ing, eager. Then another laugh, very different, a man's. And it was fat and
> lazy—ended in something like a yawn.

The result, of course, is jealous rage:

> Niel found himself at the foot of the hill on the wooden bridge, his face
> hot, his temples beating, his eyes blind with anger. (71)

Then, the second realization:

> It was not a moral scruple she had outraged, but an aesthetic ideal.
> Beautiful women, whose beauty meant more than it said. ... Was their
> brilliancy always fed by something coarse and concealed? Was that their
> secret? (72)

Cather has in mind something very exact. Even though it is "aesthetic," it is neither asocial nor apolitical. *Aesthêsis*, we should remember, means "perception."
The "aesthetic" question here is the way in which "beauty" or "brilliancy," or any
lambent, and therefore valuable, quality comes into relief, becomes perceptible. It
does so by virtue of its bitter contrast with its opposites—"something coarse," as
Cather puts it here, something faithless, or ugly, or horrible. The "aesthetic" is not
"beauty" or "brilliancy" conceived of as something in itself—a core or an essence,
for example—but the formal structure of contrast with their opposites that allows
qualities, or forms, to emerge in the first place. The aesthetic—the perceptible—
must, to be perceived at all, be a contrast, or the function of a contrast.

The psychological effects of this realization are profound. Loss and sadness now
define how Niel feels. The beloved object's presence and availability have always
been predicated on the threatened loss or absence of the beloved object. Now
loss and absence, too, become real. The "aesthetic ideal" that Mrs. Forrester violates is, precisely, that ideal in its "coarse and disheartening action." Its violation
is the very structure of its ideality. Jealousy, derived from the Oedipal situation,
thrills the spectator in a spasm of betrayal, longing, and a wish fulfilled. Mrs.
Forrester's infidelity is what also carries for Niel Mrs. Forrester's potential for loving him. Restriction becomes opportunity in this defensive dialectic. If Frank
can replace Captain Forrester, then so can he.

These contrary emotions ripple the economy of Niel's ego in waves of pleasure
and unpleasure. This dissonance dislocates him, and, by dislocating him, also
locates him, violently, and coarsely, as the object, or abject, to use Kristeva's
term, of his own desire. This is also where psychical process and the structure
of readership are identical, and where Cather's relation to Ford grows more
exact, including her greater wisdom, both technically and thematically. Cather's

technique takes advantage of a potential for betrayal to sway her reader in an agony of psychical longing for a satisfactory resolution to this erotically exhausting story. Unlike Ford, Cather informs rather than deceives, requiring her reader to tolerate conflict and contradiction rather than seek a profit from their false resolution, as a young Western businessman might do. Tolerating ambivalence and deferral in the story's anticlimactic dénouement is the narrative equivalent to Niel's learning to tolerate the ambivalence that structures love in his heart.

Pornography and the primal scene

When we turn back to the pornographic image, Cather's account is of enormous help. Niel's Oedipal position in *A Lost Lady* is the position of the pornographic spectator. What he hears, or sees, is the pornographic image par excellence: his glamorous beloved loving someone else. *A Lost Lady* is, strictly speaking, pornographic. Its technical virtuosity, especially the ways in which it frames what its characters can and cannot see, can and cannot hear, is what enables its thematic sophistication in regard to its understanding of sexuality. The object must, in the lover's mind, be imagined as unfaithful in order to be imagined as faithful.

What Cather evokes, in other words, is the family romance and, with particular clarity, the family romance's centerpiece, the primal scene. Profoundly regressive, the pornographic image does the same thing. What does the pornographic spectator's gaze make of two people having sex? What scene does it "recall," or recapitulate? The primal scene—a glimpse, or a murmur, of the parents making love. It is the unconscious fantasy on which pornography as a form is largely based. Film as a whole, as Christian Metz suggests, is based, as a form, on this kind of voyeurism, since in "the filmic spectacle," says Metz, "the object seen is ... radically ignorant of its spectator" (1977, 64). Its prototype, he concludes, is "the prohibited character peculiar to the vision of the primal scene" (65). "Pornographic films," says Fredric Jameson, "are thus only the potentiation of films in general" (1992, 1). Derived from the Oedipal situation, pornography is designed to produce in the spectator a fitful dialectic of love and jealousy. Perhaps this is why Masson and MacKinnon are so uncomfortable with psychoanalysis and pornography alike. The primal scene—I suppose it still has to be stressed—is a fantasy, not a recollection, and therefore a product of desire rather than of memory. Happy endings in literature or film are pleasing because they half complete the spectator's unconscious desire to share in what pornography actually presents: the bed of a comedy's or a romance's soon-to-be-married protagonists. The fantasy of seeing one's beloved with another lover is a recreation of the family romance, to any number of ends. Rivière regards jealousy as a principal mechanism of defense (1932).

Now we may offer a definition of pornography. Pornography is whatever constitutes for the spectator a reminiscence of the primal scene. There is precedent
for this argument, although it has not been elaborated. Steven Marcus concludes
The Other Victorians with the observation that "pornography is, after all, nothing more than a representation of the fantasies of infantile sexual life, as these
fantasies are edited and reorganized in the masturbatory daydreams of adoles-
cence" (1966, 286). Richard Randall, in 1989, also observed that "pornographic
expression is likely to reflect the complex emotion of the oedipal experience"
(1989, 27), and that "its fantasies" have "infantile counterparts" (29). It is Elizabeth Cowie, however, who has directly linked the pornographic scenario with
the primal scene, particularly to the many "positions" (1992, 141) the primal
scene provides the subject for inspecting the parents at play. If the ontology of
the photographic image is, to use Bazin's formulation, the mummification of the
human figures represented (1945), the ontology of the pornographic image is, to
use Abraham and Torok's word (1976), the "crypt" of the family romance in the
spectator's unconscious.

The pornographic image, then—unlike the literary, filmic, or pictorial image—is
neither a screen nor a mirror. It does not present objects, or even object-choices,
but object-relations. It presents, formally speaking, a more-than-partial fulfill-
ment of infantile desires because of its modality. Its content is not metonymic, or
displaced; nor even metaphorical, or condensed. Its content is, to use Umberto
Eco's terms, identical with its expression. Why? Because pornography does not
represent; it performs.

It is almost a critical commonplace to say that pornography is a kind of performance art (see, for example, Peckham 1969, 182; see especially Williams on
Annie Sprinkle, 1993). Pornography breaks down the boundaries between acting and doing, mind and body, representation and projection. The performers'
lovemaking deconstructs any notion of the image as representation. Here the
image *is* what it represents. The actors are not representing roles; they are producing discourses, or labor. Hence questions of personal motivation and public
exploitation are alike moot. If the representation is not mimetic—not representational—then it reflects no prior object-world in which cause or responsibility
can be hunted down. This performativity becomes altogether manifest with the
webcam, which, in cyberporn, allows the viewer to represent him- or herself in
the images he or she actually sees. Pornography from this point of view is our
most avant-garde form.

Pornography's key image is the same, then, as Cather's: the promise of intimacy
with the parents. We settle for a voyeur's jealous view of their copulation. This
is why pornography produces a qualitatively different kind of response in the
viewer than do the arts as such, which either block or mediate such desire in

relation to representation. The example of Hamlet is sufficient. Pornography, by contrast, does not block or mediate desire; instead, it intercepts desire at its infantile roots, reconstituting its object-relations rather than representing them. The spectator is partner, included in his or her exclusion.

Susan Sontag's assumption—the customary assumption—that pornographic excitement is based on identification with some, or all, of the figures represented (1967, 54) is therefore misleading. Even Cowie's emphasis on "position" (1992, 139) leads back to "identification" (139) as the mechanism that produces desire in the spectator (see also McClintock 1992, 125). The focus on identification leaves out the real motive force in pornographic spectatorship, the force of jealousy, which is based not on inclusion through identification but on exclusion and the pain of exile. Bloom has argued that it is, finally, sexual jealousy that is the deepest motive in all of Shakespeare. The pornographic spectator's gaze is constitutive, even interactive, not identificatory. Pornography is not "mediated sex," to use Brian McNair's phrase (1996). The notion is problematic in a number of ways. First, the originals of desire are the parents; permissible sex is therefore always mediated or surrogate sex in the first place, to avoid this outrage. Nor is pornography a naïve representation of such "mediation." Because it is performative, it generates its own referentiality. The work of directors like Bobby Rinaldi and Vince Voyeur is instructive here, since in these instances the actress actually looks at the camera while having sex with a man whose face we do not see. It appears that identification with the male figure is in order; in her dialogue, the actress even pretends that she is making love to him. The mise-en-scène, however, belies the dialogue. The spectator's actual experience is not mediated: It is what it is. The camera angles plainly reveal that he is watching the actress have sex with a third person while she looks at him.

Does such an approach also apply to less heterosexually normative scenarios? The homoerotic potential of point-of-view oral-sex pornography is obvious enough, heterosexual though it presumably is. Where is the line between straight and "transgressive" porn? Even a sexist presentation goes two ways at once, according to Anne McClintock. Says McClintock regarding the cum shot: "The penis becomes an object of critical attention at the very moment when male power is ... most impotent" (1992, 122)—when, that is, the penis has had its little orgasm. Such contradiction is endemic to representation no matter the gender and predisposition of the employees. Mrs. Forrester has already shown us how the Oedipal situation structures not only male desire but also the place of women. We should remember that the place of women also structures male desire.

Like all psychical structures, in other words, gender, too, is a chiasmus. The object is the function of its aim, which is the function of its object. This relationship is the function in turn of a return to the past that is itself enabled by the later objects that recall the object-relations that people it. The position of the subject is skewed by its choices. Positions chronologically precede the ability to make object-choices, although the object-choices precede the positions in the memories we use to account for them. Is gender a position or an object-choice? Which comes first? Like other psychical structures, these, too, are twin-born. Gender is chiasmatic because it is bisexual, or rather, it is bisexual because it is chiasmatic. Even normatively conceived, homosexuality as a narcissistic construction (the classical view) is not solipsistic but relational. Recall our reading of "On Narcissism." This gender position, too, requires a role for the subject's mother in a reconstitution of the fragile dyad between mother and child. Even here the father is never far away. The purity of gender roles in their difference from anatomical identity is especially clear.

Eve Sedgwick's work (1985, 1990), as we all know, regards gender as shifting, its possibilities laid out on a continuum in each one of us. Two men making love to the same woman in straight pornography becomes part of Sedgwick's remarkable aperçu regarding such scenarios in the novel and in film: that the men want each other. Gender, in other words, resides along a scale of images which can variously recommend different object-relations in the spectator's unconscious. The spectator's drift of fascination and revulsion toward the same-sex object is no more than the signature of a constitutive infantile bisexuality, which is organized, one way or another, with the onset of the Oedipus complex, and the belated identificatory choices that the subject makes, or refuses to make, in his or her psychical life. "Even in boys," says Freud, in "Some Psychical Consequences of the Anatomical Distinction Between the Sexes" (1925),

> the Oedipus complex has a double orientation, active and passive, in accordance with their bisexual constitution; a boy also wants to take his mother's place as the love object of his father—a fact which we describe as the feminine attitude. (19:250)

The history, or lack thereof, of looking at the camera in pornography now takes on a rich and symptomatic color. With instructive exceptions like Rinaldi or Voyeur, even hard-core commercial pornography represses pornography's own unconscious center by clinging to fourth-wall illusionism. The subjective camera has had no real history in normative cinema—Pasolini's Mary is a provocative exception—and for good reason. It does not heighten illusion; it breaks it down. In porn, however, this breakdown has a reconstructive effect, as it does not in mimetic referentiality. What porn can do is now clear. The parents, especially the mother, can look at the child in *flagrante delicto*, and so include her, or him, as a witting partner in a fearful *ménage*.

The pro-am "spread"—the video centerfold—is, of course, the great exception. The centerfold, or "spread," the staple of photographic pornography, is the stock-in-trade of pro-am video and DVD, and of customized cyberporn, where the viewer can hone his imagistic choices to a self-conscious fault. In pro-am, the model looks directly at the camera, and talks. Well made-up and wearing lingerie, or shoes, or both, she spreads her legs and arches her feet, and usually masturbates, more or less grandiosely. The spread's prototype, we should remember, is the magazine centerfold. It has a well-known history of its own. Hugh Hefner had airbrushed away the labia of *Playboy* centerfolds' genitals, once, that is, he started showing them, well after the magazine's founding in 1953. In 1969, *Penthouse*'s Bob Guccione began his competition with Hefner by showing the labia of his centerfolds' genitals flat out. By institutionalizing the full-blown "spread" in mainstream pornography, Guccione focused the second key factor in pornographic ontology—the dyad with the mother. It is as decisive—perhaps more so, because it is more originary—as pornography's relation to the primal scene.

What fantasy is at work in the spread? And what is its relation to the Oedipal fantasies presented by couples porn? When you watch, or look at, a spread, you are experiencing in fantasy the mother's absent penis; her legs and her footwork compensate for the absence of the penis by restoring it through fetishistic displacements. The goal of all fetishism, with foot fetishism as its prototype, is, as we know from Freud's essay (1927), the restoration, in fantasy, of a penis to the mother. In solo gay porn, the fantasy is fulfilled without displacement; the solo male model is himself the mother. Many gender-fluid spectators often favor gay porn because each partner in the primal scene has a penis. The glamorous female model in the straight pornographic image enhances the maternal value of the female by making even its most chic performers a trifle atavistic in dress and hair, suburbanizing their looks, or casting them in high style. Heels, stockings, makeup, and hairdo infantilize the spectator even as they elevate the tone of the image. This, of course, is Cather's "aesthetic," the contrast between the coarse and the elegant, the rough and the ready.

There is also another infantile fantasy at work in the spread. The spread exemplifies an additional scenario, one described with great exactitude by Freud. Indeed, it is the recurrent scenario that defines infantile sexuality at its earliest point of contact with others, particularly from the masculine point of view. It precedes the onset of the Oedipus complex from a developmental point of view, even though it foreshadows it, with complex ironies and apparent contradictions. These include the paradox of the phallic mother, and the shadow of the Oedipus complex even in infancy. It is worth quoting Freud's full description of this scenario, in *An Outline of Psychoanalysis* (1940):

> When a boy (from the age of two or three) has entered the phallic phase
> of his libidinal development, is feeling pleasurable sensations in his sexual

organ and has learnt to procure these at will by manual stimulation, he becomes his mother's lover. He wishes to possess her physically in such ways as he has divined from his observations and intuitions about sexual life, and he tries to seduce her by showing her the male organ which he is proud to own. (23:189)

The spread porn star, in other words, is the child/spectator's mother. Pornography is not about sex. It is about masturbation. It is, in yet another way, not representational but, in its very nature, interactive, as masturbation is, even in the crib, well before the advent of cyberporn. What pornography presents at any given moment is not a mediated account of someone else's sexual activity, but a vivid projection of the masturbator's own fantasy life in paradigmatic form. This is what accounts for taste, or market choice, in pornography, in type of pornography consumed, and in stars preferred. Male or female, straight or gay, the structure is similar in its origins, since we cannot, in all imaginative conscience, restrict Freud's scene of the masturbating child to the biologically masculine child. "In both cases," says Freud, "the mother is the original object" (25:251).

The threat of castration with which the mother threatens the masturbating child brings us back, however, to the male child, and to the presumably normative, heterosexual "spread" that appeals to him more readily than it appeals to others. The mother, says Freud, "thinks she is doing the correct thing in forbidding him to handle his genital organ" (23:189). The threat of castration is writ large in the spread itself, at once the object of the child's desire and evidence of the dangers that attach to it. The site of the mother's genitals, after all, is proof positive of the very real danger of castration. It is not only the male spectator who revolves around the presence or absence of the penis (this myth, of course, is that of the "phallus"). The female, spread open to emphasize her lack of the penis, is also captured by a fascination with the phallus, in this case by its absence. From either perspective, of course, the phallus—the penis as presence *and* absence—structures the position of the subject. Rivière (1929) well precedes Lacan (1966) on this point.

This is also the Freudian origin of the rather less fantastic Kleinian notion of the mother as double in another way: as being herself both present and absent, nourishing and withholding. Propping—Freud's *Anlehnung*—seems merely to reduplicate this split in the new sexual instincts, reflecting their continuity with the self-preservative instincts from which they have become distinct. Laplanche and Pontalis distinguish too harshly between the component instincts, and insist too categorically on the different object-choices to which they give presumable rise (1967, 29–32). In the spread, the model both gives and withholds, as in Barthes's description of the stripper, who both reveals and conceals. Indeed, she reveals *to* conceal, says Barthes. She is, in other words, both the good mother and the bad mother at one and the same time. Similarly, the porn actress embodies the ambivalence that surrounds her as an imago. She is a triumphant figure, a whole object in a precarious economy that can disintegrate at any moment. Says Brittany Andrews, to one's scientific astonishment, during a solo performance: "Suck on my nipple, like a little baby."

Of course, masturbation does not, says Freud, begin in this way. "It is to be assumed," he says, again in "Some Psychical Consequences of the Anatomical Distinction Between the Sexes," that

> masturbation is attached to the Oedipus complex and serves as a discharge for the sexual excitation belonging to it. It is, however, uncertain whether ... masturbation has this character from the first, or whether on the contrary it makes its first appearance spontaneously as an activity of a bodily organ and is only brought into relation with the Oedipus complex at some later date. ... Analysis shows us in a shadowy way how the fact of a child at a very early age listening to his parents copulating may set up his first sexual excitation, and how that even may, owning to its after-effect, act as a starting-point for the child's whole sexual development. Masturbation, as well as the two attitudes in the Oedipus complex, later on becomes attached to this early experience, the child having subsequently interpreted its meaning. It is impossible, however, to suppose that these observations of coitus are of universal occurrence, so that at this point we are faced with a problem of "primal phantasies." Thus the prehistory of the Oedipus complex, even in boys, raises all of these questions for sifting and explanation; and there is the further problem of whether a great variety of different preliminary stages may not converge upon the same terminal situation. (19:250–51)

This is an extraordinarily fluid potential. One of these "preliminary stages," as we have seen in our reading of both "On Narcissism" and Strachey's earliest essay, is the child alone with the mother, before the onset of the Oedipus complex, but after she has become an object-choice. Of course, this is itself an example of how the Oedipus complex is already at work even at the beginning of life: The mother's absence, which deepens the child's desire for suture by frustrating it, can only be blamed on the rival demands of another. Even in same-sex marriages, this structure obtains, since an imaginary division of social labor is required by the child's fantasy life to explain life's circumstances. It is only in this sense that "sovereignty," as Foucault calls it, can be said to come, to use Freud's word, "first." It is, as we saw in our look at *The Ego and the Id* in Chapter 2, first or sovereign only as an aftereffect. The child's experience gives it a shape only later on. No matter its "origin" here, it is what later contingencies will make *of* this origin that will make it the origin that it only later on will be. These include the possibility of gender management.

Freud is very clear about the sequencing of the subject's gender mythology. In "Hysterical Phantasies and their Relation to Bisexuality" (1908), Freud describes how a "purely autoerotic procedure" becomes "merged" with an "idea." "Originally," he says,

> the action was a purely autoerotic procedure for the purpose of obtaining pleasure for some particular part of the body, which could be described as erotogenic. Later, this action became merged with a wishful idea from the sphere of object-love and served as a partial realization of the situation in which the phantasy culminated. (9:161)

A "sensation," as we saw in "On Narcissism," becomes associated with an "idea." The "situation" here, of course, is masturbation for the mother, a reflexive "situation" whose economy requires no displacement, since it is its own aim. Freud calls this link or association a process of "soldering," one that Lacan will, of course, call "suture."

> When, subsequently, the subject renounces this type of satisfaction, composed of masturbation and phantasy, the action is given up, while the phantasy, from being conscious, becomes unconscious. (9:161)

The Oedipal shadow, even in the dyad with the mother, is, of course, clear to Freud himself. With the original fantasy now unconscious, to what "subsequent" fantasy does the child's dyad with the mother give way? Freud is more blunt about this unconscious fantasy and its origins in *An Outline of Psychoanalysis*. If the spread represents the presumably pre-Oedipal mother, then the more conventional pornographic views of copulation represent this next stage of fantasy development in the child's mind:

> In a word, his early awakened masculinity seeks to take his father's place with her; his father has hitherto, in any case, been an envied model to the boy, owing to the physical strength he perceives in him, and the authority with which he finds him clothed. His father now becomes a rival who stands in his way and whom he would like to get rid of. If while his father is away he is allowed to share his mother's bed and if when his father returns and he is once more banished from it, his satisfaction when his father disappears and his disappointment when he emerges again are deeply felt experiences. (23:189)

Oedipal disappointment, however, cuts two ways. It also serves, ironically, a defensive purpose. Severing the child from the mother not only keeps desire in the Imaginary. It also has the eventual benefit, says Freud, of civilizing the child, since "the catastrophe of the Oedipus complex (the abandonment of incest and the institution of conscience and morality) may be regarded as a victory of the race over the individual" (19:257). Freud describes this unconscious fantasy and its origins in "A Special Type of Choice of Object Made by Men" (1910), in a passage immediately following his first published use of the term "Oedipus complex." If the spread presents the pre-Oedipal mother, then the more conventional pornographic views of copulation address the jealousy that results from the actually defensive onset of the Oedipus complex proper. The child, says Freud,

> does not forgive his mother for having granted the favour of sexual intercourse not to himself but to his father, and he regards it as an act of unfaithfulness. If these impulses do not quickly pass, there is no outlet for them other than to run their course in phantasies which have as their subject his mother's sexual activities under the most diverse circumstances; and the consequent tension leads particularly readily to his finding relief in masturbation. As a result of the constant combined operation of the two driving forces, desire and thirst for revenge, phantasies of his mother's unfaithfulness are by far the most preferred; the lover with whom she commits her act of infidelity almost always exhibits the features of the boy's own ego, or, more accurately, of his own idealized personality, grown up and so raised to a level with his father. What I have elsewhere described as the "family romance" comprises the manifold ramifications of this imaginative activity and the way in which they are interwoven with various egoistic interests of this period of life. (11:171–72)

What conventional pornographic scenario compensates the child, most obviously the masculine child, for this betrayal? Here the role of porn's most notorious trope emerges with some clarity. The facial cum shot with which both straight and gay porn scenarios conventionally end takes on its indelicate meaning. The aim, as it were, of the semen is highly determined. Like other familiar signifiers in porn, this determination, too, gives the lie to the presumably "transgressive" nature of porn's representations. As Williams observes, the "money shot" is porn's central—and centralizing—sexist fetish. Here, the *sème*—the semen and, through the pun, the sign—is not in free play, but is, quite exactly, aim-inhibited: It is destined to repeat, endlessly, its complex capture by the maternal imago, including its wish for a revenge compatible with love. This imago—the mother's face, not her breasts, a mirror, not an object—is subjected to this double response to its own doubleness. Both mother and child are now subject and object alike.

The lack of directorial focus and imaginative vision in commercial pornography well reflects the ambivalent wishes of the unconscious in regard to the common sites of fantasy that are its focus. Pro-am and digital pornography understand the form far better by returning the spectator to the original "situation" Freud has in mind for the child, alone with the mother. This is the earlier "unconscious fantasy," as Freud puts it, that lies behind the fantasy of seeing the mother with someone else.

The pathos of the porn star

Beyond its performativity, however, lies the question of pornography's wider status as a cultural practice. Its implications for a study of Freud are perpetually surprising, especially when they help us to clarify, in a study about Freud's writing, what the notions of art that guide Freud's thinking really are. As we noted early on—and as Trilling was quick to remind us then—they are not the ones that Freud displays as a rather Ernest Jones-like critic of the arts per se. Instead, they are in his active complicity, as a practicing writer, in the kind of reflexive project that he shares with a contemporary like Joyce.

Let us once again approach the problem by recourse to our focus on pornography, and to an institutional problem that pornography shares with Freud, and, at one time, with Joyce: the problem of where to place it as a cultural practice. With Freud, the question of science and literature will not go away; with Joyce, the question of obscenity and literature did. Part now of what we like to call "popular culture," porn has a different relation to problems of "high" and "low" than does the relation of rock to classical music, say, or of film to painting. This "high" and "low" is one between what is conscious and what is repressed, which is a phrenological difference at bottom; the terms "high" and "low" in regard to culture are, historically, "highbrow" and "lowbrow" in regard to skull types (see Rubin 1992). Both kinds of "high" and "low" are to be found, of course, in the work of Andy Warhol. This is also where the boredom that often defines pornographic viewing is made the very subject of films that take the structure of attention as their subject. Pro-am is the precise oxymoron for the praxis of this tradition, which "transgresses" cultural oppositions like art and trash, original and copy. In Warhol's films, the difference between art and pornography is also deconstructed.

We will, however, be disappointed if we expect porn to be particularly transgressive unconsciously. Porn, too, has as its own unconscious fantasy a rather more familiar one than we might think, and one that derives not so much from the pop arts as from the long bohemian tradition of the bad tale, and of bad faith in love. This is the literature of the also-rans, of aspirant shopgirls and their cruel lovers. This tradition begins with Henri Murger's *Scenes of Bohemian Life* (1851); Mansfield often takes these mythologies as the very subjects of her own stories more than fifty years later on. "The Tiredness of Rosabel" (1908) is a superb emblem for this dangerous genre. Warhol's films are its the culmination. One of pornography's recurrent tropes embodies this tradition with particular faithfulness. I have in mind the raised pinky used by almost all female porn performers while masturbating, or making love. Here is Jean Harlow, lurking behind Marilyn Monroe. Whether the raised pinky is ironic or not, however, one cannot say. The situation resembles MGM's translation of "art for art's sake"—Gautier's *l'art pour l'art*—into a Latin variant it never had, not "originally": *ars gratia artis*. The pop or "amateur" striving to be "high" or "pro" makes a faux pas. The raised pinky is not so much fetishistic—a penis—as it is transformative, or dialectical. It transports the star, or attempts to, out of the realm of the working girl and into high society.

Thus emerges porn's central pathos, the intimate portrait of the star's heart, as it were, as well as her body. Her raised pinky represents her dreams—the stripper or prostitute become film star, and her ascent proclaimed. And yet the porn star's praxis deconstructs the very distinctions that make up the world in which she wishes to succeed. She has outstripped herself. Here there is no difference between art and pornography because there is no difference between representation and reality. Pornography disturbs our epistemological illusions even more than it disturbs our sexual ones. From the point of view of the primal scene, of course, these are one and the same thing anyway. Pornography is a breakdown of our faith in faithfulness itself, both in love and in representation. It violates our sexual taboos, not for moral reasons, but because of the epistemological crisis that this violation engenders.

These Flaubertian echoes bring us back to our larger themes. Where is the line—if there is one—between pornography and other discourses, particularly artistic ones? Where is the line between psychoanalysis and other discourses, between, for example, psychoanalysis and the novel? These are not so much sociological questions as they are aesthetic ones, in Cather's sense. Is there a genuine difference in aesthetic response between the kinetic, with which we associate porn, and the static, with which we associate the arts proper? We know that a reading of Freud is hardly static; it is kinetic. We know the same about Mansfield, and James, and Hardy. The terms "static" and "kinetic," taken from Kant, are Joyce's in the fifth chapter of *A Portrait of the Artist as a Young Man*, in a discussion about the difference between art and pornography (1916, 205). How useful are they? Does pornographic representation challenge the very assumptions on which Joyce's assumptions are based? We know that pornography is not representation. Perhaps the assumptions in the *Portrait* are only Stephen's. They are certainly not Andy Warhol's, with whom we like to think Joyce has much in common.

Surely Joyce himself does not share Stephen's assumptions. Here we come to the heart of the doctrinal modernist resistance to Freud, particularly in Pound, Eliot, and their school. It is the resistance to Freudian temporality, to deferred action (see Meisel 1987). Its repression is clearest in the famous definition of the Image by Pound: "An 'Image,'" he says, "is that which presents an intellectual and emotional complex in an instant of time" (1918, 4). The "instant" is to be preserved, but the history that produces it is to be repressed. As the Woolf of

To the Lighthouse well knows, moments of stasis, to use Stephen's terms, are produced by kinesis. But to admit the role of time in the chain of instants that produces epiphanies would impugn their ideality. To what aesthetic conclusion are we therefore led? Is there a difference between art and pornography? Or do they share a modality? Indeed, does the kinetic modality of pornography actually serve as a startling prototype for response and responsiveness, in art and life alike? Needless to say, the answers are both obvious and arguable. Literature is a series of screens. Pornography is not. Like psychoanalysis, pornography removes these screens, exposing what is behind them. Art swerves from capturing the infantile sites of pleasure and pain that lie there.

Freud, Bakhtin, Shakespeare

What is representation?

The ontology of the pornographic image puts us in a position to ask the question that we have been waiting to ask throughout this study: What is psychical representation? And what is representation in general? How do we conceptualize it? How do we do so with its time lag intact and its disappointments plain? The psychical representations that pornography exploits exceed both the visual and the verbal, and yet they include them both. They also include the ideational, particularly in fetishism. What notion of representation sufficiently accommodates all these aspects of the pornographic image, and, of course, of the primal scene of which it is a reminiscence? There are sights as well as sounds; there is narrative as well as iconography. The specificity of the pornographic image and its psychical context also exceeds the specificity of the linguistic resources available to us to characterize it. As we saw in Chapter 5, Freud's own distinctions among *Darstellung*, *Vorstellung*, and even *Bild* are not ones that Strachey can honor because English does not make the distinctions that German does. Pictorial (*Darstellung* or *Bild*) and imaginative (*Vorstellung*) senses of "representation" divide the semantic chain very differently than do "idea" and "representation" in English. In English, all aspects of "representation," even "idea," are functions of a similar modality that share, finally, no matter their context, a visualizing predisposition that makes representation in English one based decidedly on the image. It was probably this insufficiency in the German language that led Freud to appropriate the term *imago* from Jung, a term designed to emphasize, in Freud's use of it, the particularly visual nature of unconscious representation. This visuality is not allied with primary process because visuality is more basic to perception than language. We have already unpacked the majority of the illusions involved in that sort of perspective. No, the reason "representation" in English is largely a visual affair compared to its nonequivalent varieties in German is because the word's etymology tell us that this is the case from the point of view of the actual history of the English language.

Even in its first sense in the *OED*—"presence, bearing," as in the "air" one possesses socially—"representation" is already tainted by the predominance of the visual. The secondary meaning of "representation" in this social sense makes clear that it is the visual that really is at stake: "appearance," says the *OED*, or "impression on the sight." The word's second meaning makes this altogether clear: "An image" or a "likeness," whether "material" or a "figure"; "exhibiting in some visible image or form." Only later in the word's semantic inventory do its more familiar German cognates come into play: "the exhibitions of character and action upon the stage," which, in the single English term, includes the division between play (*Vorstellung*) and acting (*Darstellung*) made in German. And not until very late in the inventory does an equivalent for *stellen* emerge: "the action of placing a fact, etc., before another or others by means of discourse." Other vagaries of signification, especially a late one describing representation figurally—as the "substitution of one thing or person for another"—bring us at last to the question of mechanism. But this concern emerges only slowly, from under the preponderant weight of the word's visual meaning.

The etymology even draws us into wars over the status of the image from the point of view of the religious history of England, particularly in the Renaissance. A 1425 religious usage describing the "representacyone" of Christ's "blyssed passyone" is followed two centuries later, after the religious shift in England has occurred, by Sidney's view of "writings," in a text printed in 1655, as the "representationes" of "thoughts." But while the context changes from religious to literary, critical, and epistemological, the structure of assumption has not changed at all. In both cases, the representation—Jesus, or writing—is the outward form of something else inside, whether blessedness or thinking. Mimesis is the structure of assumption that binds the religious and the secular meanings of "representation" even as the two contexts stand, especially with Sidney, newly apart historically.

The religious wars were themselves wars about reference. In religion, as in myth, the question is particularly important. In psychoanalysis, it is even more so. To what does representation refer? Does it refer at all? Or does it simply repeat? Is it a re-presentation of something already in its system, as it were, rather than a copy of something external to itself? What does it re-present? A memory? A memory of what? And how does this avoid being a copy, a mimesis?

First, in other words, is the question of whether a representation is mediate or immediate. In the case of the image, the question is less absurd. Does it refer to something beyond itself, or is its power—what we might otherwise call its transcendence—its ability to be, quite precisely, exactly and only what it is?

To put it this way, of course, is the problem. For the image to be either mediate or immediate, it must, of course, be both. It must, for its power, refer only to its own specificity. But for its specificity to be, well, specific, it must emerge against all, as Stephen Dedalus puts it, that is not it. Hence its specificity is a function of the very differences that ironically constitute it. This kind of ratiocination, however, is unnecessary. The problem has a psychoanalytic pathway, and a good bibliographical terminus. Sex and literature, we should remember, share the same thrill: *knowing*, an epistemological thrill. What is this thrill? Is it seeing the mother's genitals, or the father's penis? Or is it something else, something unconscious that is reflected back to us in the ontology of the pornographic image? Pornography moves, as we have seen, from the mimetic to the projective. It becomes the eye of desire rather than a representation of what the eye sees. The "conditions of representability," as Freud calls them, have changed with pornography, at least from the point of view of a normative poetics. These "conditions" do not reflect the conditions of reality, but put in its place one's reaction to them.

What are these "conditions of representability"? How are they bound up with representation? And how, if we recall our novelists, is representation bound up with resistance? The pornographic image is valuable because it provides an efficient and useful site for asking these questions. Pornography dramatizes the question that attends all psychical representation. Its constant plaint is the one behind all projection: Do you love me? Even an answer in the affirmative can only be understood by an affirmation of the negative.

Barbara Johnson's well-known meditation on apostrophe (1987) is helpful here because it regards rhetoric and psychoanalytic process as versions of each other, particularly the rhetoric of the infant's cry. The mother's very presence, says Johnson, is a representation. More important still is the specific rhetorical device employed to make her so—apostrophe, as in "Mama." "The mother addressed," writes Johnson, "is somehow a personification, not a person—a personification of presence or absence, of Otherness itself" (1987, 198). The apostrophe that defines the child's cry is, to put it simply, a form of projective identification. It splits the object it presumably addresses, identifying with it on the one hand and with its own fear of its loss on the other. The object, in other words, is both present and absent at the origin, already an object-relation. The child's cry does not represent the mother by simply referring to her; it is the child's double response to her nearness and her otherness. It is, we must always remember, a projection. Its two accents are spun of the child's same cry. As we saw in discussing representation and resistance in the novel, representation is, from a Freudian point of view, a matter of resistance or defense from the start. Imagining what is at hand is our way of dealing with what is at hand. The breast will come, but it will also go. Representation is the very job of defense. This is true of both the verbal apostrophe and the images that structure the subject's object-relations.

If I have spoken of pornography's use of "immediate" psychical images or representations, I did so well knowing that Johnson's essay would now explain what I meant by "immediate"—a temporal lag designed to indicate, not a Bergsonian living present, but the nature of any image, necessarily memorial in way or another. An image always returns the mind to what it feels to be a primal moment. Such a moment is never more than nostalgic. Of course, here the primal also achieves a new kind of dignity. Even feeding becomes a symbol, since the satisfaction it provides includes, among other things, that of a fantasy of hunger being satiated. Feeding, in other words, is already subject to insertion in a chain of symbolizations at the earliest moments of life.

This splitting at the origin by personification is, to translate Johnson's terms back into those of Paul de Man, the intentional structure of the Romantic image (1984). Here Freud's affiliation to Wordsworth is inescapable. So is the fact that apostrophe and splitting are the same in structure and effect. Like chiasmus and constancy, they are rhetorical and psychoanalytic twins. They form the experience of the newborn into a single rhythm of pain and pleasure, gain and loss. Klein is no schismatic. Projective identification is what is needed, notionally, to sharpen Freud's own notion of representation. It underlines what is always plain in Freud himself. Projective identification is always ambivalent. Ambivalence is its very mode of being. It produces a double or split series of personifications, like a Victorian novel, or like the discourse of "myth." If "myth," with its ambivalent petulance, has any mechanism at all—such a mechanism has often been obscure to us, shrouded behind claims of unmediated mimesis—it, too, is projective identification. That is Mann's argument. Myth and religion split the world very neatly in half to defend against the most frightening and toxic of the gods, death and loneliness. Projective identification can take the form, most typically, of good and bad things—good breast/bad breast, of course, is the prototype—but it can also, as we have seen, take the form of fluid gender.

Projective identification can also take the form of reader-response, or, rather, reader-response can take the form of projective identification. Projective identification is a good way of describing the defensive nature of the reader's activity as I described it earlier in Mansfield and in James, and in what Hardy actually has his characters do to each other in *Jude the Obscure*. In fact, Sue and Jude's many conversations are the concrete conjunction of the frustrations of love and reading alike. These conversations, especially their own "second, silent" ones, are a bitter exchange of projective identifications, both speaking only to themselves. Projective identification also has a moral dimension, as the pain rather than the pathos of Hardy's characters suggests it does. Projective identification is narcissistic in motivation—this is perhaps what is irksome in Hardy and his disciple Lawrence both—even in its attempt to master the bad as well as the good. Projective identification precedes narcissism, of course, but it is its prototype. It allows us to identify with our parents by taking ourselves as our own objects of love. However pathologically, this retrospective conceit corrects any failing in the real parental bond by idealizing it. Parental love—by parents and child alike—is an object-relation rather than love toward real objects.

Like the psyche, pornography produces a text beyond representation. Like Freud's text and its objects, pornography exists in the spectator's response to it. Regarded traditionally, or mimetically, pornography is an intensification of subjectivity by means of the subject's exclusion from the primal scene. Regarded aesthetically or performatively, and through the lens of deferred action, pornography is instead a means of revisiting this site, and rewriting it. "Point-of-view" pornography splits the viewer quite precisely between the illusion of participation—mimesis—and a manifest voyeurism—aesthesis—in regard to the primal scene or the mother's face. Is she looking at me while I make love to her, or while someone else does? This is not just Oedipal voyeurism at the primal scene. It is also an example of the splitting that results from the projective identification that structures one's response to it. This is the split tonality of the family romance as a whole. The family romance is actually a salad of projective identification by parents and children alike. Splitting propels the unconscious from its very beginnings. It is also—and more crucial to our argument—what motivates representation. Now representation itself should be redefined not only as resistance, but as ambivalent resistance.

Freud and Bakhtin

We need a critical term with which to characterize psychical representation more fully. Identification is the key to Freudian representation, although not as we typically conceive of identification. Identification is an exclusionary medium, one that produces its identificatory effects at two removes. By excluding the subject from the scene in which he or she wishes to participate, it shifts the subject's desire to a new position, that of the jealous seeker who reconfigures desire as voyeuristic instead of as palpable in its aim. How can you identify with that which excludes you? This is the position of both the pornographic and the colonial subject. This is also the position of all subjects in the Oedipus complex. The abject only exacerbate and make overtly political the latter's normative circumstances.

Still fugitive, however, is what it is that excludes the subject. As in James, say, or Hardy, or Mansfield, what kind of representation is necessary and sufficient to generate resistance? Freud's German and Strachey's English are alike insufficient in being able to produce as exact a description as we need. Bakhtin's Russian provides one. If identification is the pivotal trope for the psyche, its measure must be wide. Bakhtin's notion of "stylization" is a way of making it particularly expansive. Readily translatable into English, and readily translatable as a notion, "stylization" is, quite simply, an exaggeration of any kind. What Bakhtin calls the conventionality of stylization (1929, 193) is the name for stylization's achievement of transparency by means of imitation and practice. Stylization is the common element in all representation, whether verbal, visual, or ideational. Without exaggeration—without transgression—there would be no norm to seek, no constancy to have. This endless difference—Freud calls it the difference between ideal ego and ego-ideal—is the source of the power that representation has in affecting us. After "On Narcisissm," ego and libido coexist uneasily in a single field of libidinized identifications or "stylizations," no longer opposed, as they are in the early Freud, but producing one another. Pornography is the concrete externalization of this paradigmatic site. By presenting material reminiscent of the family romance, pornography situates the viewer at the crossroads of his or her identificatory mechanisms *in statu nascendi*. These identifications—these "stylizations," as I will call them now—structure object-choice. The subject desires what his or her idealizations desire. This is how pornography returns its viewers to their infantile or "primal" scenes of gender emergence in a manner far less displaced than do other modes of representation. Stylization well describes how the mind stores influences, particularly identifications, while also remaining open to new influences or identifications. It provides an additional model for what Derrida sees Freud searching for in the *Project*. To regard the "residua" of the unconscious as a grid of "stylizations" is to give them both a ready status as identifications and a slumbering one as socially and historically derived. Their functioning is a fine example, in daily life, of Mann's mythic identification. *Skaz*, the kinds of oral speech that often give narrative its verisimilitude, is a kind of stylization, too. Its folksiness or down-homeness is an ironic function of its conformity to type. It is, to use another of Bakhtin's terms, a kind of self-parody as a social praxis. No wonder Boris Eichenbaum, who first draws attention to *skaz*, described Gogol's *skaz* as "contrived" (1918, 283).

Stylization readily shows what is at stake in psychoanalytic interpretation. What is a dream a distortion of? We rejected the notion of repression as a form of distortion earlier because the notion of distortion was understood mimetically. But if we regard distortion dialogically—as a form of stylization—repression becomes instead a form of editing on a continuous field of signification. The topographical model is unnecessary. Manifest content is not structured in relation to latent as copy to original, but as a hypostasis of something continuous with it discursively which it (and because it) condenses or displaces. The subject is not distinct from the field of discourse phenomenologically, but only as *parole* is to *langue*, as speech is to language.

So useful is stylization from the point of view of symptomatology that Bakhtin inadvertently identifies it with a surprisingly familiar clinical form in Freud. Bakhtin's description of the structure of stylization sounds like Freud on the structure of melancholia:

> The stylizer uses another's discourse precisely as other, and in so doing casts a slight shadow of objectification over it. To be sure, the discourse does not become an object. After all, what is important to the stylizer is the sum total of devices associated with the other's speech precisely as an expression of a particular point of view. He works with someone else's point of view. Therefore a certain shadow of objectification falls precisely on that very point of view, and consequently it becomes conditional. (1929, 189–90)

By "objectification," Bakhtin means the defamiliarization that another point of view brings to the subject. This is identification's ironically alienating effect, which binds one to someone else and, in so doing, makes one feel less rather than more at home. As with *skaz*, "defamiliarization"—Freud's "uncanny"—is that which is at once strange and familiar. "Objectification" is the depressive position par excellence. For the reader, thrust into the role of observer, or for the analyst, this "shadow" of identification is indeed objective; it is what he or she sees that the speaker, or patient, does not. "Objectification" is also the exclusionary moment in pornography. It draws one in as it pushes one away. This is also the Hegelian moment in the play of narcissism and identification. In a Hegelian vocabulary—it is not inappropriate to employ one in a Marxist context—"objectification" is a kind of knowledge of knowledge.

Stylization is also the technical link between the novel and psychoanalysis, both of which house the subject in a storehouse of stylizations. Bakhtin's notion of the "double-voicedness" of novelistic texts is the same in structure as what in Freud is the structure of the ambivalence that identification breeds: "the intersection within it of two voices and two accents" (192), the speaker's voice and its influences. "Stylization," says Bakhtin, "stylizes another's style in the direction of that style's own particular tasks" (193). The ego of the stylizer can easily get lost in the shadow of the stylization.

This bit of deferred action in reading Freud through a reading of the belatedly available Bakhtin is, of course, another example of how literary history, like the psyche, also doubles Freud's texts. Thanks to Lacan, Freud and Bakhtin are consistent. Particularly amusing is the account of Freud by Bakhtin's colleague and friend, V.N. Vološinov, in *Freudianism: A Critical Sketch* (1927). For Vološinov, psychoanalysis is subjectivist and biologistic; it has no social dimension. A period and ideological stylization in its own right, *Freudianism* is a classical Marxist misreading of psychoanalysis. But it is also self-contradictory. Despite its polemicism, it sees what it does not want to see: a Bakhtinian Freud. That some Bakhtin scholars believe that Bakhtin wrote *Freudianism* under the cover of Vološinov's name (as, presumably, he did *Marxism and the Philosophy of Language* [1929]) makes its double posture more understandable. When Vološinov corrects his own assumption that Freud describes no more than a struggle of natural forces by concluding instead that what he really describes is a struggle of ideological motives, one wonders whether or not Bakhtin did indeed have a hand in the text:

> Every utterance is *the product of the interaction between speakers* and the product of the broader context of the whole complex *social situation* in which the utterance emerges. … It is essential to reconstruct all those complex social interrelations of which the given utterance is the ideological refraction. … Inner speech, too, assumes a listener and is oriented in its construction toward that listener. Inner speech is the same kind of product and expression of social intercourse as is outward speech. … The psychical "mechanisms" readily disclose their social derivation to us. (1927, 79–80)

It is 1927, and Vološinov has followed Freud through his changes very scrupulously. Vološinov—Bakhtin—describes a social Freud, a Freud whose sociality depends on the subject's relation to representations, whether from family life or from the life of civil society. The key, for Bakhtin as it is for Freud, is identification, which encompasses object-choice—we might as well admit it—together with identification in its classical sense (47). As I noted, even the distinction between narcissistic and self-preservative object-choice runs into the same structure of exclusion; both reside in the mother, who splits (see Laplanche and Pontalis 1967, 29–32).

The classical Marxist question regarding psychoanalysis, however, still requires an answer. Why, in a polyformal world, does Freud insist on the "castle" (1927, 90), as Vološinov calls it, of the family romance as the single determinant of psychical life? The metaphor of the castle is helpful. From a Marxist point of view, the family romance has a familiar structure. The grant of authority to the father for the sake of protection tolls reminiscent bells. This is feudalism, although a feudalism that has, as it were, been internalized. It is a feudalism of the unconscious, a mutualism of vassal and lord, knight and king. It is the baleful landscape of Bloom's Romanticism. Incorporation is included in the mix because of the king's two bodies and the knight's eucharistic one. This is the totemic arrangement of *Totem and Taboo*. In the case of the family romance, it is also historically specific. For the modern subject—the subject as such—feudalism is the Imaginary mode of thought that misreads or represses the Symbolic order of capitalism. The family romance is its representative. It preserves feudalism in the bourgeois home by making every man a king. In point of fact, value or authority, in wealth or in kinship, is in capitalism no more than a position in a system of exchange. The feudal unconscious masks the Symbolic in a more grounded mythology of rule. In so doing, it unmasks it. The sociality that narcissism has uncovered is radically historicizing. Most important, the family romance has a particular discursive form. Like feudalism, it is monological. It has only one tale to tell. Medieval carnivalesque is the foil of the family romance, not its repressed meaning. It augurs the world of capitalism, which is dialogical. Capitalism is a babble of tongues. Freud—modernity—structures the psyche by putting these two discursive modes at odds. Their strife provides us with a picture of the psyche's social history. The tension between them is, from the point of view of literary models, the tension between, in Bakhtin's terms, epic and novel.

Shakespeare and Freud

The unexpectedness with which Bakhtin's central preoccupation brings us back to Freud's should come as no surprise. The tension between epic and novel is Shakespeare. Shakespeare is the hinge, both historically and generically, of the change from the one to the other. Indeed, Shakespeare *is* that change. An admixture of heroic and courtly love poetry with prose of all kinds, Shakespeare's forms reflect his themes. Shakespeare's endless subject is also Freud's: the family romance. The passing authority of fathers and kings is what Shakespeare is about; the absolute authority of time alone is how we know that. Bakhtin, curiously, retreats from Shakespeare, despite Shakespeare's centrality to his project. For Bakhtin, Shakespeare's "polyphony" is insufficient. Drama has a "plurality" of voices, but as a form it has "only one valid voice, the voice of the hero" (1929, 34). This may be true of normative drama, including that of Oscar Wilde and Beckett, but it is not true of Shakespearean drama.

As a discourse, Shakespearean drama is novelistic. As in *Moby-Dick*, its heroic plots are set within a wider social matrix that tests and assaults them. Shakespeare the playwright—Shakespeare the novelist—thrives on the interruption of poetry by prose, and of fine poetry by self-consciously middling or even bad poetry. This is the continuous stuff of Shakespearean dialogue, comedies and tragedies alike. Discourse, as a rule, overwhelms genre. The irregularities are not between characters so much as within them. Shakespeare collides whole discursive worlds within presumably single minds, producing the riot of forms that character is. Tone is crucial—it is our only guide—but tone is as much a function of the reader or spectator as it is of character in an intentional mode. Character in an intentional mode is what Shakespeare's characters try to be, but cannot. Bolingbroke surrenders his personality to be king; Prince Hal will do the same.

Rule and consciousness are not only not identical; they are mutually exclusive. Falstaff, of course, is the carnivalesque that cannot be controlled. Carnivalesque in Shakespeare is not, as it is in Bakhtin, redemptive; it is dangerous, for mental health and politics alike. This is the source of Falstaff's Lawrentian vitality. He does not conform to the categories that everyone else is happy to embrace to escape chaos. Falstaff is a universe, Hal and his father a world. When rule is at issue, Falstaff must simply be banished, as is the poet from Plato's republic.

This is Hamlet's very activity—to sustain the kinds of generic distinctions that discourse disrupts: "To be or not to be." Unlike his Greek counterpart, Oedipus, Hamlet deals in no dead certainties. Oedipus has indeed killed Laius, but for Hamlet what has happened is all inference about what someone else did. Shakespeare, too, has rejected the seduction theory. Unlike Oedipus, Hamlet is part of a complex, not a rivalry. He is the odd man out. Exclusion is what defines him, not guilt. Shakespearean drama as a whole is a mirror of Hamlet's exclusion. Hamlet is a spectator, and so, perpetually, are we. Drama as a form has as its very condition the exclusion of the audience, which participates only by looking on. It is the formal embodiment of both Bakhtin's "objectification" and Freud's primal scene. In Shakespeare, they are one and the same.

Bakhtin is not interested in Shakespeare. He flees from the scene of his own best exemplification. Freud, of course, does not. The Shakespearean primal scene is Freud's chief anxiety because it is his chief influence. For Freud, inventing the family romance means finding a place to put Shakespeare. Shakespeare becomes the Freudian unconscious. This is how Shakespeare disappears in Freud even as he remains visible. Unlike Locke's or Hegel's, Shakespeare's shadow always remains to "objectify" the proceedings. Locke and Hegel, thanks to James and Bergson, have become part of the machinery. Shakespeare is Freud's apostrophic ghost. Without him, there is no family romance; because of him, it must be made unconscious. Freud has turned the problem of Shakespeare into its own solution. It is called the psychoanalytic model of mind. There is no better instance of Freud's own dialogism, and no better instance of the literary Freud.

Works cited

Abraham, Nicolas, and Torok, Maria. 1976. *The Wolf Man's Magic Word*. Trans. Nicholas Rand. Minneapolis: University of Minnesota Press, 1986.

Althusser, Louis. 1964. "Freud and Lacan." In *Lenin and Philosophy*. Trans. Ben Brewster. New York: Monthly Review Press, 1971 189–219.

Amacher, Peter. 1965. *Freud's Neurological Education and Its Influence on Psychoanalytic Theory*. Madison, CT: International Universities Press.

Armstrong, Richard H. 2005. *A Compulsion for Antiquity: Freud and the Ancient World*. Ithaca: Cornell University Press.

Auden, W. H. 1935. "Psychology and Art To-Day." In *The English Auden: Poems, Essays, and Dramatic Writings, 1927–39*. Ed. Edward Mendelson. New York: Random House, 1977, 332–42.

Bakhtin, Mikhail. 1929. *Problems of Dostoevsky's Poetics*. Trans. Caryl Emerson. Minneapolis: University of Minnesota Press, 1984.

Barthelme, Donald. 1970. "Paraguay." In *City Life*. Rpt. New York: Pocket Books, 1978, 29–40.

Barthes, Roland. 1959. *Mythologies*. Trans. Annette Lavers. New York: Hill and Wang, 1972.

——. 1968. "The Death of the Author." In *Image/Music/Text*. Trans. Stephen Heath. New York: Hill and Wang, 1972, 142–48.

Bazin, André. 1945. "The Ontology of the Photographic Image." In *What is Cinema?* Vol. 1. Trans. Hugh Gray. Berkeley: University of California Press, 1967, 9–16.

Bell, Clive. 1914. *Art*. Rpt. London: Chatto & Windus, 1949.

Bergson, Henri. 1889. *Time and Free Will: An Essay on the Immediate Data of Consciousness*. Trans. F. L. Pogson. Rpt. New York: Dover, 2001.

Berkeley, George. 1709. *A New Theory of Vision*. Rpt. London: J.M. Dent and Sons, 1910.

Bettelheim, Bruno. 1983. *Freud and Man's Soul*. New York: Knopf.

Bhabha, Homi K. 1994. *The Location of Culture*. London: Routledge.

Bloom, Harold. 1968. "The Internalization of Quest Romance." In *Poetics of Influence*. Ed. John Hollander. New Haven, CT: Henry R. Schwab, 1988, 17–42.

——. 1978. "Freud and the Poetic Sublime." In *Poetics of Influence*. Ed. John Hollander. New Haven, CT: Henry R. Schwab, 1988, 187–212.

Bodkin, Maud. 1934. *Archetypal Patterns in Poetry: Psychological Studies of Imagination*. Rpt. New York: Oxford University Press, 1974.

Borch-Jacobsen, Mikkel. 1996. *Remembering Anna O*. New York: Routledge.

Borges, Jorge Luis. 1941. "Tlön, Uqbar, Orbis Tertius." In *Ficciones*. Trans. Alistair Reid. Ed. Anthony Kerrigan. New York: Grove Press, 1962, 17–35.

Brooks, Peter. 1984. *Reading for the Plot: Design and Intention in Narrative*. New York: Knopf.

——. 1994. *Psychoanalysis and Storytelling*. Oxford: Blackwell.

Burke, Kenneth. 1939. "Freud—and the Analysis of Poetry." In *The Philosophy of Literary Form: Studies in Symbolic Action*. 3rd ed. Berkeley: University of California Press, 1973, 258–92.

Butler, Judith. 1990. *Gender Trouble: Feminism and the Subversion of Identity*. New York: Routledge.

——. 1997. *The Psychic Life of Power: Theories in Subjection*. Stanford: Stanford University Press.

Cather, Willa. 1922. "The Novel Démeublé." In *Willa Cather on Writing*. Lincoln: University of Nebraska Press, 1988, 33–43.

——. 1923. *A Lost Lady*. Rpt. New York: Vintage, 1990.

——. 1936. "Katherine Mansfield." In *Willa Cather on Writing*. Lincoln: University of Nebraska Press, 1988, 105–20.

Chaudhuri, Amit. 2003. *D. H. Lawrence and Difference*. Oxford: Oxford University Press.

Chertok, Leon, and Saussure, Raymond de. 1973. *The Therapeutic Revolution: From Mesmer to Freud*. Trans. R. H. Ahrenfeldt. New York: Brunner/Mazel, 1979.

Cousineau, Diane. 1984. "Division and Difference in *A Lost Lady*." *Women's Studies* 11:305–22.

Cowie, Elizabeth. 1992. "Pornography and Fantasy: Psychoanalytic Perspectives." In *Dirty Looks: Women, Pornography, Power*. Ed. Pamela Church Gibson and Roma Gibson. London: British Film Institute, 1993, 132–52.

Daley, Kenneth. 2001. *The Rescue of Romanticism: Walter Pater and John Ruskin*. Athens: Ohio University Press.

Deleuze, Gilles. 1957. *Bergson: Mémoire et vie*. Paris: Presses Universitaires de France.

——. 1966. *Bergsonism*. Trans. Hugh Tomlinson and Barbara Habberjam. New York: Zone, 1988.

——, and Guattari, Felix. 1972. Anti-Oedipus. Trans. Robert Hurley et al. New York: Viking, 1977.

de Man, Paul. 1984. "The Intentional Structure of the Romantic Image." In *The Rhetoric of Romanticism*. New York: Columbia University Press, 1984, 1–18.

Derrida, Jacques. 1967. "Freud and the Scene of Writing." In *Writing and Difference*. Trans. Alan Bass. Chicago: University of Chicago Press, 1978, 198–231.

——. 1975. "Le facteur de la vérité." In *The Post Card: From Socrates to Freud and Beyond*. Trans. Alan Bass. Chicago: University of Chicago Press, 1987, 411–96.

Donagan, A. 1966. "Wittgenstein on Sensation." In *Wittgenstein: A Collection of Critical Essays*. Ed. George Pitcher. New York: Doubleday, 1966, 324–51.

DuBois, W. E. B. 1903. *The Souls of Black Folk*. Rpt. New York: Penguin, 1996.

Edel, Leon. 1953–72. *Henry James*. 5 vols. Philadelphia: Lippincott.

Eichenbaum, Boris. 1918. "How Gogol's 'Overcoat' is Made." In *Gogol from the Twentieth Century*. Ed. Robert A. Maguire. Princeton: Princeton University Press, 1974, 269–91.

Eliot, T. S. 1919. "Tradition and the Individual Talent." In *Selected Essays*. London: Faber, 1951, 13–22.

——. 1921. "The Metaphysical Poets." In *Selected Essays*. London: Faber, 1951, 281–91.

——. 1922. *The Waste Land*. In *Collected Poems* (1963). Rpt. New York: Harcourt, Brace & World, 1970.

———. 1923. "*Ulysses*, Order, and Myth." In *Selected Prose of T. S. Eliot*. Ed. Frank Kermode. New York: Harcourt Brace Jovanovich, 1975, 175–78.

———. 1928. "Freud's Illusions." *Criterion* 8 (31): 350–53.

Ellenberger, Henri F. 1956. "Fechner and Freud." *Bulletin of the Menninger Clinic* 20:201–14.

———. 1970. *The Discovery of the Unconscious: The History and Evolution of Dynamic Psychiatry*. New York: Basic Books.

Erikson, Erik. 1958. *Young Man Luther*. New York: Norton.

Fechner, Gustav. 1860. *Elements of Psychophysics*. Vol. 1. Trans. Helmut E. Adler. New York: Holt, Rinehart and Winston, 1996.

Fetterley, Judith. 1978. *The Resisting Reader: A Feminist Approach to American Fiction*. Bloomington: Indiana University Press, 1978.

Fish, Stanley. 1967. *Surprised by Sin*. London: St. Martin's.

Foucault, Michel. 1954. *Mental Illness and Psychology*. Trans. Alan Sheridan. New York: Harper Colophon, 1976.

———. 1961. *Madness and Civilization: A History of Insanity in the Age of Reason*. Trans. Richard Howard. New York: Vintage, 1973.

———. 1966. *The Order of Things: An Archaeology of the Human Sciences*. Trans. Alan Sheridan. New York: Vintage, 1970.

———. 1969. "What is an Author?" In *Language, Counter-Memory, Practice: Selected Essays and Interviews*. Ed. Donald F. Bouchard. Ithaca: Cornell University Press, 1977, 113–38.

———. 1975. *Discipline and Punish: The Birth of the Prison*. Trans. Alan Sheridan. New York: Pantheon, 1977.

———. 1976. *The History of Sexuality*. Vol. 1: *An Introduction*. Trans. Robert Hurley. New York: Pantheon, 1978.

Freud, Anna. 1936. *The Ego and the Mechanisms of Defense*. Trans. Cecil Baines. New York: International Universities Press, 1966.

Freud, Ernst L., ed. and trans. 1970. *The Letters of Sigmund Freud and Arnold Zweig*. New York: Harcourt Brace Jovanovich.

Fry, Roger. 1924. *The Artist and Psycho-analysis*. London: The Hogarth Press.

Gearhart, Suzanne. 1995. "Foucault's Response to Freud: Sado-Masochism and the Aestheticization of Power." *Style* 29 (3): 389–403.

———. 1997. "The Taming of Michel Foucault: New Historicism, Psychoanalysis, and the Subversion of Power." *New Literary History* 28 (3): 457–85.

Gide, André. 1931. *Pretexts*. Trans. Justin O'Brien et al. New York: Meridian, 1959.

Gilbert, Sandra, and Susan Gubar. 1979. *The Madwoman in the Attic: The Woman Writer and the Nineteenth-Century Literary Imagination*. New Haven, CT: Yale University Press.

Gilman, Sander L. 1993. *Freud, Race, and Gender*. Princeton, NJ: Princeton University Press.

Girard, Réné. 1961. *Desire, Deceit, and the Novel: Self and Other in Literary Structure*. Trans. Yvonne Freccero. Baltimore, MD: The John Hopkins University Press, 1965.

Greenblatt, Stephen. 2004. "Me, Myself, and I." *The New York Review of Books* 51 (6): 32–36.

Grünbaum, Adolf. 1984. *The Foundations of Psychoanalysis: A Philosophical Critique.* Berkeley: University of California Press.

Hardy, Thomas. 1895. *Jude the Obscure.* Rpt. New York: Riverside, 1965.

Hartley, David. 1749. *Observations on Man.* 2 vols. Rpt. London: J. Johnson, 1791.

Hegel, G.W.F. 1807. *The Phenomenology of Mind.* Trans. J.B. Baillie. Rpt. New York: Harper Colophon, 1967.

Helmholtz, Hermann von. 1847. "The Conservation of Force: A Physical Memoir." In *Selected Writings.* Ed. Russell Kahl. Middletown, CT: Wesleyan University Press, 1971, 3–55.

——. 1861. "The Application of the Law of the Conservation of Force to Organic Nature." In *Selected Writings.* Ed. Russell Kahl. Middletown, CT: Wesleyan University Press, 1971, 109–21.

Hume, David. 1748. *An Essay Concerning Human Understanding.* Rpt. Oxford: Oxford University Press, 1999.

Huxley, Aldous. 1925. "Our Contemporary Hocus-Pocus." *The Forum* 73 (1925): 313–20.

Hyman, Stanley Edgar. 1962. *The Tangled Bank: Darwin, Marx, Frazer and Freud as Imaginative Writers.* New York: Atheneum.

Inman, Billie Andrew. 1981. *Walter Pater's Reading: A Bibliography of His Library Borrowings and Literary References, 1858–1873.* New York: Garland.

——. 1990. *Walter Pater and His Reading, 1847–1877. With a Bibliography of His Library Borrowings, 1878–1894.* New York: Garland.

Jakobson, Roman, and Morris Halle. 1956. *Fundamentals of Language.* The Hague: Mouton.

James, Henry. 1877. *The American.* Rpt. New York: Holt, 1967.

——. 1903. *The Ambassadors.* Rpt. Cambridge, MA: Riverside, 1960.

——. 1904. *The Golden Bowl.* Rpt. New York: Meridian, 1972.

James, William. 1890. *Principles of Psychology.* 2 vols. Rpt. New York: Dover, 1950.

Jameson, Fredric. 1992. *Signatures of the Visible.* New York: Routledge.

Johnson, Barbara. 1987. "Apostrophe, Animation, and Abortion." In *A World of Difference.* Baltimore, MD: The John Hopkins University Press, 184–99.

Johnson, Samuel. 1779–81. *Lives of the Poets.* "John Milton." In *Selected Writings.* Ed. Katherine Rogers. New York: New American Library, 1961, 309–72.

Jones, Ernest. 1910. "The Oedipus Complex as an Explanation of Hamlet's Mystery." *American Journal of Psychology* 21 (1): 72–113.

——. 1949. *Hamlet and Oedipus.* New York: Norton.

Joyce, James. 1916. *A Portrait of the Artist as a Young Man.* Rpt. New York: Viking, 1974.

——. 1922. *Ulysses.* Rpt. New York: Modern Library.

Jung, C.G. 1912. *Psychology of the Unconscious: A Study of the Transformations and Symbolisms of the Libido.* Trans. Beatrice M. Hinkle. Princeton, NJ: Princeton University Press, 1991.

——. 1913. "The Theory of Psychoanalysis." In *Freud and Psychoanalysis.* Trans. R.F.C. Hull. New York: Pantheon, 1961, 83–226.

——. 1919. "Instinct and the Unconscious." In *The Structure and Dynamics of the Psyche.* Trans. R.F.C. Hull. Princeton, NJ: Princeton University Press, 1960, 129–38.

Kazin, Alfred. 1961. "The Language of Pundits." In *Contemporaries*. Boston: Little Brown, 1962, 382–93.

Kendrick, Walter. 1977. "The Sensationalism of *The Woman in White*." *Nineteenth-Century Fiction* 32 (1): 18–35.

———. 1987. *The Secret Museum: Pornography in Modern Culture*. Rpt. Berkeley: University of California Press, 1996.

Kerouac, Jack. 1958. "The Essentials of Spontaneous Prose." *Evergreen Review* 2 (5): 72–73.

Kofman, Sarah. 1970. *The Childhood of Art: An Interpretation of Freud's Aesthetics*. Trans. Winifred Woodhull. New York: Columbia Univeristy Press, 1988.

Kristeva, Julia. 1995. "Le scandale de hors-temps." *Revue Française de Psychanalyse* 59 (4): 1029–44.

———. 2000. *Melanie Klein*. Trans. Ross Guberman. New York: Columbia University Press, 2001.

Kuhn, Thomas. 1962. *The Structure of Scientific Revolutions*. Chicago: University of Chicago Press.

Lacan, Jacques. 1932. *De la psychose paranoïaque dans ses rapports avec la personnalité*. Rpt. Paris: Seuil, 1975.

———. 1966. *Ecrits*. Trans. Bruce Fink. New York: Norton, 2002.

Laplanche, Jean, and Pontalis, J. B. 1967. *The Language of Psychoanalysis*. Trans. Donald Nicholson-Smith. New York: Norton, 1973.

Laplanche, Jean. 1970. *Life and Death in Psychoanalysis*. Trans. Jeffrey Mehlman. Baltimore: The John Hopkins University Press, 1976.

Laqueur, Thomas. 2003. *Solitary Sex: A Cultural History of Masturbation*. New York: Zone Books.

Lawrence, D. H. 1921a. *Women in Love*. Rpt. New York: Viking, 1966.

———. 1921b. *Psychoanalysis and the Unconscious*. Rpt. New York: Viking, 1962.

———. 1927. "Four American Novels." In *Selected Literary Criticism*. Ed. Anthony Beal. New York: Viking, 422–28.

———. 1936. "Study of Thomas Hardy." In *Phoenix: The Posthumous Papers of D. H. Lawrence*. Rpt. New York: Viking, 1980, 398–516.

Leavis, F. R. 1932. *New Bearings in English Poetry*. Rpt. London: Penguin, 1967.

Lewis, David Levering. 1993. *W. E. B. DuBois: Biography of a Race 1868–1919*. New York: Holt.

Lodge, David. 1985. "Lawrence, Dostoevsky, Bakhtin." In *After Bakhtin*. London: Routledge, 1990, 45–56.

Lukacher, Ned. 1986. *Primal Scenes: Literature, Philosophy, Psychoanalysis*. Ithaca, NY: Cornell University Press.

Luria, A. R. 1973. *The Working Brain: An Introduction to Neuropsychology*. Trans Basil Haigh. New York: Basic Books.

Mahony, Patrick J. 1986. *Freud and the Rat Man*. New Haven, CT: Yale University Press.

———. 1987. *Psychoanalysis and Discourse*. London: Tavistock.

———. 1989. *On Defining Freud's Discourse*. New Haven, CT: Yale University Press.

Mailer, Norman. 1957. *The White Negro*. In *Advertisements for Myself* (1959). Rpt. New York: Berkley Medallion, 1966, 311–31.

Mann, Thomas. 1929. "Freud's Position in the History of Modern Thought." In *Past Masters and Other Papers*. Trans. H. T. Lowe-Porter. Freeport, NY: Books for Libraries Press, 1933, 165–98.

——. 1936. "Freud and the Future." In *Essays of Three Decades*. Trans. H. T. Lowe-Porter. New York: Knopf, 1947, 411–28.

Mansfield, Katherine. 1918. "Bliss." In *Stories*. New York: Vintage, 1956, 145–58.

——. 1919. "Je ne parle pas français." In *Stories*. New York: Vintage, 1956, 159–88.

Marcus, Steven. 1966. *The Other Victorians: A Study of Sexuality and Pornography in Mid-Nineteenth-Century England*. New York: Basic Books.

——. 1974. "Freud and Dora: Story, History, Case History." In *Freud and the Culture of Psychoanalysis*. New York: Norton, 1984, 42–86.

Masson, Jeffrey Moussaieff. 1984. *The Assault on Truth: Freud's Suppression of the Seduction Theory*. New York: Farrar, Straus.

McClintock, Anne. 1992. "Gonad the Barbarian and the Venus Flytrap: Portraying the Female and Male Orgasm." In *Sex Exposed: Sexuality and the Pornography Debate*. Ed. Lynne Segal and Mary McIntosh. London: Virago, 1992, 111–31.

——. 1993. "Maid to Order: Commercial S/M and Gender Power." In *Dirty Looks: Women, Pornography, Power*. Ed. Pamela Church Gibson and Roma Gibson. London: British Film Institute, 1993, 207–32.

McNair, Brian. 1996. *Mediated Sex: Pornography and Postmodern Culture*. London: Arnold.

Meisel, Perry. 1980. *The Absent Father: Walter Pater and Virginia Woolf*. New Haven, CT: Yale University Press.

——. 1987. *The Myth of the Modern: A Study in British Literature and Criticism after 1850*. New Haven, CT: Yale University Press.

Meisel, Perry, and Kendrick, Walter, eds. 1985. *Bloomsbury/Freud: The Letters of James and Alix Strachey, 1924–25*. New York: Basic Books.

Metz, Christian. 1977. *The Imaginary Signifier: Psychoanalysis and the Cinema*. Trans. Celia Britton et al. Bloomington: Indiana University Press, 1981.

Miller, James. 1993. *The Passion of Michel Foucault*. New York: Simon & Schuster.

Mitchell, Juliet. 1974. *Psychoanalysis and Feminism*. New York: Random House.

Modell, Arnold H. 1990. *Other Times, Other Realities: Toward A Theory of Psychoanalytic Treatment*. Cambridge, MA: Harvard University Press.

Mosse, George L. 1964. *The Crisis of German Ideology: Intellectual Origins of the Third Reich*. New York: Grosset and Dunlap.

——. 1978. *Toward the Final Solution: A History of European Racism*. New York: H. Fertig.

Ornston, Darius. 1982. "Strachey's Influence: A Preliminary Report." *International Journal of Psychoanalysis* 63 (1982): 409–26.

——, ed. 1992. *Translating Freud*. New Haven, CT: Yale University Press.

Pater, Walter. 1873. *The Renaissance*. Originally published as *Studies in the History of the Renaissance*. All references and citations from Pater are from the New Library Edition. 10 vols. London: Macmillan, 1910.

——. 1874. "Wordsworth." In *Appreciations*, 39–64.

——. 1878. "The Child in the House." In *Miscellaneous Studies*, 172–96.

——. 1889. "Style." In *Appreciations*, 5–38.

Peckham, Morse. 1969. *Art and Pornography: An Experiment in Explanation*. New York: Basic Books.

Pound, Ezra. 1918. "A Retrospect." In *Literary Essays of Ezra Pound*. Ed. T. S. Eliot. Rpt. New York: New Directions, 1968, 3–14.

Randall, Richard S. 1989. *Freedom and Taboo: Pornography and the Politics of a Self Divided*. Berkeley: University of California Press.

Ransom, John Crowe. 1924. "Freud and Literature." *The Saturday Review of Literature*, October 4, 1924: 161–62.

Read, Forrest, ed. 1967. *Pound/Joyce*. New York: New Directions.

Richardson, Alan. 2001. *British Romanticism and the Science of Mind*. Cambridge: Cambridge University Press.

Ricks, Christopher. 1988. *T.S. Eliot and Prejudice*. Berkeley: University of California Press.

Ricoeur, Paul. 1970. *Freud and Philosophy*. Trans. D. Savage. New Haven, CT: Yale University Press, 1977.

Rieff, Philip. 1959. *Freud: The Mind of the Moralist*. Rpt. Chicago: University of Chicago Press, 1979.

Rivière, Joan. 1929. "Womanliness as a Masquerade." In *The Inner World and Joan Rivière: Collected Papers, 1920–1958*. Ed. Athol Hughes. London: Karnac, 1991, 89–101.

———. 1932. "Jealousy as a Mechanism of Defense." In *The Inner World and Joan Rivière: Collected Papers, 1920–1958*. Ed. Athol Hughes. London: Karnac, 1991, 103–15.

Roazen, Paul. 1971. *Freud and His Followers*. New York: Knopf.

Roudinesco, Elisabeth. 1993. *Jacques Lacan*. Trans. Barbara Bray. New York: Columbia University Press.

Rubin, Joan Shelley. 1992. *The Making of Middlebrow Culture*. Chapel Hill: University of North Carolina Press.

Rudnytsky, Peter. 1991. *The Psychoanalytic Vocation: Rank, Winnicott, and the Legacy of Freud*. New Haven, CT: Yale University Press.

Sacks, Oliver. 1998. "Sigmund Freud: The Other Road." In *Freud and the Neurosciences*. Ed. Giselher Guttmann and Inge Scholz-Strasser. Vienna: Verlag der Österreichen Akademischer Wissenschaften, 11–22.

Sartre, Jean Paul. 1966. "Jean-Paul Sartre répond." *L'Arc* 30: 87–96.

Schivelbusch, Wolfgang. 1977. *The Railway Journey: The Industrialization of Time and Space in the Nineteenth Century*. Berkeley: University of California Press.

Schur, Max. 1972. *Freud: Living and Dying*. New York: International Universities Press.

Sedgwick, Eve. 1985. *Between Men: English Literature and Male Homosocial Desire*. New York: Columbia University Press.

———. 1990. *Epistemology of the Closet*. Berkeley: University of California Press.

Solms, Mark. 1997. "What is Consciousness?" *Journal of the American Psychoanalytic Association* 45: 681–703.

Solms, Mark, and Oliver Turnbull. 2002. *The Brain and the Inner World*. New York: Other Press.

Sontag, Susan. 1967. "The Pornographic Imagination." In *Styles of Radical Will*. New York: Farrar, Straus & Giroux, 1969, 35–73.

Spence, Donald. 1982. *Narrative Truth and Historical Truth: Meaning and Interpretation in Psychoanalysis*. New York: Norton.

Stephen, Leslie. 1875. "Art and Morality." *Cornhill Magazine* 32 (July): 91–101.

Straayer, Chris. 1993. "The Seduction of Boundaries: Feminist Fluidity in Annie Sprinkle's Art/Education/Sex." In *Dirty Looks: Women, Pornography, Power*. Ed. Pamela
Church Gibson and Roma Gibson. London: British Film Institute, 1993, 156–75.

Strachey, James. "Some Unconscious Factors in Reading." *International Journal of Psychoanalysis* 11 (1930): 322–31.

——. "The Nature of the Therapeutic Action of Psychoanalysis." *International Journal
of Psychoanalysis* 15 (1934): 127–59.

Sulloway, Frank. 1979. *Freud: Biologist of the Mind*. New York: Basic Books.

Sussman, Henry. 1982. *The Hegelian Aftermath: Readings in Hegel, Kierkegaard, Freud,
Proust, and James*. Baltimore: The Johns Hopkins University Press.

Taylor, Dennis. 1993. *Hardy's Literary Language and Victorian Philology*. Oxford: Clar-
endon Press.

Trilling, Lionel. 1940. "Freud and Literature." In *The Liberal Imagination*. Rpt. New
York: Doubleday, 1953, 32–54.

——. 1945. "Art and Neurosis." In *The Liberal Imagination*. Rpt. New York: Doubleday, 1953, 155–75.

——. 1955. "Freud: Within and Beyond Culture." In *Beyond Culture*. Rpt. New York:
Harcourt Brace Jovanovich, 1978, 77–102.

Valentine, Kylie. 2003. *Psychoanalysis, Psychiatry, and Modern Literature*. New York:
Palgrave.

Vološinov, V. N. 1927. *Freudianism: A Critical Sketch*. Trans. I. R. Titunik. Bloomington:
Indiana University Press, 1976.

Williams, Linda. 1990. *Hardcore*. London: Picador.

——. 1992. "Pornographies on/scene, or Diff'rent strokes for diff'rent folks." In *Sex
Exposed: Sexuality and the Pornography Debate*. Ed. Lynne Segal and Mary McIntosh. London: Virago, 1992, 233–65.

——. 1993. "A Provoking Agent: The Pornography and Performance Art of Annie
Sprinkle." In *Dirty Looks: Women, Pornography, Power*. Ed. Pamela Church Gibson and Roma Gibson. London: British Film Institute, 1993, 176–91.

Williams, Raymond. 1978. "The Bloomsbury Fraction." In *Problems in Materialism and
Culture*. London: Verso Editions and NLB, 1980, 148–69.

Winter, Sarah. 1999. *Freud and the Institution of Psychoanalytic Knowledge*. Stanford:
Stanford University Press.

Wittgenstein, Ludwig. 1953. *Philosophical Investigations*. Trans. G. E. M. Anscombe.
Rpt. New York: Macmillan, 1968.

Whitehead, Alfred North. 1925. *Science and the Modern World*. Rpt. New York: Free Press,
1967.

Woolf, Leonard. 1914. "Everyday Life." *The New English Weekly*, June 13, 1914.

Woolf, Virginia. 1919. "Modern Fiction." In *Collected Essays*. 4 vols. New York: Harcourt, Brace and World, 1967, 2:103–10.

——. 1920. "Freudian Fiction." In *Contemporary Writers*. London: The Hogarth
Press, 1965, 152–54.

Wordsworth, William. 1800, 1802. "Preface 1800 (with 1802 variants)." *Lyrical Ballads*.
Rpt. London: Methuen, 1965, 241–72.

Žižek, Slavoj. 1989. *The Sublime Object of Ideology*. New York: Verso.

Index